NORTH PACIFIC OCEAN

WAKE I.   ← To Viet Nam

160°   170°   180°   170°

The Voyage of the VANCE under Captain Arnheiter

1. *Pearl Harbor:* Captain Arnheiter takes command, December 22, 1965.

2. *On the way to Guam, December 28, 1965, to January 7, 1966:* Captain Arnheiter summons first War Council—and sees to the spiritual well-being of the crew.

3. *Guam, January 7 to 14, 1966:* The mess night, the silver candelabras and a coffee server, the sandbags and the oil drums. Captain Arnheiter holds his first public captain's mast.

4. *Under way for Viet Nam, January 14 to 20, 1966:* Captain Arnheiter exercises the Special Fire Team, and the engines protest. The Boner Box appears and "Hellcats Reveille" sounds.

5. *On Market Time patrol off central Viet Nam coast, January 27, 1966:* Captain Arnheiter reports he has discovered submarine smuggling point and sends landing party ashore under Lieutenant Mason to capture guerrilla porters.

6. *January 29, 1966:* Captain Arnheiter supposedly decimates a company of Viet Cong hard-core soldiery.

7. *January 30, 1966:* Captain Arnheiter says he blasted a group of Viet Cong guerrillas who shot at the *Vance.* Chief Petty Officer Cornejo sees some chickens.

8. *February 1, 1966:* Captain Arnheiter announces he has demolished enemy stone machine-gun bunker with *Vance's* 3-inch cannons.

9. *Early February 1966:* Captain Arnheiter tows the motor whaleboat at night in choppy seas with a crew embarked.

10. *To February 18, 1966:* Patrolling off Gulf of Siam coast, water rationing and Captain Arnheiter's twenty-minute showers. Lieutenant Generous despairs. Guerrilla warfare.

11. *February 20 to 24, 1966:* Ashore in Bangkok.

12. *February 28 to March 14, 1966:* Chaplain Dando pays a visit. Boiler Tender MacSaveny has had enough.

13. *March 19 to 22, 1966:* The secret search for the Chinese submarine. Captain Arnheiter directs water-skiing festivities.

14. *En route to Manila Bay, March 23 to 26, 1966:* An Audie Murphy movie and a Silver Star.

15. *March 29, 1966:* Leading Boatswain's Mate Smoot sent to the psychiatric ward. Two days later Captain Arnheiter is relieved of command.

THE ARNHEITER AFFAIR

RANDOM HOUSE
NEW YORK

THE
ARNHEITER
AFFAIR

by
Neil Sheehan

For Susan

ACKNOWLEDGMENT

This book could not have been written without the assistance given me in the course of my research by numerous officers and enlisted men of the United States Navy. They must go unnamed because some are still on active service.

N. S.

CONTENTS

PROLOGUE

The end crowns every action, stay till that.

—Thomas Randolph, *The Muses' Looking-Glasse*

I first saw Lieutenant Commander Marcus Aurelius Arnheiter in May 1968, in a crowded hearing room in the Ray-
burn House Office Building, a pile of Stalinesque marble on
the southwest slope of Capitol Hill. The late Representative Joseph Y. Resnick, a brassy Democrat from upstate New
York, wanted to run for the Senate against Senator Jacob
K. Javits, that fixture of New York politics. Resnick had
seized upon Arnheiter's case as an appealing issue and had
become his congressional champion. He was holding a public
hearing to try to force the Navy to convene a formal court
of inquiry into "the Arnheiter Affair," as Arnheiter's dispute
with the Navy hierarchy was commonly called.

   Commander Arnheiter preferred to give another title to
his travail. He described it as "the *Vance* Mutiny." For the
previous two years he had been telling anyone who would
listen that he was the victim of a clever conspiracy that
amounted to the first successful mutiny in the history of the
United States Navy. He had been abruptly removed by the
Navy on March 31, 1966, from his position as captain of
the U.S.S. *Vance,* a warship assigned to coastal patrol off

South Viet Nam. Arnheiter contended that his dismissal had been secretly engineered by a campaign of rumor and innuendo fomented against him by his subordinate officers. They had surreptitiously made false complaints to chaplains and other outsiders about the way he had been running the ship, he said. His superiors panicked at the complaints and relieved him without warning in violation of Navy regulations. To justify their unethical act, these superiors then ordered an investigation of his conduct as captain. They rigged the inquest against him into "a fantastic fishing expedition" for make-believe evidence of misbehavior. He had since gathered proof of the conspiracy, Arnheiter said, and had presented the evidence to the admirals responsible for his dismissal to show them their mistake. They had refused to believe him. Arnheiter argued that in what constituted a second conspiracy, officially sanctioned by the Navy, he was being sacrificed by the admirals, his career ruined, to preserve an appearance of infallibility.

By whatever name, the Arnheiter Affair had already consumed as much time and energy within the United States Navy as the loss at sea in April 1963 of the nuclear submarine *Thresher*, with her entire crew of 129 men, the worst peacetime submarine disaster in Navy history. No one was known to have suffered any physical harm in the Arnheiter Affair. Its protagonist, a forty-two-year-old graduate of Annapolis, was now exiled to a backwater post as a communications staff officer at the Treasure Island Naval Base in San Francisco. The warship he had commanded for a brief ninety-nine days, the *Vance,* a relic of World War II and the Cold War called a destroyer escort radar, was still working her monotonous trade of guarding the South Vietnamese coast. Yet, curious as it may sound, the Arnheiter Affair was of more abiding and essential interest to the Navy, and to much of America at large, than the submarine disaster. For it had to do with prized traditions: command of a warship at sea, the loyalty and respect a ship's subordinate officers and crew owe to their captain, the integrity of the Navy officer corps—human matters both enduring and complex.

The easy capture of the intelligence ship U.S.S. *Pueblo* in January 1968 by North Korea's ship-in-a-bottle navy had focused more attention on the Arnheiter Affair. The *Pueblo* disgrace had seemed a failure of just those human qualities. The highest admirals had obviously not foreseen the North Korean coup. When the emergency occurred, the *Pueblo* was abandoned to her fate without any effort at rescue by planes or other United States warships. The *Pueblo*'s captain, Commander Lloyd M. Bucher, surrendered his ship and crew after little or no resistance, an unprecedented act of timidity in a navy that had prided itself on never striking its colors while a vessel could maneuver and a gun could fire.

Arnheiter had become captain of the *Vance* in a ceremony at Pearl Harbor on December 22, 1965. She was his first command. He took the ship on a patrol off the South Vietnamese coast during which she three times bombarded enemy gun positions along the shore. Arnheiter was recommended by two of his officers and an enlisted man for the Silver Star for gallantry, the Navy's third-highest combat decoration. He was then summarily relieved on March 31, 1966, in Manila Bay for an investigation of "certain irregular practices" he had allegedly followed as captain. The next morning he was put off the ship in disgrace. The investigation convened five days later, on April 6, 1966, at Subic Bay Naval Base in the Philippines. For six and a half days a senior Navy captain took sworn testimony from Arnheiter, his subordinate officers and several sailors. The Navy subsequently accepted the findings as evidence that Arnheiter had destroyed the morale of his crew and that he had "exercised bad judgment and lack of integrity in so many important matters" that he should never again be given command of naval officers or seamen, either ashore or at sea.

Arnheiter had refused to accept ruin. He had devoted his life to obtaining restitution. In the next two years he wrote tens of thousands of words in rebuttal of the investigation and appealed his case to every echelon of naval authority, including the civilian Secretary of the Navy at the time, Paul R. Ignatius. Rebuffed in these official channels, he turned to the law courts and was suing the Navy for violation of its own regulations and his constitutional rights. He and his supporters, including several retired admirals with distinguished World War II records and an active-duty officer whose career had formerly been one of the most promising in the Navy, Captain Richard G. Alexander, had also been waging a campaign in Congress and in the press to reverse the Navy's verdict.

The House Armed Services Committee usually handled these military squabbles. It had conducted a private staff inquiry earlier in the spring of 1968. The conclusion was that the Navy had been justified in relieving Arnheiter. The committee therefore refused to hold the hearing that Arnheiter and his partisans had been demanding. Since the committee's chairman then was Representative Confederate Americana, the late Lucius Mendel Rivers of South Carolina, a man who loved all uniforms, but Navy blue best, the committee's determination was suspect, to say the least. Although Representative Resnick's congressional duties in the military domain were limited to a lowly membership on the House Veterans Affairs Committee, he had convened an unofficial hearing on his own authority, a privilege of any legislator. His act seemed a courageous one, defying the congressional seniority system that placed issues of such importance in the hands of replica Calhouns like Rivers.

Arnheiter led off the testimony, punctiliously dressed in a khaki uniform. The conspiracy against him had been instigated and led, he said, by "a Berkeley campus type of Vietnik/beatnik" named William T. Generous, Jr., the *Vance*'s operations officer, a Phi Beta Kappa graduate of Brown University who had obtained his commission through the Naval Reserve Officer Training Corps. Generous had been motivated by political opposition to the Viet Nam war, personal cowardice and a psychotic impulse to oppose any established authority, Arnheiter said. Arnheiter's short black hair, flecked with the gray of his forty-two years, was brushed into place with the same precision shown by the press of his uniform. His eyes were large and dark, set in a round, boyish face. His voice had a nasal burr. The questioning was friendly. The interrogator was a prominent San Francisco trial lawyer, a pleasantly florid man in a deep-green suit with shawl lapels and an off-gold tie. He was the attorney representing Arnheiter in his civil suit against the Navy for alleged violation of his constitutional rights. Resnick permitted the lawyer to act as hearing counsel. Arnheiter startled the audience by accusing Vice Admiral Benedict J. Semmes, Jr., then commander of the Second Fleet in the Atlantic, of lying to Congress to defend his decision that Arnheiter's dismissal had been warranted. Semmes had been Chief of Naval Personnel at the time Arnheiter was relieved. This was an extraordinary charge for an active-duty naval officer of median rank to level against a senior admiral.

If they were so disloyal, why hadn't Arnheiter reported the behavior of his junior officers to his own superior, the squadron commodore, before they could engineer his removal with a cunningly staged mutiny? "I did not desire immediately after taking command of a ship to start complaining," he said. "Lord Nelson," Arnheiter continued, leaning across the witness table as he pronounced the hallowed name of the British naval hero Horatio, Viscount Nelson, "said that he could take any lout and make a naval officer out of him and I daresay that it occurred to me that I should really attempt to follow through with the Nelsonian tradition as best I could." This and other answers appeared as carefully rehearsed as the questions. Both questions and answers were designed to produce headlines. None of this disturbed me. The technique was common enough in Washington, and the hearing was admittedly intended to present Arnheiter's side of the case and to force the Navy to hold a formal court of inquiry, an action that would lay Arnheiter's dismissal open to question once more. His answers might be true, for all I knew. While he spoke, he puffed with the regularity of a metronome on a thin cigar with a wooden tip.

The appearance the next day of Captain Richard G. Alexander evoked instant respect and some slight awe in the hearing room. Here was a storybook naval officer, elegantly slim and handsome, like a figure from a Gainsborough painting. He testified as a man of unquestioned integrity, a blameless and selfless officer. He had sacrificed a career of virtually certain pre-eminence because he believed Arnheiter had been done an injustice that would undermine the entire structure of authority within the Navy if it were not corrected. Alexander's public defense of Arnheiter six months earlier had lent a sense of respectability and passionate righteousness to Arnheiter's crusade for restoration to command. In November 1967, shortly after he was appointed captain of the 54,000-ton U.S.S. *New Jersey*—a coveted command, of the world's only operational battleship, then being refitted for Viet Nam war service—Alexander had spent an hour personally pleading Arnheiter's cause to Secretary Ignatius. He left a twenty-seven-page summary of his views with Ignatius and then quickly distributed copies to congressmen and several reporters. His plea had been an eloquent polemic that endorsed all of Arnheiter's accusations of conspiracy and unjust removal. It defiantly condemned the manner in which the naval hierarchy had handled the case. Arnheiter, Alexander had told Ignatius, was "a dedicated professional officer . . . of great energy, ability and high standards." His subordinates had been a pack of "liars and disloyal officers bent on assassinating the captain professionally." Why? Because he had disturbed "their slovenly and unseamanlike lives" by enforcing discipline. Worse, they had "succeeded in stampeding" the squadron commodore and the two admirals immediately above him into throwing Arnheiter off the ship. Alexander accused Arnheiter's superiors of behaving almost as culpably as his subordinates. They had failed to observe "elementary common sense in pursuing impartial justice." Acting "without a shred of substantiation," they had accepted at face value a passel of "damning, ruinous allegations" and had removed Arnheiter "by flawed and extra-legal means." The squadron commodore had been unwilling even to inform Arnheiter of the accusations against him before requesting his summary relief, Alexander noted to Ignatius. "His conduct was so unmanly as to inspire instant contempt." The two admirals had shared in this "improper, cowardly and peremptory action" by approving the commodore's request. Subsequent evidence proved that the allegations against Arnheiter were nothing but "rumor and falsehood," Alexander had written.

"Mr. Secretary, what all of your officers will demand to know is just how in hell this could happen in the United States Navy!" Alexander had cried out in a denunciation widely quoted in the press. He urged Ignatius to summon a court of inquiry. As for himself, Alexander told the Secretary, he had already concluded that the proceedings against Arnheiter should be extinguished, full restitution granted and Arnheiter's subordinates court-martialed for conspiracy and mutiny.

Had this philippic instantly been secreted in the drawers of the Navy bureaucracy, life would still have been grim for Richard Alexander. Publicity was the knife of professional hara-kiri. Admiral Thomas H. Moorer, a pine-knot Alabamian who was then Chief of Naval Operations, had been enraged and insulted. He summoned Alexander back to Washington from the Philadelphia Navy Yard, where the *New Jersey* was being refurbished. Any officer who could write and publicize "such an emotional, intemperate statement" to influence the Secretary of the Navy on a sensitive issue "raised serious questions" about his judgment, Moorer told Alexander in an arctic voice. He was specifically worried, he said, about how Alexander might behave in command of the *New Jersey*'s 16-inch-gun batteries if he happened to disagree with an order from his superiors. Alexander had responded like a gentleman. He offered to relinquish the *New Jersey* if the admiral continued to doubt his judgment. Within six weeks Alexander was called back to Washington to the Bureau of Naval Personnel and handed a typed form to sign. Ignatius had ruled against Arnheiter and a court of inquiry in the meantime. The form requested a transfer "for personal reasons" to a lackluster staff job at the Boston Naval District headquarters, "the Elephants' Graveyard" in Navy slang.

The self-sacrifice of a man of Alexander's stature had fostered the impression that the admirals must indeed have blundered in relieving Arnheiter. Ignatius had made the Navy look sillier by announcing that Alexander's exile had no connection with the Arnheiter Affair. No one had believed this, of course, and Resnick made sure that the true story of Alexander's demise found its way into the newspapers. Shortly afterward, the Navy released a letter to Chairman Rivers in which Admiral Moorer acknowledged the real circumstances of Alexander's banishment to Boston, but the damage had been done.

Alexander's tossing down of the gauntlet in November had also occurred against a backdrop of publicity on the Arnheiter Affair that had been rising relentlessly over the previous months. Almost all of the press accounts had portrayed Arnheiter as a patriotic victim of a cabal of mutinous juniors and inept seniors. The accounts included several nationally syndicated "Washington Merry-Go-Round" columns by Jack Anderson, the late Drew Pearson's associate columnist. The two exceptions unfavorable to Arnheiter, articles in *Time* and *Newsweek* magazines, came a few weeks after Alexander's press release. The *Time* story reflected most closely the official Navy version. It described Arnheiter as a whimsical tyrant, an incarnation of Queeg, the paranoid captain of Herman Wouk's novel *The Caine Mutiny*. Arnheiter sued *Time* for libel, and the broadside had done nothing to improve the Navy's credibility or to diminish sympathy for the former captain of the *Vance*. The fallibility of the country's military leadership had been revealed too conspicuously by the Viet Nam war for anyone to take the Navy's word. Besides, Arnheiter's cause had a kind of double-edged appeal to both liberals and conservatives. To the liberals, he was a little man who had been victimized by an impersonal military institution. The suspicious circumstances surrounding his disgrace were symbolic of a lack of integrity and good judgment in high places. To the conservatives, the mutinous behavior of Arnheiter's subordinates was a manifestation of the general disorder and mockery of authority that was polluting the quality of national life, a symptom of the weakening of the institutions of family, university, government and the military under the assault of anarchistic forces. In March 1968, two months before the Resnick hearing, a lengthy article on the case by the right-wing columnist James Jackson Kilpatrick had appeared in the *National Review*. The article was entitled "He Might Have Been Another Halsey." It left no doubt that Arnheiter possessed those traits of resoluteness, imagination and independence that had enabled Fleet Admiral William F. Halsey to humble the Imperial Japanese Navy. If a right-wing writer like Kilpatrick had taken up Arnheiter's cause, perhaps the Navy had really bungled, after all?

Alexander's calm and deliberate testimony in the hearing room added plausibility to this conclusion. He rested his elbows on the witness table while he talked, propping his chin on folded hands. He made no harsh accusations this time and did not seek to blame his superiors for his own consignment to oblivion. A simple matter of principle had arisen, he said, and he had felt honor bound to take a stand. The captain of a ship, he explained, "is required to display a considerable amount of moral courage in getting the job done . . . And that moral courage has got to be matched upstairs where the seniors are, who laid these requirements on the ship in the first place . . . If they cave in at this point and decide that the captain is no good because in attempting to reach the goals they established he has made people unhappy, the moral courage shown by the captain is not matched by the moral courage of the seniors, and cases of this nature result."

Other testimony during the three-day hearing was just as persuasive.

A sailor, Seaman John Cicerich, Jr., who had boarded the *Vance* four months after Arnheiter's relief, testified that the ship was "a living hell . . . there was absolutely no military discipline there." Seaman Cicerich told a story of gangs of bullies who used him and other sailors as punching bags and burned their bodies with the lit ends of cigarettes. He spoke of "unkempt officers" who tolerated this brutality. Lieutenant Generous, the operations officer whom Arnheiter had accused of masterminding his downfall, had acted like a psychotic intellectual, belittling the ordinary sailors with the bric-a-brac of his university education by habitually asking them arcane questions about "history, literature, plays, et cetera, et cetera," Cicerich said. Lieutenant George W. Dando, the chaplain Arnheiter had also charged with carrying false tales about him to his superiors, was a fat slob who did nothing but "eat, eat, eat and watch movies" instead of listening to legitimate complaints from victimized sailors like himself, Cicerich continued. (Dando was a young Presbyterian minister. He had been the squadron chaplain and had visited the *Vance* in the course of a circuit around the ships off Viet Nam. A very critical report he had given the squadron commodore on the morale of the *Vance*'s crew had been a major reason for Arnheiter's summary dismissal. At the time, Dando's Navy experience had been limited to a mere six months of active service.) From what other sailors told him, Cicerich said, the *Vance* had been a hell ship prior to Arnheiter's arrival. Arnheiter had brought a brief reign of law and decency, but the *Vance* relapsed into her old anarchic ways after his disgraceful removal.

Arnheiter's attorney introduced the most damaging testimony at the hearing from the official Navy records of the case. An examination of the records revealed, he said, that one active-duty admiral, Rear Admiral Walter H. Baumberger, the Commander, Cruiser-Destroyer Force Pacific, who ranked in the chain of judicial review just below the admiral commanding the entire Pacific Fleet, had exonerated Arnheiter on all but three of the forty accusations against him. He had dismissed these remaining three as trivial and had twice recommended that Arnheiter be given the command of another ship, only to be overruled by Admiral Semmes (the Chief of Naval Personnel) and other superiors.

The Navy boycotted the Resnick hearing. Its silence seemed to bespeak the weakness of whatever refutation it might offer. For three days I wrote articles for *The New York Times* which contributed more favorable publicity to Arnheiter's campaign for redress. I decided that although he might be a difficult man to get along with and to serve under, he appeared to have been stuck with milksops and neurotics who were posing as naval officers. His own prickly personality had created a crisis and his superiors had made him the scapegoat instead of disciplining his juniors. In a review of the hearing for the Sunday *Times,* I was tempted to begin with a remark that if Marcus Aurelius Arnheiter had stood on the bridge of the *Pueblo,* the North Koreans would have met bullets instead of compliant surrender. I remembered the testimony of Vice Admiral Thomas G. W. Settle, a wizened, peppery retiree with forty-five years of service and a Navy Cross, the second-highest combat award, for commanding the cruiser U.S.S. *Portland* against the Japanese in the Pacific. Admiral Settle had said that he had known the former captain of the *Vance* for years and that Arnheiter's personality made him "particularly competent for a sea command in war."

The day after the hearing ended, I received a telephone call from a captain in Navy Public Information. Since Arnheiter was washing his dirty linen in public, he said, the Navy had decided to release the transcript of the testimony given at the six-and-a-half-day investigation at Subic Bay. If I cared to read this and the subsequent reviews by admirals up the line, I could see them at the office of a Navy lawyer in the Judge Advocate General's office.

A reporter for a morning newspaper has only a few hours in the day before 5 P.M. tolls and he must begin writing his story for the first-edition deadline. The Subic Bay transcript was a tome of 429 pages. The Navy lawyer pointed out that I might find most interesting the section where Lieutenant Ray Sterling Hardy, Jr., the *Vance*'s executive officer, accused the captain of coercing him and Generous into recommending Arnheiter for the Silver Star for gallantry. As I read I had that sense of excitement a reporter feels when he makes a discovery. Although Arnheiter denied coercion in his reply to Hardy's accusation, his testimony at the investigation was curiously evasive. Attached to the hearing transcript was a copy of the proposed citation for the Silver Star. Its style was similar to other writings of Arnheiter's that I had read during the three-day Resnick hearings.

I drove back to my office, and before writing, telephoned Arnheiter to see what he had to say. His answer had the same tenor of equivocation as his testimony at Subic Bay. Hardy's accusation was a lie, he said. Hardy and Generous had suggested recommending him for the medal. He had merely consented to their wish. He had not written the proposed citation. He had simply referred them to the Navy administrative manual, where models for such citations could be found. "I didn't even see that citation after it was written," he said indignantly. But he didn't let it go at that. "You don't understand how these things are done," he said. "You get put up for a higher medal and then they reduce the recommendation and award you a lesser one. That's how it's done." The next day Arnheiter and Resnick denounced the Navy for releasing the Subic Bay transcript, which they had previously been taunting the Navy to make public, accusing the admirals of "character assassination." Then Arnheiter wrote a letter to *The Times* "to correct an erroneous impression" the Silver Star story might have created among readers. My story had already included his denial. The letter seemed a bit unnecessary, a hint of "doth protest too much." Had Arnheiter actually coerced his officers into proposing him for the Silver Star? I wondered. What kind of man would do this?

As soon as the Resnick hearing ended, Arnheiter had begun importuning my editors for more publicity about his case. Should we go on? I asked myself. I decided that if we did anything, it ought to be a fairly thorough investigation of the whole affair. I wrote a memorandum to my editors asking to be freed from routine assignments for two weeks to interview Arnheiter and some of the officers and sailors who had served

under him. By this time many of them had returned to civilian life; the remainder were strewn about the country at
Navy posts. "The Arnheiter Affair is one of those very complicated cases to which we simply cannot do justice under
the pressure of a daily file," I said in the memorandum. Permission came back from New York for two weeks of research.

I began by telephoning Arnheiter at his home in a San
Francisco suburb, explaining that I intended to write as defini-
tive a story as possible on his case. I intended to interview
him and his former subordinates to get both sides of the story,
and could not tell him how the article would turn out, only
that I would search carefully before writing. Would he cooperate? Of course, he replied enthusiastically, a thorough
story in *The Times* was what he wanted to help force the
Navy to convene a court of inquiry. He said that he would
expect me, in fairness, to talk to his opponents, but he had
no doubt that I would emerge among his partisans. He would
be glad to furnish whatever I needed—an interview of any
length, documents, anything I desired. Before the interview,
I said, I wanted to learn as much as I could about his background. The handiest source of information would be his
personnel file, including his fitness reports, at the Bureau of
Naval Personnel. (The Navy keeps a dossier on every officer from the day he is commissioned. The fitness reports,
periodic evaluations of an officer's performance over the years
by his immediate superiors, can often be very revealing.)
Since the Navy will not grant outsiders access to the file
unless the officer consents, I asked Arnheiter to telegraph
permission from California. That wouldn't be necessary, he
explained, because he had already written Representative Resnick a letter of consent and I could read the fitness reports
and other records in Resnick's office.

A drive to Capitol Hill the next morning revealed that
Resnick had not bothered to obtain the fitness reports. Also,
Arnheiter's letter of consent applied only to reports by superiors who had recommended him for command at sea. This
constraint presumably consigned to silence any superior with
a less complimentary opinion of Arnheiter. I wanted to see

all the reports. Another long-distance call to Arnheiter and an explanation of the problem. Would he please wire the Bureau right away because I wanted to get started. I reminded him that I had to fly to California in two or three days to begin the interviews. He promised to send a telegram that evening and assured me that it would arrive by the following morning. He had no objection to letting me read the entire file. "There's nothing in there I wouldn't trust you with," he said. "When you read some of those early reports you'll see that I had some personality clashes with some people. The judgment section of the Navy fitness report needs a major overhauling, anyway. The easiest way to axe someone is to question his judgment."

I telephoned the Bureau at 9 A.M. There was no telegram. Another long-distance call to Arnheiter. "The telegram didn't come. What happened, Commander?"

He had talked to Admiral Settle and his lawyer, he said, and they had advised him not to let me see the file. "It's just that I don't trust the Navy. If I open that file to you, they might pull a fast one on me and slip one of those fitness reports from somebody I had a personality conflict with to the *Navy Times,* that house organ of theirs, or to the Chicago *Tribune.* They'd print it out of context and I'd look bad." I said I could understand his concern, but I still wanted to read the file. I pointed out that if he did not let me read the reports, I would have to assume that he wanted to conceal something. "I want to assure you that I have nothing to hide," he said. A telegram arrived shortly. I rushed to the Navy Annex Building, rows of corridors stacked atop one another in functional military style on a hill at the south end of Arlington Cemetery, across the highway from the Pentagon. The captain in charge of the personnel records there explained with a seasoned smile that Arnheiter had, in effect, consented to my continuing ignorance. The telegram granted me permission to read Arnheiter's Selection Board Jacket. This held the details of his academic career at Annapolis and subsequent Navy schools, the records of his annual physical examinations, requests for assignment and similar miscellany. It comprised only one segment of the personnel file and did not include the fitness reports.

This time, when I called Arnheiter, the telephone line from California sang with a tirade against the Bureau of Naval Personnel. "Those people in BuPers are a bunch of damned obstructionists. They're always trying to harass me, to make me look bad," he said. He swore the term "Selection Board Jacket" encompassed everything "relevant" in his file, including the fitness reports. Would he please dispatch another telegram, I asked, and word it precisely to say that I had his consent to read "my entire personnel file." I repeated the required wording. He vowed to send a telegram by the next morning. It never came. When yet another long-distance call elicited more spleen against beadledom in the Bureau and a repetition of the argument that the Selection Board Jacket contained his fitness reports, I decided to leave for California to start the interviews and to resume the skirmish of the personnel file later.

The Arnheiters' redwood house on a hillside overlooking San Rafael north of the Golden Gate Bridge joggled with the kind of tumult only five young children—three daughters and two sons—can generate. They seemed a reasonably happy family despite the father's troubles. Even the overwrought dedication to her husband's cause of Janice Vaughn Arnheiter, a chunky woman who frequently interrupted the interviews with remarks of her own, had apparently not disturbed the children. The first evening, Arnheiter greeted me for dinner attired in dress blues with the same meticulous press I had remarked in his uniform at the Resnick hearing. He had a pleasantly trim, athletic build, marred only by the slight paunch of beginning middle age. His tastes were those a civilian might expect of an authentic naval officer. He smoked an elegant Irish pipe with a silver band around the stem. Over the fireplace hung a fine nineteenth-century primitive of a Yankee sailing ship.

That evening, and on several subsequent days, Arnheiter put no limit on the time he would spend with me. The problem was what we would do with it. I wanted to ask him about

his background and his experiences on the *Vance*. He wanted
to talk while I sat more or less mute until I was convinced of
his rightness. His answer to a question had a way of switching back into the reading of a lengthy testimonial on his behalf in the *Congressional Record* by Resnick or some other
sympathetic congressman. Or he might read a similar perora-
tion by one of his retired-admiral partisans urging the Navy to
"clear its escutcheon of this stain," or a "memorandum for
file" on some aspect of his case (he had written many and
they were clearly not meant to be filed away), or a detailed
recital of numerous violations of Navy regulations by Admiral Semmes and other members of the Navy hierarchy.
The tugging of wills would end in compromise, of course,
and we would wend our way back to my line of questioning,
if only to veer off once more. By 1 or 2 A.M., when we were
both too exhausted to continue, I would drive back to my
hotel, disturbed by a sense of incompleteness. I would feel
that though I had been with him ever since midmorning, I
had not mined nearly as deeply into the personality and the
life of this man as I wanted. He always agreed politely to see
me the next morning. I would come back and we would resume the interview. The strain was further increased by the
fact that I was forced to work in time to interview two of the
leading figures on the opposite side, Generous and former
Ensign Luis A. Belmonte, the first lieutenant in charge of the
Vance's deckhands. Both had left the Navy and were living
in the San Francisco area. Arnheiter also took to constantly
telephoning me at the hotel. An hour or two I had meant
to spend reading some of the hundreds of pages of documents the case had accumulated would be used up in a conversation about his civil suit against the Navy or about some
other momentary fracas with the hierarchy. On days when I
was not scheduled to see him, Mrs. Arnheiter usually extended an invitation to dinner. At last I resorted to having
the hotel operator tell all callers I was out, whether I happened to be or not.

How had he learned that he had been toppled by a conspiracy? I asked one evening. "Oh boy, was I groping at first!"

he said. "I just couldn't understand why I'd been relieved. I'd keep racking my brains and I couldn't find the answer. Then I got that letter." Recapitulating his testimony at the Resnick hearing, he described a letter that Generous had written to a Roman Catholic chaplain at the Pearl Harbor Naval Base, the *Vance*'s home port, claiming that Arnheiter was forcing the crew to attend Protestant religious services. In the letter Generous asked the chaplain to intervene without disclosing that he, Generous, had made the complaint. He had written the chaplain that Hardy, the executive officer, "advised me not to jeopardize myself" by a formal protest to the captain, the forthright and officially sanctioned procedure in such situations, "but to seek outside help anonymously." A copy of the letter was attached to a twelve-page denunciation of Arnheiter that Generous had submitted to the investigating officer at the Subic Bay hearing. "That provided the fuel for me to start thinking," Arnheiter said. "That letter was prima facie evidence there'd been a conspiracy to undermine the captain." As the defendant at the investigation, Arnheiter had been given copies of Generous' denunciation and the letter. "From then on I started to put things together and nail them down. Every time I'd come up with another piece, I'd raise my hand and say, 'Look, Teacher, I've got some more.'"

As he narrated the unfolding of the conspiracy that had contrived his disgrace after a fleeting ninety-nine days in command, Arnheiter reminded me not of a student, but of one of my Latin teachers at boys' school. His language had a kind of Victorian redundancy. "A chuckle" did not suffice, it was "a mirthful chuckle." "Despair" was not despairing enough, it was "the doldrums of despair." He had a way of wagging his forefinger stiffly at you, wrinkling his brow and pursing his lips into a stern frown to emphasize an argument, then reversing into a boyish grin when he felt that he had laid out some particularly telling evidence. There was even a classic, professorial absent-mindedness. We wandered into his study and I asked him to show me a bone-handled revolver that I had noticed slung on his hip in several photographs of the voyage. He took the pistol from a drawer and twirled it on his forefinger while he told me how his subordinates had lied in accusing him of leaving loaded rifles and submachine guns strewn about the bridge, a hazardous practice, since one might go off accidently when the ship rolled in a trough. I noticed that he became completely absorbed in what he was saying and was apparently oblivious to the fact that now I was uncomfortable standing in front of a pistol being pointed at me.

He had since discovered, he said, that the conspiracy germinated soon after he took command of the *Vance* at Pearl Harbor three days before Christmas in 1965. The initial motive was simple. His predecessor, Commander Ross W. Wright, had been "an easygoing skipper." The *Vance* had degenerated into "a roach-infested yacht" with little discipline and fewer fighting qualities. The officers lazed about every afternoon "watching matinée movies." Arnheiter immediately began to rehabilitate the ship and to transform it into "a man-of-war." The officers could not abide the necessary discipline, so they started plotting against him. The conspiracy gained impetus and further motives after the *Vance* reached her coastal patrol station off South Viet Nam. Arnheiter operated aggressively, taking the *Vance* close to shore to bombard enemy gun positions. Inevitably, there was the risk that the Viet Cong guerrillas or the North Vietnamese troops fighting in South Viet Nam would shoot back. His subordinates quickened their clandestine efforts to frustrate him because they were politically opposed to the Viet Nam war and were cowards. "They wanted to physically thwart me from seeking out and destroying the enemy," Arnheiter said. "They were afraid for their own damn skins."

Generous was the instigator of the conspiracy and the guiding intelligence throughout, Arnheiter continued, now describing his junior officers in more colorful language than he had used at the Resnick hearing. "Generous has an abundance of brains, but so did Professor Moriarty, the criminal genius Sherlock Holmes matched wits against. Perhaps that's the best description of Generous. He's twisted. He has a diabolical mind. He is a psychotic. He has a compulsion to push established authority as far as he can to see if he can get away with it. No matter what was proposed, you could count on Generous to dissent. He had to oppose the captain."

Given the determination of Arnheiter to reform the *Vance* and the reluctance of the junior officers to relinquish their comfortable habits, Generous had no difficulty stirring them up against the captain. Once this had been accomplished, Arnheiter said, Generous found a natural ally and puppet in Hardy, the executive officer and the hinge between the captain and the crew, the man who was supposed to translate the captain's commands into action and to administer the ship. "I should have seen Hardy's weakness as soon as I met him," Arnheiter said. "He was so polite, so affable. I remember saying to Janice, 'The only trouble I'm going to have with that fellow is that he's obsequious.' What makes Hardy tick and without which he would be in the doldrums of despair is his drive to be popular." Arnheiter explained that as soon as Generous had incited the other junior officers, this dominant psychological trait led Hardy to join the plot to get rid of the captain. "Hardy jumped on the bandwagon," Arnheiter said, "because he's got to be popular." Instead of enforcing discipline as the captain's alter ego, Hardy began deceiving Arnheiter about the clandestine mutiny which the other officers were mounting and Hardy was now aiding, Arnheiter said.

Personality traits had also made Ensign Belmonte, the officer who ran the ship's deck hands, the third major conspirator, Arnheiter said. Belmonte had been a very disparaging witness against the captain at the Subic Bay investigation. "He's a high-pressure-salesman type," Arnheiter said. "He's reckless and extremely immature. In wartime situations, a reckless individual is sometimes useful. There was a place for Belmonte. But he's an individual with no scruples, as evidenced by his testimony—an astonishing record of lying and gross exaggeration in a malicious way."

The inquest at Subic Bay had been a kangaroo court. "My God, it was incredible," Arnheiter said. "Every time I'd start getting at those rascals and exposing their lies, the hearing officer would turn off the tape recorder and we'd go 'off the record.' The man was maddening. I was beside myself."

A graver insult, Arnheiter continued on another afternoon at his home, was that Admiral Semmes, the deciding judge and jury as the Chief of Naval Personnel, had accepted this charade as an impartial investigation. He had overruled Admiral Baumberger, the Commander, Cruiser-Destroyer Force Pacific, who had recommended that Arnheiter be given another ship to command, and had waved away the conspiracy as a bubble of Arnheiter's imagination. (Semmes, a slim, white-haired man, is a sober and somewhat strait-laced descendant of the daredevil Confederate Navy raider Admiral Raphael Semmes, who captured or sank sixty-nine Union vessels during the Civil War.)

Arnheiter told me how he had flown to Washington to plead his case at Semmes' office in the Bureau. His description of his reception by Semmes was the same he had given at the Resnick hearing. "He ushered me in and said, 'All right, I will give you fifteen minutes to state your case. My mind is made up.'" Their first meeting had developed into a lengthy confrontation, ending in a standoff, however, Arnheiter now explained, and he had come back for a second session, which he also recounted to me in detail. As Arnheiter was ending his narration of this second face-down with Semmes, the telephone rang. It was Macon Reed, the Pentagon correspondent for the vaguely official *Navy Times*. Arnheiter motioned to me to pick up the receiver in the kitchen while he talked on the bedroom phone. Reed had run across a press release Arnheiter had disseminated while captain of the *Vance*. It described one of his engagements with the Viet Cong. A paragraph of biography at the end mentioned that Arnheiter was a "grandson of the late Baron Louis von Arnheiter, an early pioneer in manned flight." Reed wanted to know more about Baron von Arnheiter.

"I don't want to get involved with anything that is not focused on the rudiments of the problem, Macon," Arnheiter replied. "Answering tangential questions like that is a waste of my time and a waste of the public's time." Reed said he under-

stood, but that his question was a legitimate one. Would Arnheiter please tell him more about the baron?

"I will answer any question having to do with a court of
inquiry," Arnheiter said, "but I'm not going to get bogged
down in useless trivia." Arnheiter cut Reed off when he tried
to speak once more. "Why don't you publish some of the testimony given at the Resnick hearing?" he asked.

In the machine-gun fashion I had come to know so well,
Arnheiter read from the transcript over the telephone, focus-
ing on a section where Admiral Settle suggested that Admiral
Semmes ought to be court-martialed for allegedly lying to Congress about the circumstances of Arnheiter's dismissal. "You
could have a field day here, Macon," Arnheiter said. Reed
tried to interrupt several times. His weak "Now Marc, now
Marc," was to no avail. "Boy, what a banner headline you
could make with that, Macon," Arnheiter said, reading with
more animation. "What a challenge! The Navy would really
be in your debt for telling the truth."

"Well," Reed said, "I asked you the question. Give my
best to your wife, Marc. Good-bye."

"By the way," I asked, "who was Baron von Arnheiter?"

"He was my great-grandfather," Arnheiter said, correcting
his reference to the baron and pioneer aviator as his grand-
father in the press release. Arnheiter's father, I learned, had
been a musician—a tenor soloist who played the violin and
piano. He had worked as a voice instructor at the Hasbrouck
Institute in New Jersey and had written pantheistic poetry in
his spare time. He had also been choirmaster at St. Matthew's
Church in Jersey City, a lower-middle-class Episcopalian parish, for many years before his death on New Year's night of
1951, the year prior to his son's graduation from the Naval
Academy at Annapolis.

Arnheiter invited me to go for a swim at a neighboring
tennis club where his family was spending the afternoon.
Afterward he decided to drive his ten-year-old son, Jeffrey,
into the Marin County hills for some pistol practice. Wayne
H. Farnum, a petty officer who had been the second-ranking
signalman on the *Vance* and who had rallied to Arnheiter's

side since his dismissal, signing letters to newspapers and affidavits for congressmen like Resnick, had gone swimming with us. An angular young man of twenty-five, Farnum was a guest at Arnheiter's home that weekend, apparently for my benefit. Over breakfast with Arnheiter, he had told me he was convinced that Generous, Hardy and Belmonte had staged an ingenious mutiny by slandering the captain.

Now, as we were getting ready to leave the club, Farnum smiled at me, glanced toward Arnheiter, who was momentarily looking the other way, and rubbed the fingertips of his right hand against the palm in a rolling motion. His gesture was an unmistakable mimicry of Queeg, the captain in *The Caine Mutiny,* rubbing together the steel ball bearings he habitually carried in his palm. Farnum's act puzzled me, in view of his announced sympathies. I was embarrassed, and hoped that Arnheiter had noticed nothing.

Driving through the brown, layered hills above San Rafael, Arnheiter told me about his life before he had taken command of the *Vance.* His talk of his youth and the books he had read centered around an idea that clearly fascinated him —the concept of the military hero who lives above the rules that govern ordinary men. Lord Nelson, the greatest of all sea captains and the hero of the Napoleonic Wars, had won glory on several occasions by following his own instincts in battle and disregarding the orders of lesser men who happened to be his superiors. Nelson was his favorite hero, his model and his inspiration, Arnheiter said. He recalled the particular pleasure as a youth of reading C. S. Forester's Captain Horatio Hornblower novels, an adventure series inspired by Nelson's life. Most of his other youthful reading had also consisted of adventure stories and biographies of military leaders, especially naval figures such as John Paul Jones, Preble, Decatur, Truxtun and Farragut. As they grow older, most men lose the romanticism this kind of literature evokes. Arnheiter seemed to have retained his. Listening to him, you sensed that the romantic impressions of this man's youth had deepened with the years. And Nelson, whose unique genius in war had compelled him to defy the commonplace men set over him, had remained Arnheiter's central interest, an ideal that had carried through his Naval Academy years into adulthood.

"Nelson had a tremendous number of enemies," Arnheiter said. "He was only forty-seven when he was killed at Trafalgar, and he had this top-heavy group of fat admirals sitting on him who were dreadfully unhappy because this young upstart was winning all those victories. It's a wonder Nelson got anywhere at all, but the British needed someone who could drive Napoleon's fleets from the seas and those stodgy old plush bottoms couldn't do it.

"Oddly enough, I didn't disobey any orders while I was commanding officer of the *Vance*," Arnheiter added quickly, seemingly worried that I might think he was drawing parallels with his own career.

That evening over dinner, Arnheiter elaborated on a service intrigue he had been involved in as a junior staff officer in the Pentagon. He had testified about it during the Resnick hearing and had said that it might have contributed to his disgrace once his subordinates fomented the campaign of rumor and innuendo against him. At the turn of the decade, he explained, the "black-shoe" surface-ship sailors and the "brown-shoe" Navy aviators had been engaged in a feud over the adequacy of defenses against submarine attack by the Soviet Union. The black-shoe faction argued that the antisubmarine weaponry of the destroyer force had been completely outmoded by technological advances in nuclear submarine design and that nothing was being done to overcome this weakness because the aviators and their aircraft carriers consumed whatever money was available. The aviators countered that air superiority would take care of any submarine menace. Arnheiter said that in order to dramatize publicly the submarine threat, the black-shoe faction had him ghostwrite a book that purported to be the diary of a Soviet submarine commander who had defected to the United States. Among various harum-scarum exploits, the Russian submariner told how he had guided his sub undetected into New York Harbor and later nearly torpedoed the space capsule containing Colonel John Glenn, the first American astronaut, as it floated in the Caribbean waiting to be recovered at the end of Glenn's earth orbits. "The original scheme," Arnheiter said, "was to palm off the book on a publisher as a real diary and tell him we'd obtained it through Naval Intelligence. The Russian submariner was supposed to have written it in a hideout in Switzerland. They tried to do that through a businessman from the Midwest who was doing a two-week reserve tour at the Pentagon. But the publisher was suspicious and so they told him the book was fiction. I later discovered that the book's sponsor was a four-star admiral who was the Vice Chief of Naval Operations. I didn't know that at the time, though. The captain I worked for kept me in the dark as much as possible." Arnheiter said he was attached to an organization in Navy headquarters called the Progress Analysis Group. "It was a kind of super propaganda outfit. We wrote speeches, scripts for films, and tried to plant articles on subjects the Navy wanted to promote, like oceanography, in civilian magazines and newspapers. I remember doing one paper attacking all the money the Air Force was spending on intercontinental ballistic missiles. I called it 'the American Maginot Line.' We tried to get *Time* magazine to run the paper as an article. They wouldn't do it."

Arnheiter wrote the book during a thirty-day leave in June 1962 at his home in McLean, Virginia, on a Navy IBM typewriter. "I wrote a chapter a day," he said. "A lot of the material came from my own experiences as gunnery officer on the destroyer *Abbot* during the Lebanon landing in 1958. I went down to the Pentagon library and got the logs of the ships involved to make sure the maneuvers I described would check out historically. The captain I worked for fed me stacks of newspaper clippings, and a submarine officer in Progress Analysis who'd carried out some secret reconnaissance missions off the Russian coast gave me ideas and technical advice. I had a neighbor whose father had been an officer in the Russian army in the days of the Czar. He provided the information on Russian customs. It was easy to reconstruct the ship movements in New York Harbor the day the Soviet sub was supposed to have penetrated. Janice did it for me from the sailing schedules published in *The New York Times.*"

The book was published in 1963 by Doubleday & Company as fiction—*Shadow of Peril*, ". . . a novel of the deadly underseas struggle between the Soviet Union and the United States . . . a story that could have happened." Arnheiter chose the pseudonym Aleksandr I. Zhdanov as the name of the Soviet submarine captain. "It was the name of a cruiser in the Russian navy," he said. "I took it from the list in *Jane's Fighting Ships.*"

Although his authorship had been kept as secret as possible, Arnheiter said he was afraid that enough rumors of who Aleksandr I. Zhdanov really was had spread among the admirals to earn him the lasting anger of the aviators. He had already made himself an object of their resentment by publishing several articles under his own name in military affairs magazines on weaknesses in the submarine defenses. "The Navy has a long memory," he said. "Maybe when Generous and Hardy started to sabotage me, somebody in the hierarchy said, 'Here's that fellow Arnheiter making trouble again and now we've got something on him.' The four-star admiral who was the sponsor of the book died before I was relieved."

Janice Arnheiter commented that exposure to the moral compromises and Byzantine rivalries of the military elite while a relatively junior officer might have hurt her husband in a more subtle way. He was a thirty-five-year-old lieutenant when he entered the Pentagon in 1960. "A lot of Marc's friends said he shouldn't have seen all that intrigue while he was still so young and impressionable," she said.

The next day Arnheiter and I resumed the skirmish over his personnel file. I had scheduled a morning flight to San Diego to interview other former crew members of the *Vance* who were now stationed there. Arnheiter had again assured me that he had no objection to letting me see his complete record, including his fitness reports. As we parted after dinner that evening, he promised to have a letter of permission ready for me early in the morning. The letter would state that

I had his consent to see his entire personnel file, including all fitness reports. We agreed on the phrasing the Bureau of Naval Personnel required to open the file to an outsider.

I checked out of my hotel in a sleepy scramble and drove across the Golden Gate Bridge to San Rafael. I would barely have time to pick up the letter and drive back to the San Francisco airport for the plane. Where was the letter? Arnheiter apologized. He had been too tired the night before to write it. He would type it immediately. On the way to the typewriter in his study, however, Arnheiter found a fresh copy of the *Congressional Record* on a side table and stopped to read me another testimonial in his behalf by Congressman Resnick. Then he found a copy of a memorandum he had written on fifty-one separate violations of Navy regulations by Admiral Semmes. We had to go over these. They were vital to his case.

"Commander," I protested, "I've already missed the plane I planned on taking. I've got to catch the next one to San Diego. Please type the letter."

More and more memoranda came out of his drawers. He was stalling, of course, but he became so mesmerized by his words that he seemed to lose consciousness of time. He appeared genuinely unsensing of the inconvenience he was causing me. Hours went by. I began to feel a prisoner of this man and his voice. Yet I could not leave. I was determined to get that letter.

I finally maneuvered him into the chair in front of the typewriter. Arnheiter writes as fast as he talks. His fingers tripped across the keys and the sentences bobbed onto the paper. Reading over his shoulder, I could see that he was transforming even this supposedly banal letter of permission into a diatribe against the "character assassination" the Navy was committing by making public the Subic Bay transcript. The necessary phrases of consent were scattered here and there, though, and the addition of whatever else he had to say was his privilege. Midway through the last paragraph at the bottom of the page the words suddenly alarmed me. I would be allowed to see his fitness reports only for my personal edification and "not for publication."

"Wait a minute, Commander," I said. "The letter's no use to me that way. If you give us access to your file, you've got to let us publish what we see fit. We can't accept any restriction. You keep telling me you haven't got anything to hide."

He resumed the argument I had heard over the phone in Washington. Although he was willing to trust my judgment, if he allowed *The Times* to publish from the fitness reports in the Bureau file, the Navy might bootleg some uncomplimentary report to Macon Reed at the *Navy Times* or to another captive publication, where it would be printed out of context. I reiterated that if he wanted to be open with us, he would have to take that risk. The assurances of candor I had been hearing for the past several days now vanished. He flatly refused permission without the restriction on publication. By this time I had missed several planes for San Diego, but I knew I had to give up. The stalemate was complete.

"Well, Commander, that's your decision," I said. "I guess I'll have to be content with the fitness reports you've given me and try to find out what's in the others on my own." Under prodding, he had provided me with copies of several from files in his study. Some were surprisingly critical. Arnheiter had plausible explanations, however, that attributed each disparaging comment to the caprice of a superior rather than to any shortcoming of his own.

We shook hands and I drove off, with a promise to call and clear up any details we had not been able to touch on over the past week.

The interviews with Generous and Belmonte which I had crowded into that week in San Francisco had not borne out the portraits of them Arnheiter had drawn for me. Generous was an intellectual, it was true, and since his discharge in June 1967 he had been studying for a doctorate in history at Stanford University, in Palo Alto. He was high-strung and seemed more temperamental and neurotic than the average man, but I could find no evidence that he was "a psychotic" and an evil genius with Professor Moriarty's talents for machination. Arnheiter had described Generous as an atheist and a leftist radical, a determined opponent of the Viet Nam war. Generous said he was a practicing Roman Catholic. His politics seemed decidedly conventional. While he was, like most Americans, fast losing enthusiasm for the war, he said he had supported the Johnson Administration's Viet Nam policy and still more or less agreed with it. He had believed in fighting the war during Arnheiter's brief tenure as captain and during the eighteen months he served on the *Vance* off Viet Nam after Arnheiter had been dismissed.

Belmonte, another Viet Nam dissenter according to Arnheiter, claimed to be a war hawk. After Arnheiter's departure, he had spent a year with the Marines in central Viet Nam as a naval gunfire spotter, a hazardous occupation that consists of directing shellfire onto the enemy with a portable radio from an uncomfortably close position. Belmonte said that he'd enjoyed the work and had thought seriously about joining the Marine Corps. When Arnheiter had not spoken of Belmonte as "ruthless and unscrupulous," he had described him as "a beatnik." Belmonte did seem to lead a casual and somewhat disorderly life. He earned a minimal living buying and renovating Victorian houses in San Francisco. He was tough (he confessed he had once supervised while a boatswain's mate beat up a seaman who had repeatedly refused to work and had deserted in port), boisterous, profane, and given to some exaggeration. None of these qualities appeared to be the extreme traits Arnheiter had attributed to him.

I spent the better part of a week in San Diego interviewing others who had been officers or enlisted men on the *Vance*. On the plane back to Washington I read Arnheiter's novel, *Shadow of Peril*. I understood immediately why it had not been a commercial success. The book was badly flawed by its hasty composition. Arnheiter's prose was overblown, and the tale hinged on the fear syndrome of the Cold War that was fading by the time the novel was published in 1963. Yet none of this mattered at the moment. Against the background of what I had just heard in California, the novel was eerie. Some of the characters and events bore an uncanny resemblance to those connected with Arnheiter's captaincy of the *Vance* and his narrative of the conspiracy against him. Aleksandr Zhdanov, the narrator and purported Soviet submarine captain, was a figure from the mirror in which Arnheiter saw himself. Zhdanov was the natural aristocrat of Arnheiter's self-image—sophisticated, fond of impeccably tailored uniforms. But curiously, Zhdanov had the fundamentalist religious instincts of a Holy Roller. The transcending event in his life was a flash of inspiration in the Washington National Cathedral when he heard the words of the Protestant hymn, "Once to every man and nation,/Comes the moment to decide/In the strife of truth with falsehood/For the good or evil side . . ." The memory of that "soul-searching Christian hymn" later gave him the courage to disregard instructions from Soviet naval headquarters implying that he should blow John Glenn's space capsule out of the water with a special electric torpedo. Arnheiter had denied any religious zealotry to me. Generous had lied in accusing him of forcing the crew to attend Protestant services, he had said. The meetings were the usual moral-guidance lectures the Navy expects its captains to give to crews at sea.

The account of the end of Zhdanov's career in the Soviet navy was remarkably prescient of Arnheiter's own professional demise. After a dangerous and successful ninety-day reconnaissance cruise off the American coast that included the penetration of New York Harbor, Zhdanov was summarily relieved of command. The immediate pretext was an investigation of "alleged irregularities" in the way he had been commanding the submarine. (The language was almost the same the United States Navy was to use in convening the investigation of Arnheiter's ninety-nine days as captain of the *Vance*.) Zhdanov soon learned that his downfall had been secretly engineered by a malicious and conniving political commissar named Sverdlov, whose resemblance to the Generous of Arnheiter's description was remarkable. There were other disquieting aspects to the book. In an effort at comic relief of a melodramatic tale, Arnheiter had inserted a strange brand of humor that involved practical jokes with the submarine's commodes. He had evidently thought the anecdotes amusing. They came off in distinctly bad taste.

I put down the novel. The officers and men I had interviewed in San Diego had told me a story of the *Vance*'s voyage which agreed in essentials with that of Generous and Belmonte and starkly contradicted Arnheiter's narrative. Moreover, I had discovered that I was the first reporter to talk to these men. Although Generous and Belmonte had once been interviewed briefly by a reporter from *Time* magazine and another from the Columbia Broadcasting System, little of what they had to say had been printed or broadcast. Those journalists who had preceded me as students of the case had apparently not gotten beyond Arnheiter and the hundreds of pages of documents he had compiled to prove the conspiracy. It was possible that Generous, Belmonte and the other officers and sailors had all been lying to me, but they would have had to expend an extraordinary amount of time matching their stories to lie this well. I remembered Arnheiter's boyish smile across the dinner table a week earlier and his voice telling me how he had composed his fictitious voyage of the Soviet submarine, and the subsequent downfall of her captain, using a random assortment of facts and a liberal imagination.

The two weeks I had requested from my editors to research and write the story were already gone and I knew I was just beginning the work. It took me another two months to learn what had happened on that ninety-nine-day voyage. The story I eventually wrote for *The Times* was much more bizarre than the tale I had envisioned in the memorandum to my editors about the individualist, Arnheiter, "the oddball" who inevitably gets into trouble in a tradition-bound institution like the Navy. Here is that story, as well as I have been able to reconstruct it from the accounts of the men who sailed on the *Vance* and the documentary material I accumulated in the course of researching the Arnheiter Affair.

Most of the interviews with the principal participants were tape-recorded and each lasted several days. The typed transcripts of these interviews, together with the documents—the ship's plans of the day, the war diary and other records, the transcript of the testimony at Subic Bay and the subsequent official reviews and related correspondence, letters the men wrote home to their wives and families and written statements they made at Subic Bay which were not incorporated into the official record, affidavits from officers on other ships off Viet Nam who had observed the activities of the *Vance* and her captain, even the transcripts of radio transmissions by Arnheiter which had been tape-recorded by another destroyer captain—grew as my research progressed into a stack of source material four feet high. The problem was to select from this material the elements of a coherent narrative that would accurately tell the story of the voyage. During the interviews I had asked each of the men to recall his actual thoughts and feelings and conversations as the events unfolded. The documents provided dates and other hard facts against which to check the veracity of the interviews and to resolve the inevitable conflicts in memory. Where there were conflicts, such as the date on which a particular incident occurred or the precise roles on the various participants, I compared the interviews with each other and with the documents, attempted to discern the truth and put it into narrative form. The conflicts were of detail, not of substance. The evidence from both the interviews and the documents weighed overwhelmingly in the direction the following chapters of this book will take. This technique of reconstruction, I believe, most truly reflects the reality of those ninety-nine days on the United States Ship *Vance*.

1

THE CAPTAIN

From the morning one can tell
whether the night will be clear.

—Burckhardt, *Arabic Proverbs*

Tales of a man's youth reveal something of the man. Marcus
Aurelius Arnheiter was born in Jersey City, New Jersey, on
November 8, 1925, one of twin boys. He spent most of his boyhood in New Jersey and in Manhattan, where his family
moved to an apartment. His summers passed pleasantly in the
foothills of the White Mountains in southern Maine; there
his parents converted an old red schoolhouse near Kezar Lake
into a vacation home. Although his father, Theodore Arnheiter, and his mother, Dorothy Schuhardt Arnheiter, named
him after the Roman Stoic and emperor, Marcus Aurelius,
Arnheiter never developed any taste for a philosophy of quiet
endurance. He was an activist, and early showed the traits
of a man who seeks to dominate his fellows and to win by
refusing to conform to established rules.

Neighbors who lived in the same apartment house as the
Arnheiters, at 48 East Eighty-ninth Street, remembered one
of young Marcus' displays of will power. He joined the
Boy Scout troop at the fashionable Episcopal Church of the
Heavenly Rest, at Fifth Avenue and Ninetieth Street. He became a patrol leader and then persuaded a number of the
other boys to stop going to meetings at the church and to

attend Scout gatherings at his family's apartment instead. Forming his own troop out of these schismatics, Marcus led the boys in marching, knot tying, bugle practice and other scouting skills. His mother, a stocky, forceful woman who practices metaphysics and prefers to be addressed as "Dr. Arnheiter," encouraged him, according to the neighbors. When the scoutmaster discovered the reason for the abrupt drop in attendance at church troop meetings from some of the boys who had declined to join Arnheiter's troop, he and the church rector, the curate and several Boy Scout officials from the area formed a court of inquiry to investigate. The boys of the church troop and of Arnheiter's ad hoc troop were the audience. The neighbors remember that young Marcus was not intimidated by the proceedings. He defended his division of the church troop, accused the scoutmaster of incompetence, and claimed that he could handle the boys better. "We never faced anyone like this young man," the rector is said to have remarked. The court drummed Arnheiter out of the Boy Scouts. He soon rejoined and attained the highest rank—Eagle Scout. In California, he still wore his scout knee socks around the house and led one of the nearby troops on weekend camping trips into the mountains northeast of San Francisco.

Later, at another fateful turn in his life after graduation from New York's Stuyvesant High School, Arnheiter's will to dominate got him into trouble again, this time with his equals. His boyhood reading stimulated him to become a naval officer, but his mind would not grasp technical subjects like mathematics and engineering. The entrance examination for Annapolis, replete with questions on these topics, frightened him off. A couple of his friends managed to get into West Point, however, and their success at the Army academy encouraged him to follow. In 1944 he gained admission to the Army's Specialized Training Program at Amherst College, in Massachusetts, a wartime route to the Point. He spent the next two years there and at Fort McClellan, Alabama, and Fort Benning, Georgia, as a rifle instructor and enlisted troop indoctrination and education specialist, while awaiting an appointment to the Military Academy. By the time he received one in 1946, several of his former Army companions had preceded him. He had, unfortunately, made enemies of them. His manner had irritated them and they had resented the way he brandished his authority in the enviable jobs of rifle instructor and education specialist. During his plebe year they subjected him to more than the usual amount of harassment from upperclassmen. This hazing and his difficulty with technical subjects, notably military topography and graphics and analytical geometry, put Arnheiter in the bottom ten percent of his class by the end of the year. In the slang of West Point, he had been "found"—flunked out. He was permitted to resign, and told the records clerk he "did not wish to devote life to military service." When he filled out a biographical data form for a top-secret security clearance thirteen years later, he did not mention this West Point experience; the omission was not discovered by Naval Intelligence agents, who are supposed to investigate thoroughly any officer to whom such a clearance is granted.

Despite what he had told the records clerk at West Point, Arnheiter entered a famous Southern military academy, The Citadel, at Charleston, South Carolina, in the fall of 1947. He studied political science there and is said to have done well academically, well enough to encourage him to attempt Annapolis now, despite its forbiddingly technical curriculum. The following summer he obtained an appointment. He entered in July 1948 and graduated four years later, 628th in a class of 793 midshipmen.

Arnheiter was a considerable success as a member of the Annapolis debating team. His class yearbook predicted that he was marked for leadership. But by sophomore year he managed a confrontation with the Academy's commandant of midshipmen, a senior captain. Arnheiter decided that another student magazine, the *Trident*, needed "spicing up" to promote circulation. His hero worship of Horatio Nelson was supple enough for him to write an article for the magazine entitled "The War Crimes and Illicit Love Affairs of Lord Nelson." The commandant sent a copy for vetting before publication to a professor of naval history who was the resident Nelson scholar. The elderly professor was apoplectic at the article. It was not published and Arnheiter received a verbal keelhauling from the commandant.

In his senior year, when he inherited the power of a first-class midshipman over the rest of the student body, Midshipman Arnheiter became a famous devotee of the sport of "running plebes"—hazing the freshman students. Commissioned an ensign in the summer of 1952, he married Miss Janice Blair Vaughn, of New York City and Miss Hewitt's, a blue-chip girls' school.

He went to sea in the battleship U.S.S. *Iowa*, on shore-bombardment duty off Korea. Ensign Arnheiter is remembered by his shipmates for his smart appearance, for carrying a swagger stick, and for enthusiastically berating midshipmen who visited the *Iowa* on student training cruises for any lapses in performance or military etiquette.

Ill luck chose his next assignment—electronics material officers' school. He graduated thirty-ninth in a class of thirty-nine men and was sent to the destroyer U.S.S. *Fiske* as electronics material officer. The next two years were the unhappiest in his naval career until his summary relief from command of the *Vance* in 1966. His work was uncongenial, he did not get along with some of his fellow junior officers, and he fell into the bad graces of the captain. His fitness reports were unsatisfactory, and repeatedly questioned his judgment. In 1955 he suffered the disaster of being passed over for promotion to full lieutenant, a misfortune that befalls a rare five percent of all naval officers. When he was detached from the *Fiske* on August 30, 1955, his fitness report contained another rarity for a naval officer. It said that Arnheiter had received nonjudicial punishment for being absent without leave, AWOL. Shipmates recalled that Arnheiter had walked off his post as the officer in charge of a work party of sailors ashore to spend an evening with his wife. He was sentenced to a week "in hack"—confinement to his compartment on the ship except for trips to the toilet. Every afternoon during that week he wrote his captain a letter protesting that the punishment was unjust. This fitness report predicted that Arnheiter would "never make a naval officer."

His next skipper, the captain of the destroyer U.S.S. *Coolbaugh,* to which Arnheiter was assigned as gunnery officer, thought otherwise. He was a tolerant man who was amused by Arnheiter's unconventional behavior and admired his enthusiasm, his brashness and his willingness to act on his own initiative. Lieutenant Junior Grade Arnheiter organized and led a special marching detachment from the ship's crew in parades at the Key West Naval Base, the *Coolbaugh*'s home port, and at Mobile, Alabama, when the destroyer was invited there for a Mardi Gras. He was given a collateral duty as public information officer, and his imaginative press releases got the *Coolbaugh* regular attention in the local newspapers. He had an insatiable appetite for gunnery practice. On one occasion his avidness led him to construct a gunnery target that would not float upright and had to be rammed and sunk as a hazard to navigation. Whatever Arnheiter's faults, the *Coolbaugh*'s captain felt that he would make a fine senior officer and an excellent combat leader in wartime if he survived his junior years. The captain wrote a special fitness report that secured Arnheiter a tardy promotion to full lieutenant in October 1956.

This roller-coaster pattern of condemnation and praise was to persist throughout Arnheiter's career until his assignment as captain of the *Vance*. Some superiors were, like the captain of the *Coolbaugh,* highly impressed with his energy, imagination, and writing and speaking skills, while others were irritated to the point of serious doubt about his judgment and common sense.

At the Pentagon, where Arnheiter spent three years starting in May 1960, his verbal talent came to the fore: he served as a briefing officer in Naval communications headquarters and as a writer for a Navy propaganda brain trust, the Progress Analysis Group. More important, Arnheiter displayed an aptitude for the kind of corporate politics that help a young man to scrabble upward in any large organization. He parlayed his facility with words into some high and useful connections. He kindled the wrath of the aviation admirals with his ghost-written novel and his magazine articles on the billions that were being spent on super carriers and jet planes while the Soviet submarine menace grew and American submarine defenses went a-begging, but he aroused the admiration of surface-ship admirals and leading submariners. Several wrote or telephoned congratulations, including, ironically, the man who was later to seal Arnheiter's ruin, Benedict J. Semmes, Jr. On August 2, 1962, the chief of the Progress Analysis Group wrote a letter expressing "sincere appreciation for the excellent services rendered by Lieutenant Arnheiter during the period 15 March to 31 July, 1962. These services included research and writing in the fields of: oceanography, nuclear deterrence (mobile systems), anti-submarine warfare, hydrofoils." The letter's mention of "nuclear deterrence (mobile systems)" was presumably a reference to "The American Maginot Line," the article Arnheiter remembered writing for planned publication in *Time*. This was the article that had adversely compared the vulnerability of the Air Force's fixed, intercontinental-ballistic-missile installations with the virtual invulnerability of the Navy's mobile, Polaris missile submarines. Arnheiter's last fitness report at the Pentagon commented favorably that "he has frequently provided special research services to the Opnav Progress Analysis Group and flag officers in the Department of Defense in connection with highly sensitive projects of great importance to the Navy."

The magazine articles also gained Arnheiter the friendship and assistance of the retired vice admiral who was henceforth to be his professional mentor—Thomas G. W. Settle. Like Arnheiter, Settle was an unusual man. The admiral had begun his forty-four-year career during the 1920's as a destroyer ensign in the old Asiatic Fleet. "Those were comfortable years for a white man in Asia," the admiral reminisced in an interview. "You didn't need to carry money. You signed a chit for everything. At the end of the month, the chit coolies came around and you paid your bills. A man could even go into a bordello and sign a chit for a piece of tail." In between the world wars, Settle had helped organize the Navy's now-defunct blimp antisubmarine patrol squadrons. His politics had become very right-wing in his old age. He had taken to writing circular letters to his friends to encourage an invasion of mainland China by Chiang Kai-shek's forces on Formosa, and had very pronounced views on the need for adequate defenses against the Soviet submarine threat. In 1961 he was working for a California firm that was attempting to sell the Navy a remote-controlled hydrofoil boat that would attack submarines with torpedoes. Arnheiter promoted the idea in one of his articles, to which Settle wrote the introduction.

Settle, in turn, assisted Arnheiter and the Progress Analysis Group with the fictitious diary of the Soviet submarine commander by impressing a Doubleday editor with the novel's plausibility and patriotic purpose. Richard Nixon, then a defeated candidate for governor of California, endorsed the book when it was published in 1963. He said he hoped that it would be "widely circulated and read. In this period of 'phoney peace' I believe that any volume, like this one, which informs the American people about continued Soviet espionage activities serves a vital purpose." The ghosted praise of a future President notwithstanding, about half of the eight thousand copies printed were returned by the booksellers. Doubleday lost money.

By March 1964 Arnheiter had worked his way up to the job that is for destroyer officers traditionally one step away from command of a ship of their own. He reported aboard the destroyer *Ingersoll* at Kaohsiung, Formosa, as her new executive officer. Within eight months the captain of the *Ingersoll* was so pleased with the changes his deputy had wrought in the life of the ship that he reported he had the "best DD [destroyer] executive officer in the fleet." In a perfect fitness report, he praised Arnheiter for "magnificent leadership" in achieving "the extraordinarily high new standards set and met by the ship in matters of military smartness of personnel, in cleanliness and in overall readiness . . . I attribute such brilliant accomplishments very largely to Arnheiter's careful, exhaustive planning and tremendous drive." He endorsed "without hesitation or reservation" a request by Arnheiter to the Bureau of Naval Personnel for the captaincy of a destroyer-type ship. The division and squadron commanders concurred, and the admiral in charge of the destroyer flotilla forwarded the request "highly recommending approval."

"Lieutenant Commander Arnheiter's zeal and intellectual abilities are well known to the flotilla commander through personal observation," the admiral wrote.

The Navy values ponderousness as much as speed, depending on the circumstances, and the Bureau of Naval Personnel does not lightly confer commands. Arnheiter had to wait for another year. In December 1965 Arnheiter kissed his wife and children good-bye in San Diego and settled comfortably into the seat of a big jet bound for Hawaii. In the inside pocket of his dress-blue jacket were the orders he had sought since the day he entered Annapolis. He was to take command of the U.S.S. *Vance* at Pearl Harbor.

2

THE SHIP

The ship is the horse of the sea.

—Shaw, *Heartbreak House*

The U.S.S. *Vance* was one of those workaday ships of the fleet that rarely appear in newspaper columns and are forever outstyled by their glorious big sisters—the aircraft carriers and the heavy cruisers. In her twenty-two years of existence before Marcus Aurelius Arnheiter became her captain, she had taken part in no memorable naval actions. None of her previous captains had gained fame or notoriety.

The *Vance* was an ungainly-looking vessel. Her dull gray superstructure was replete with radar masts, domes, rotating-screen antennas, and needlelike high-frequency aerials that gave her the top-heavy appearance of a seagoing Conestoga wagon. Twin 3-inch guns in stern and bow turrets and two .50-caliber machine guns mounted forward on the highest level of the superstructure proclaimed her a warship. She was a destroyer escort radar (the *Vance* was DER 387), the smallest class of destroyer, bastardized with enough long-range radar sets, high-frequency radios and teletypes to create a picket ship that can loiter for weeks or months far out on the ocean to provide early warning of attacking enemy aircraft or missiles. A DER has other uses. She can serve as a communications relay ship, a weather ship or a navigational beacon. She can vector American fighter aircraft to approaching enemy bombers or guide American bombers toward foreign cities. In the Viet Nam war, the *Vance* became simply a coastal patrol ship whose mission was to intercept North Vietnamese sampans and junks smuggling infiltrators and arms and ammunition into the South.

In her first incarnation, the *Vance* had been a plain destroyer escort, a DE, and lacked these trappings of the electronic age. Her origins were undistinguished. She was hurriedly constructed in Houston, Texas, in 1943, with the minimum attributes of a convoy escort. Nazi U-boats were sinking Allied merchantmen like ninepins, and any escort that could drop a depth charge on a submarine would do. A full-fledged destroyer gets its high maneuverability and pirouettes of speed from a smoothly operating steam-propulsion plant that can respond within seconds to a demand for power. But the *Vance* was driven by four Fairbanks-Morse diesel engines that had to be laboriously shifted from forward to reverse and accelerated gradually to avoid lacerating their innards. At her commissioning in November 1943, she was named after a young naval officer, Lieutenant (j.g.) Joseph William Vance, Jr., of Memphis, Tennessee. He had been killed at his battle station aboard the Australian cruiser H.M.A.S. *Canberra* while serving as a liaison officer at the Battle of the Coral Sea in 1942, and went down with the ship.

Armed with depth charges and 3-inch guns, the *Vance* passed the first two years of her life shepherding merchant ships through the Atlantic and the Mediterranean. She sailed under Coast Guard officers and men—"the Coasties," in derisive Navy slang. Nevertheless, the Coast Guard gave the *Vance* her feistiest days. On May 11, 1944, she joined in the killing of a Nazi submarine off Oran, Algeria. A year later to the day, on May 11, 1945, she was escorting some merchantmen near the Azores when one of her sailors spotted a light in the blacked-out convoy. The *Vance* bore down on the light with as much speed as her diesels could muster and caught a surfaced U-boat in the glare of her searchlights. Someone yelled a few orders in German over a bullhorn from the deck of the *Vance,* and the crew of the *U-873* accepted the better part of valor. A prize crew under a Coast Guard lieutenant boarded the submarine and the *Vance* led her trophy to captivity at the naval base at Portsmouth, New Hampshire. The war ended before the *Vance* could see combat service in the Pacific. In November 1945 she was decommissioned and retired to the reserve fleet at Green Cove Springs, Florida.

She spent the next ten years in mothballs, until the Cold War and the growing nuclear threat from the Soviet Union inspired naval architects to transmogrify the DE into the DER. At the Mare Island Naval Shipyard in California in 1955, a plethora of surface-search, air and height-finding radars, weather instruments and high-frequency communications gear was installed on the *Vance*'s superstructure.

This paraphernalia took up a great deal of room and required technicians to operate it. The entire section of the main deck amidships, previously open with gangways, as on normal destroyer escorts, had to be enclosed with aluminum sides to provide enough living space. The Navy pronounced the cumbersome result "one of the most livable ships in the fleet." This description becomes distinctly relative when you remember that 135 sailors and 15 officers were confined to a ship 306 feet long and 37 feet at the beam, the widest part amidships. In such close quarters a man's bodily aroma, the noise he makes and his personal eccentricities impinge on the sensitivity of his fellows in a way they would never do on land.

Her refitting completed, the *Vance* went off to four and a half years of solitary picket duty in the arctic waters of the North Pacific near the Aleutian Islands chain, the approach route Soviet bombers and missiles were expected to take from their bases and launching pads in Siberia. A lonely tour as an ocean navigation station below New Zealand for aircraft flying supplies to Operation Deep Freeze, a scientific expedition on Antarctica, followed, and then the *Vance* went back to picket duty off the Aleutians. By early 1965 she was marked for decommissioning and scrapping.

The discovery of a hundred-foot steel-hulled trawler unloading arms and ammunition at Vung Ro Bay on the central coast of South Viet Nam that February gave the *Vance* a new lease on life. This evidence of extensive arms smuggling by sea from North Viet Nam and the imminent commitment of United States ground combat forces to the Viet Nam war made the Johnson Administration decide to organize a large-scale American patrol operation off the South Vietnamese coast.

In March 1965 the *Vance* was ordered to Viet Nam from Pearl Harbor. She reached there in April and was the first DER to take part in what was officially called Operation Market Time. She arrived in a cocky mood. On the way the crew had rescued an Air Force pilot who had bailed out of his F-100 Super Sabre jet when it caught fire over the Pacific during a ferry flight to the air base at Da Nang, South Viet Nam. Congratulations were radioed from the Air Force and the commander of the Seventh Fleet. The sailors tied a broom to the *Vance*'s mast to signify a clean sweep as she sailed into the task force of super carriers in the Tonkin Gulf to deliver the pilot.

Monotony and frustration, interrupted by tidbits of anticipation, ruled the remainder of this first, six-month patrol off Viet Nam. *Vance* crewmen were the first Americans to board and search a Vietnamese coastal junk when this was permitted in June, but no arms or infiltrators were found on this or any of the other 184 junks and sampans searched thereafter. In mid-August the crew watched from their appointed station several miles out at sea while the Marines fought, scores of them for the last time, on the Van Tuong Peninsula in the first major battle of the war involving American troops. Not a shot was fired at the *Vance* on this or any other occasion.

Bored with their role in the conflict, the men of the *Vance* brought their ship back to Pearl Harbor in September for repairs and shore leave. They were there to greet their new captain when he flew in three months later.

3

PEARL HARBOR,
CAPTAIN ARNHEITER TAKES COMMAND

> The captain of a Navy ship is the most
> absolute monarch left in this world!
>
> —*Mister Roberts*

On December 21, 1965, the day before the new captain was
formally to take charge at a change-of-command ceremony,
Lieutenant (j.g.) Edward Hopkins Mason was worried about
his engines. "Hoppy" Mason, a calm, handsome twenty-
seven-year-old Georgian, was the *Vance*'s engineering officer.
He spent most of his waking hours in his grimy domain in
the engine rooms belowdecks coddling the *Vance*'s cranky
diesels. The World War II diesels in the DER's were notorious
for breakdowns, and since a ship is useless if it cannot move,
Mason and Commander Wright, the *Vance*'s departing skipper, had worked out an elaborate system to keep the engines
going.

Ross Wright had been a difficult man to live with. He had
also been a good captain, as far as Mason and the other subordinate officers were concerned. None had much personal
affection for Wright; all respected him. He was small and
balding at thirty-nine years, with a frequently hard manner.
When he assigned a task, his inflection said the job should

have been done five minutes before. His greatest weakness was a violent temper that burst loose at any provocation. That November, the *Vance* had been sent to qualify in shore bombardment against a deserted islet in the Hawaiian chain. The gunner's mates on the twin 3-inch guns had missed the target several times on the first run past the islet. Wright had tossed his steel helmet down on the deck of the bridge and screamed and cursed at Lieutenant (j.g.) Thomas D. Williams, twenty-six, a compact and laconic Texan who was the ship's weapons officer. On the second run the gunner's mates put the shells on the target. After these fits of temper, Wright bore no grudges. He would calm down and help the subordinate to solve whatever problem was troubling him. Since Mason and the other junior officers had only a year or two of sea duty at most, they were dependent on the captain's knowledge.

Wright knew the sea well. He was not a Naval Academy graduate. He was a practical sailor who had been a chief mate in the merchant marine and had entered the Navy during the Korean War as a lieutenant junior grade. He insisted on personal cleanliness among the officers and sailors, but otherwise cared little for spit and polish. He had concentrated on making the *Vance* as efficient and well-operating a ship as possible. Wright had what amounted to a friendship for nuts, bolts and screws. He was always nosing about, checking for cracked paint, rust or salt deterioration, tapping the deck plates under the engines to make certain they were not rotting, and poking into corners where no one else would think to look. This attitude worked to Mason's advantage. Besides caring for the engines, the engineering officer is also in charge of the shipfitters, who do general maintenance and repair work. If Mason was in need, Wright responded. Together, they had developed preventive maintenance checks, a thoughtfully assembled stockpile of spare parts, and careful running procedures to protect the engines from unnecessary strain. The *Vance* consequently had fewer breakdowns than any of her sister ships. When the squadron had been ordered to Viet Nam in March, the *Vance* was the only one of four DER's that left Pearl Harbor to make it all the way to Viet Nam on the initial voyage. One DER rammed a pier on the way out to sea, a second had a serious engine breakdown en route to Guam, and the third tore the sonar dome off her bottom passing through the San Bernardino Straits in the Philippines. In August the *Vance* had received the squadron award for engineering excellence. "Hoppy" Mason was understandably proud of this record.

Lieutenant Ray Hardy, the executive officer, had arranged for Mason and the other leading officers to brief the new captain on the workings of their departments. Hardy had set up the briefings in the wardroom, the officers' combined dining room, lounge and conference room on the main deck. Arnheiter was settled in the captain's chair at the head of the table. At his turn, Mason was anxious both to display his own efficiency and to convince Arnheiter of the necessity of maintaining these careful engineering procedures in the months ahead. He had prepared a written report, setting forth his allowance for spare parts from the ship's operating budget, his current stockpile, how many enginemen and shipfitters he had and how many he would like to have, and the other details of what was, to him, a meaningful occupation. In the middle of his briefing Mason noticed that the new captain had a kind of blank, billiard-ball expression on his boyish face. "This guy hasn't been listening to a word I've said," he thought. "He's a million miles away." Arnheiter suddenly interrupted him.

"Were your parents divorced?" he asked.

Mason was startled. He explained that his parents had been divorced when he was in the third grade and that he had moved from Chicago back to Georgia with his mother. Mason resumed his briefing, puzzled at what relevance his parents' divorce could have to the *Vance*'s balky engines, but the captain interrupted again. He pointed to the wardroom extension of the ship's internal telephone system, attached to a wall—or "bulkhead" in Navy terminology—across the room.

"Why isn't that phone on this bulkhead over here so I can

reach it without getting out of my chair?" he demanded. He dwelt on this, asking three or four questions about it. He seemed perturbed that the phone extension had not originally been placed right next to the captain's chair. Moving the phone extension to within easy reach of the new captain's hand became Mason's "first real hot project" after Arnheiter was officially installed the next day.

The briefing over, Mason escorted Arnheiter belowdecks to the engine rooms for what Mason had anticipated would be a lengthy familiarization tour. They walked into the upper level of the main control space, where the throttles and master gauges were located. Mason tried to explain to Arnheiter the antiquated clutching mechanism for the engines. The clutches were one of the principal annoyances of the diesels. If the ship was moving forward and the bridge ordered the engine room to back up, the diesels had to be shut down and re-started to reverse the propellers. To restart the engines, the clutches had to be used, and the clutches operated on air pressure. Abrupt maneuvering—sudden reverses and shifts forward again—caused the clutches to lose air pressure and the ship to go dead in the water until the pumps could build up air in the clutches once more. Destroyer captains think nothing of switching propellers back and forth to maneuver alongside a dock or another ship, because with a steam plant the enginemen simply throw steam pressure from one turbine to another. Mason wanted the new captain to understand that he could not do this with the *Vance*'s diesels. Arnheiter did not appear attentive.

They climbed down the ladder to the lower level of the compartment. A generator was running there, and the loud noise irritated the new captain. He wrinkled his brow and squeezed his face into a funny little frown Mason was to see on subsequent occasions. Mason continued to explain the quirks of the *Vance*'s power plant in the shouting voice engineers use to overcome the generator racket and other din of their world. Arnheiter's irritation grew. He flipped his hand stiffly beside his ear and started back up the ladder to the wardroom. His visit to the engine spaces had lasted about five minutes. He did not go into the other three compartments, including the two where the diesels themselves were housed. Mason was more worried than he had been before the briefing. Arnheiter did not seem to care about Mason's beloved diesels. At the back of Mason's mind was a thought he did not dare to dwell upon: the new captain could not understand the mechanics of the engines and so he was unwilling to listen.

Lieutenant (j.g.) Tom Generous had a similar experience when his turn came to brief Arnheiter on the operations department. Generous used the diminutive of his middle name, Thomas, as a familiar form of address. He was a lightly boned man of twenty-six. His pale complexion was accentuated by large black-rimmed glasses and closely cut black hair, which had an unfortunate way of springing up at the back of his head, however much it was combed. As the *Vance*'s operations officer, he was responsible for planning the training exercises, patrols and other daily activities the ship conducted. He had charge of the communications section and the combat information center, with its radar gear. In battle, the operations officer transmits the information these devices acquire to the captain on the bridge so that he can maneuver and fight the ship. Generous had likewise excelled at his work under Wright, who had held an operations billet in his junior days and had taught Generous the trade. Generous had also prepared a detailed briefing for the new captain. By the time he walked into the wardroom, it was far into the afternoon, nearing dinnertime.

"It's pretty late," Arnheiter remarked from his chair at the head of the table.

"My time is yours, Captain," Generous replied. "I'm ready to proceed."

"Never mind. Just forget it. Go on home," Arnheiter said. "There's only one thing I want to know," he added, as Generous turned to leave. "Do you know the rules of engagement?" These were the rules, listed in the *Vance*'s operations order from higher authority, that spelled out the conditions under which the ship was permitted to shell enemy positions along the Viet Nam coast or to take any other aggressive action.

"I know the rules of engagement from our operations order during the last patrol, Captain," Generous said, "and I don't think they've been changed."

"Okay, fine," Arnheiter said. "I want you to know those rules of engagement."

That evening Generous, Mason and the other subordinate officers compared impressions of the new captain. With the exception of Generous, all had been disquieted by the experiences of the day. Their concern was understandable to anyone familiar with the Navy. A warship's captain has far more control over his officers and enlisted men than the commander of a military unit on land. The manner in which he runs the ship affects virtually every aspect of their lives. The captain no longer has the power of life and death over his crew that he once had, but the authority he retains is the closest thing to ultimate power that the modern Navy dares permit. In the Navy, the concept of command at sea is treated as having sanctity. Squadron commanders and the heads of other multiship units rarely interfere with the "prerogatives of the captain," the way each captain under them rules his individual vessel. Living and working within the confines of a small ship on the ocean is unnatural to man. It is an art that has been learned by trial and error over the centuries. The art is a delicate warp and woof of traditions, rules and laws designed to keep the sexual deprivation, the fear of the elements and the discomfort of the crowded living and working conditions from destroying men emotionally and provoking them to violence.

The captain is the high priest of this art. It is he, as the arbiter, judge and commander, who must keep the fragile system in balance. The junior officer is taught to regard the captain as a father figure, a man whom he will always address as "Captain," even long after both have left the ship. He is instructed to give his captain advice when he can, but to accept the captain's judgment once it is rendered and to be confident that the decision is a correct one. The junior officer's ignorance reinforces the relationship. When he is the officer of the deck, the OOD, on the bridge at night and another ship is approaching on what seems to be a dangerous course, he calls the captain on the ship's telephone and describes the situation to him. The captain either tells him what to do, or in unusual circumstances, comes to the bridge and handles the problem himself. Regardless of whether they like him personally, the junior officers and the sailors must believe that the captain's knowledge, his intuition and the acquired wisdom of his years at sea will bring them through any hazard. In this sense, the captain retains the mastery of life and death. He is responsible for the safety of the ship and everyone on it. "At sea there is God and the captain," said Chief Petty Officer Hector Cornejo, a brassy Mexican-American who was the *Vance*'s chief medical corpsman. "If you can't find God, you turn to the captain."

Implicit in Cornejo's remark is another reason why the captain is held in awe. The loneliness of command at sea, the sense of omnipotence that arises from the total responsibility a captain has for the ship and crew, can exaggerate traits in a man's personality that were muted and restrained on land. In Wright, the headiness of a captain's power had unbridled his violent temper. This fault had been balanced, however, by Wright's other attributes and by the quite different make-up of Hardy, the executive officer. Hardy, thirty years old, stood between the captain and the other officers and sailors, executing in detail his superior's orders and administering the ship. Hardy was likewise short in stature, yet without the self-assertiveness of many small men. His bland, even features bespoke a personality that was slow to anger. He was firm, but deft and fair and very polite, sometimes too polite, a man who avoided a harsh word or gesture whenever possible. He and Wright had made a fine team.

Now the emperor they knew was leaving, and the lack of interest the new autocrat had shown in the details of the ship's life unsettled the subordinate officers. Arnheiter's coming had also been preceded by some worrisome rumors. The rumors had their source in his service reputation, a second and unofficial dossier one would not find among the fitness reports in the Bureau of Naval Personnel. A man's service reputation is a collection of memories and garbled anecdotes, the sea stories that accumulate about an officer over the years within his own branch of the Navy. They meld into a kind of invisible portfolio he carries with him everywhere, a portfolio whose details always tend to be more colorful than those recorded in the measured language of the fitness reports. Arnheiter's service reputation was colorful indeed.

There were many legends afloat within the destroyer fleet about Marcus Aurelius Arnheiter. Ensign John J. Hannigan III, broad of shoulder, hefty of arm, a twenty-five-year-old University of Maryland football halfback who was the *Vance*'s combat information center officer, had it from an ensign on a destroyer that Arnheiter was so obsessed with the niceties of uniform that he had once complained to a port commander because a sailor guarding a trash dump near the dock was not wearing white leggings. The scuttlebutt also had it that Arnheiter had gained command of the *Vance* in some sort of irregular fashion. Was the new captain a martinet who would let the engines rust while he had them all shining their belt buckles? Generous told the others not to worry. "We're the best-operating ship in the Pacific, but we could use some spit and polish. Every captain has his quirks. This guy will be just what we need."

During Arnheiter's rousing speech at the change-of-command ceremony the next day, Generous decided the new captain was "in for a big disappointment" about the nature of the *Vance*'s patrol duties off South Viet Nam. As soon as Wright had formally passed him the command, Arnheiter strode, resplendent in tailored tropical whites, to a microphone erected in front of an audience consisting of the flotilla commander and other ship captains seated in folding chairs on the *Vance*'s bow. The sailors were drawn up in ranks on the dock alongside. Arnheiter announced that life under him was going to be "different." He promised to take the crew "where there is lots of action." He vowed that the enemy would feel the presence of the *Vance* off Viet Nam and that the ship would make a major contribution to the war effort. "He's got a tremendous misconception of what's going to happen," Generous said to himself. Generous and the others had also believed at the beginning of the first patrol that the Vietnamese junks the *Vance* inspected would be chock-a-block with Viet Cong guerrillas, pistols cocked and knives clenched in their teeth. They knew better now. Instead of guerrillas, the boarding parties had found malodorous fishermen.

"Make the signal, Mr. Hardy!" the new captain ordered with a flourish at the end of his speech. Hardy shouted a command and Signalman First Class Wilbert Boson, a tall, stocky black sailor who was the ship's leading signalman, ran two flags up the yardarm. They signaled "Splice the main brace," a traditional British navy term to order a ration of rum for all hands or to declare a celebration. The signal is not normally flown in the United States Navy because drinking is forbidden aboard ship. Most of the *Vance*'s sailors did not know what the signal meant. Arnheiter had carefully rehearsed the gesture with Hardy the day before. "I want the men to know that life under my command will be fun as well as work and action," he had explained. He had instructed Hardy to set up a keg of beer for the seamen at the enlisted men's club ashore, and beer and whiskey for the chief petty officers at their club. "I want the crew to have a drink on me," he had said. A few days later the new captain told Hardy to pay for the beer and whiskey out of the crew's recreation fund, the accumulated profits from the ship's store.

During a cocktail reception for the officers, the guests and their wives after the ceremony, Hardy overheard the flotilla commander make an uncomplimentary remark about the fact that Arnheiter had taken the center of attention away from Ross Wright at the change of command. Hardy was embarrassed. The departing captain is usually the dominant personality at such ceremonies. The occasion is his valedictory, and the captain who is relieving him customarily confines himself to reading his orders and making a brief remark. Since he has not yet accomplished anything, he leaves the speechmaking to his predecessor.

The next morning Arnheiter was reading on his bunk in the captain's cabin when a cockroach crawled down from the bulkhead and ran across his chest. He leaped off the bunk and yelled for Hardy. "Good God," he shouted, as Hardy ran into the cabin, "look at that thing!" The roach was now walking across the deck. "This ship is infested. Fumigate it right away." The *Vance* had bred an excess population of cockroaches as a result of Viet Nam's tropical climate and the carelessness of the cooks in disposing of waste food. Chief Cornejo, the ship's medical corpsman, had also noticed the roaches but was new to the ship and had not yet had time to exterminate them. At Hardy's instructions he telephoned a preventive-medicine specialist on the Pearl Harbor Naval Base staff and they set about fumigating. The fumigator was not pleased at being put to work during the Christmas holiday, but within a few hours he and Cornejo had the roach population back to normal.

The new captain set a brisk pace. At lunch in the wardroom on Christmas Eve, Arnheiter turned to Hardy and asked if a quorum of the ship's recreation council was present. (A recreation council is a committee of officers which considers entertainment projects proposed by the crew's recreation committee. The council forwards the proposals to the captain with recommendations for approval or disapproval.) Hardy, perplexed, looked around the table at the other faces and answered yes. Arnheiter said he was concerned about the fact that the *Vance* possessed only a slow motor whaleboat for small-boat operations. He could foresee many uses for a second boat on Viet Nam patrol—a sixteen- or seventeen-foot runabout with a powerful outboard motor. A speedboat would increase the ship's mobility and extend its range while inspecting junks, he said.

"How much money is in the crew's recreation fund?" he asked Hardy.

"About thirteen hundred dollars, Captain," Hardy said.

"Don't you all agree," Arnheiter resumed, "that the ship is hampered with only one boat and that it really needs another?" He glanced around the table. There was silence. He took it for assent.

"Who can buy us a boat?" he asked.

Ensign Luis Belmonte, twenty-five, the first lieutenant whose deck gang manned the whaleboat, volunteered to buy a speedboat at a marina near Waikiki Beach.

"Fine, Mr. Belmonte," Arnheiter said. "You get that boat on board before we sail."

Belmonte found a second-hand, sixteen-foot fiber-glass runabout that afternoon and bargained the owner down to $950 from his asking price of $1,100. Hardy was surprised that Arnheiter had not consulted the crew's recreation committee before spending their fun-and-games money for operational purposes, a violation of Navy regulations.

Earlier that morning Belmonte had fulfilled another special mission for the new captain. His direct boss, Tom Williams, the weapons officer, told him Arnheiter wanted an additional fifteen M-1 rifles, besides the fifteen authorized for the ship. As weapons officer, Williams was responsible for the deck gang and the manning of the ship's entire armament, the 3-inch guns, the machine guns, the depth charges, the hedgehogs (a second type of underwater explosive the *Vance* carried to attack submarines), the torpedoes and the sonar gear. Belmonte was the *Vance*'s acknowledged "cum shaw" expert, the man (there is one on every ship) who does the semilegal horse trading for items the ship wants and cannot obtain through regular supply channels. Belmonte took naturally to haggling. He had the physical form and agility of a bantamweight boxer, and a face that alternated pixielike innocence with unabashed pugnacity. Williams knew a lieutenant at one of the arsenal warehouses who would cooperate and not ask for the required approval from the squadron commander. Lieutenant (j.g.) Robert H. Gwynn, the sober, solidly built young man of twenty-five who was the *Vance*'s supply officer, gave Belmonte a simple requisition form with a request for fifteen rifles typed on it, and he set off for the warehouse. In questionable undertakings such as this, the captain will often co-sign the papers involved so as to share responsibility with his juniors. Belmonte noticed that the only signatures on the requisition were his own and Gwynn's.

Some of the new captain's out-of-the-ordinary requests were interfering with the officers' ability to get their mandatory work done and still find time for holiday leave before departure, but they were managing. Mason, for example, had to divert his shipfitters to raising the sink in the private bathroom off the captain's cabin so that Arnheiter would not have to bend over when he washed his hands and shaved. The shipfitters were installing a telephone extension beside the commode so that Arnheiter could talk over it while he sat. The new captain had also instructed Mason to weld steel chairs onto both wings of the bridge, with bar rests for his feet, because he wanted to sit out in the open air while the *Vance* was underway or pulling alongside other ships or junks. And Mason was to string a hammock for sunbathing on the exposed O-3 deck that roofed the captain's cabin, the sonar compartment and the two segments of the enclosed bridge—the pilothouse, where the helmsman stood, and a space in front with wide Plexiglas windows looking out over the bow. The O-3 deck was the highest level of the superstructure, three tiers above the main deck. Mason appropriated two chairs from the "ensigns' locker," the junior officers' compartment aft where Belmonte and the other ensigns lived. Mason, Belmonte and the rest of the officers carried out the tasks energetically. They were eager to please the new captain, on the theory that a favorable impression now would make life easier in the months ahead.

Belmonte did not feel quite so cooperative after December 26. That morning he and Ensign James M. Merkel, twenty-four, a cautious, soft-spoken youth from Columbus, Ohio, who was the *Vance*'s antisubmarine-warfare officer, were moving their belongings out of a one-bedroom apartment in Honolulu which they and some of the other bachelor officers had rented since September. Belmonte had a date that afternoon with Merkel's sister, who had flown to Hawaii with Merkel's mother to see the ship off. Belmonte was looking forward to the occasion. It would be his last liberty and his

last date before the *Vance* sailed. He went back to the ship
at noon to pick up some odds and ends. There was a telephone call for him. It was from Captain Arnheiter.

"Where the hell have you been?" he asked Belmonte in
a harsh voice. "I've been trying to reach you all morning."

"Well, sir, I don't have the duty today," Belmonte replied.

"I expect my officers to be on duty at all times," the new
captain said. Arnheiter informed Belmonte that he and Mrs.
Arnheiter were at the Reef Hotel beach at Waikiki. They
wanted him to demonstrate the speedboat and to take them
water-skiing with it. Belmonte was to appear with the boat
at 1:30 P.M.

"The boat is still at the marina, Captain," Belmonte said.
"I haven't had time to move it to the ship yet, and I'm sure
the marina's closed today."

"Well, get hold of the owner and have him open it up,"
Arnheiter said.

"Yes, sir," Belmonte replied and hung up. He telephoned
Merkel's sister at another hotel near the Reef, where she and
Merkel's mother were staying. He said he would be late for
the date but promised to appear by 1:45 P.M. The boat shop
was closed, he told himself, and he was goddamned if he was
going to spend his last day ashore taking the captain and his
wife water-skiing. When he got to the shop, the proprietor of
a bait shop next door told Belmonte the owner was away skin-
diving. Belmonte continued on to the Reef Hotel beach and
found Arnheiter and his wife there in bathing suits.

"The place is closed, Captain," Belmonte said, "and the
owner is skin-diving."

"That's all right," Arnheiter answered cheerfully. "We'll be
on the beach all afternoon. You just keep trying and bring
that boat here when you locate him."

The new captain asked Belmonte if, before he left, he
would mind taking a picture of the Arnheiters in an outrigger
canoe in which they were about to go for a ride. He handed
Belmonte a camera. Belmonte backed up the beach a dozen
paces and took a photograph. Janice Arnheiter called to Belmonte that he could not possibly arrange a decent shot with-

out having the sun at his back. To accomplish this, Belmonte would have to wade into the water. He was wearing a sports coat and slacks, and the slacks were the only pair of clean civilian trousers he had left. He looked at the captain's wife, assuming she was joking. The set expression on her square face told him she was not. "Jesus Christ," he said to himself, "she means it." When he hesitated for a moment, the captain impatiently flipped his right hand at Belmonte several times, with that stiff flip from the wrist Mason had seen, motioning Belmonte toward the water. Belmonte took off his shoes and socks, rolled up his slacks to his knees and waded out. He could not seem to put the sun properly at his back close to shore, however, and Mrs. Arnheiter called to him again. He got a couple of more flips of the hand from the captain. "Screw it," Belmonte decided. He backed up until the water lapped his thighs. He felt that the several hundred bathers on the beach were watching him. He waded back and handed the camera to Arnheiter. "Thank you very much, Mr. Belmonte," the captain said politely. Belmonte stared at Arnheiter's smiling face and thought in amazement, "He doesn't seem to realize he's annoyed me."

He rolled down his now wet slacks, put on his socks and shoes, and walked to the hotel for his date with Merkel's sister. As he entered the room, Merkel and his sister and mother were laughing. "That son of a bitch—" Belmonte started to say.

"Never mind," they interrupted. "We saw it." They had been watching from the balcony.

"We're going to have real problems with this guy," Belmonte told Generous the next morning.

"Why, Luis? What's wrong?" Generous asked.

"There are just too many little things happening that aren't normal," Belmonte said.

"You're too edgy, Luis," Generous said. "This guy is going to be just what we need." Generous had attended Brown University on a Naval Reserve Officer Training Corps scholarship after a year and a half as an enlisted Navy aircraft crewman. He had graduated with military as well as academic honors, had received a regular line officer's commission, and was enthusiastic about making the Navy a career.

"Tom," Belmonte said, "you're so goddamn gung ho, you make me sick."

The *Vance* sailed for Guam the following morning, December 28. Arnheiter did not guide the ship out of Pearl Harbor. Most new captains would have done so at their first chance, to display a prowess at ship-handling to their officers and sailors. Arnheiter retired to his cabin and let Williams, under Hardy's eye, shepherd the *Vance* to sea.

4

SQUARING AWAY

I'll be careful not to boo. I won't pick
my nose and I'll dress good.

—Ensign James M. Merkel on etiquette
in an opera box

On the way to Guam, the new captain summoned a "war council." The participants would be restricted to himself, Hardy and the other principal officers, Arnheiter told the executive officer. They would all wear pistols, the proceedings would be secret, and armed sailors would be posted at the front and back doors to the wardroom, where the council would be held, to maintain security. Hardy thought the captain was arranging some sort of elaborate jest.

"There's no Viet Cong out here, Captain," he said. "We're still about seven thousand miles from Viet Nam. Why do the officers have to wear pistols?"

"They're to emphasize that this is a warlike gathering," Arnheiter said.

Hardy laughed. The captain wrinkled his brow and squeezed his face into that odd little frown Mason had noticed during the abbreviated tour of the engine compartments. The "war council" was not a joke. "You don't understand the program, Mr. Hardy," he said.

"The war council is now meeting in the wardroom," the

captain had the boatswain's mate of the watch announce to the crew as the gathering got under way. The announcement was repeated every fifteen minutes thereafter. *"Keep silence in the area of the wardroom and on the weather decks above. The boatswain's mate of the watch stands armed guard at the wardroom door."*

Inside, the officers were listening to a three-hour monologue. The captain explained how he intended to use the sixteen-foot speedboat he had purchased with the crew's money as bait to draw fire from the Viet Cong guerrillas on the coast or in junks near the shore. To illustrate the scheme, he sketched an elaborate diagram on a blackboard as he talked.

"My plan has three phases, gentlemen," he said. He drew the speedboat dashing close to shore, with the larger motor whaleboat stationed between it and the *Vance,* which was lurking just out of sight over the horizon. The day before, Arnheiter had supervised the painting of fierce shark's teeth on the speedboat's bow by Belmonte's deck hands. He had also had Mason's shipfitters mount a .30-caliber machine gun on a pipe in the middle and fix a three-by-five-foot American flag to a staff near the stern. Mason was afraid the gunner might cut down the flag or kill another crew member if he swung the machine gun around while firing. The captain now explained the ingenuity of these devices. The longer he talked, the more buoyant he became. The nasal quality of his voice was sweetened by enthusiasm. "The Viet Cong will see the flag, and the Stars and Stripes will fire up all their hatred and bitterness," he said. "They'll look at this little fiber-glass runabout with only one machine gun and they'll think they can chop it up. But we'll have another machine gun in the whaleboat, and we'll fill the whaleboat with sailors armed with M-1's and Tommy guns. They'll radio us for help while they go in and support the speedboat with their heavier fire power. We'll steam in to the rescue and blow the guerrilla junk out of the water with our three-inchers. If the Viet Cong are in fortified bunkers along the shore, our armor-piercing shells will hole them like a Gruyère cheese.

"There's only one problem," he said, turning to Hardy. "We've got to find an officer and some seamen audacious enough to get shot at in that speedboat."

Because he was a bachelor and the officer in charge of the deck force, and because he had more than his share of moxie, Belmonte volunteered. He also "volunteered" several of his deck hands and gunner's mates.

"You're an audacious young officer, Mr. Belmonte," Arnheiter said with pleasure. The officers had already learned that "audacious" was one of the new captain's favorite words. "There'll be a Bronze Star in this for you," he promised Belmonte.

The rules of engagement in the *Vance*'s operations order, which Arnheiter had discussed with Generous, were designed to discourage shore bombardment or any other participation by Market Time vessels in the land war. The rules made it clear that except in emergencies, the ship was to confine herself to the dull business of inspecting junks and sampans for contraband and infiltrators. The captain explained to the officers that he considered these rules of engagement "unfair and overly restrictive."

"My plan will provide us with a means of getting around them so that we can shoot our guns at the beach," he said. "The rules of engagement and Navy regulations state specifically that we are to fire back in self-defense. I interpret self-defense to include the ship and its small boats, plural."

From time to time Arnheiter had interrupted his monologue, and pointing toward a door, had said to Hardy, "Ray, go check on that sentry."

"Everything all right there, sentry?" Hardy would ask, poking his head into the passageway. "Yes, sir," the sentry would reply. "All clear, sir."

"You are not to tell anyone, including your fellow officers who have not been permitted to attend, what we have discussed here," the captain said sternly at the end of the meeting. "This plan is classified. The other officers and the crew will be told later, on a strictly need-to-know basis."

The repeated announcement that a "war council" was un-

der way sounded "pretty ridiculous" to Radarman Third Class
William J. Sides, twenty, a placid, muscular country boy from
Benton, Wisconsin. Like most of the other officers and sailors,
Sides had been to Viet Nam before and knew he was not
sailing back to shot and shell. "What in the hell is going on?"
he wondered.

And every day or so for the next week, one of Mason's
senior enginemen would ask him what had transpired at the
"war council." Some of Mason's "snipes," as the engine crew
were called in Navy slang, were fairly salty sailors with half
a dozen or so years of sea duty behind them. "I can't tell you,"
Mason would reply. "It's classified."

"Planning a big operation, eh, Mr. Mason?" the petty officer
would say with a knowing smile before sauntering back to
his gauges.

On the afternoon of the first day at sea, Arnheiter had
called the executive officer to his cabin. He handed Hardy a
manila folder with about forty single-page memoranda inside,
explaining that each described one of the "very successful
programs" he had conducted while executive officer of the
Ingersoll. He instructed Hardy to issue similar memoranda in
his own name and to begin carrying out these "programs" on
the *Vance.* Back in his compartment, Hardy read the memoranda. The great majority dealt with matters of military and
social etiquette and details of uniform. Various memoranda
specified on what occasions junior officers were to wear
swords, how they were to "call upon" the captain and his wife
at their home, how a formal meal was to be served in the
wardroom. Hardy was something of a practical sailor, as
Ross Wright had been. He did not see how these "programs"
merited general application on a working Navy ship, particularly one preparing for patrol duty off Viet Nam. It was unlikely that anyone would have an opportunity to call on the
captain and his wife at home, Hardy thought, since Mrs.
Arnheiter was in San Diego and the *Vance* was headed the
other way. Hardy also was preoccupied at the moment with
the task of again familiarizing the officers and sailors with

identification-and-search procedures for junks and sampans. But Arnheiter was the captain, and whatever he wanted, Hardy would have to provide.

As he was musing over how he would conduct the mundane training lessons the crew needed to accomplish their work and still see that the captain's Emily Postisms were taught, Arnheiter solved his problem. The captain sent down a separate two-and-a-half-page memorandum of items he wanted enforced immediately "to square away the ship." The list was long and the items were all minor. Sailors and officers were always to answer, "Aye, aye, sir," to an order and "I'll find out, sir," to a question, if they did not already know the answer. They were never to reply with "Yes, sir," or any variant thereof. The captain and the executive officer were to be saluted every time they were met, and other officers were to be saluted on the first encounter each day. Sailors were to wear clean uniforms with shined belt buckles and shoes at all times, even when they were working. Officers were to be clean-shaven and attired in unsoiled khaki shirts at all meals and were to appear at dinner every evening in a freshly pressed and starched shirt. These aspects of military etiquette and dress are taught sailors in boot camp and officers at cadet school. Under working conditions on a small ship at sea they are usually enforced with discretion. The demand for invariably clean uniforms, for example, was a minor matter ashore but a major burden for the *Vance*'s tiny laundry at sea in the tropics.

The memoranda were issued over Hardy's signature, and the captain stalked the decks to monitor their enforcement. Whenever he spied a sailor with a dull belt buckle or scuffed shoes, or an officer at a meal with an oil spot or sweat stain on his shirt, the sound-powered phone extension in Hardy's compartment would shake with a *whup, whup, whup*. The captain had a characteristic way of twisting the hand-crank caller, the substitute for the ring on a conventional telephone, with a quick twirl. Hardy could always tell when Arnheiter was on the line. "Mr. Hardy," the burred voice would say, "please come to my cabin immediately." Hardy would climb the ladder to the captain's cabin for a precise account of the violation and a lecture on the need to eliminate such failings, accompanied by much wrinkling of the brow and wagging of the captain's right index finger. Hardy would then summon the responsible officer and reprimand him on his own appearance or that of one of his sailors. The officer would in turn castigate the sailor.

Belmonte's deck gang, the "deck apes" in nauticalese, were repeated objects of the captain's irritation. Arnheiter could not seem to understand that they grew dirty chipping paint and handling machinery. The sight of one of Mason's enginemen, filthy with grease and oil from his work, stung the captain like a hornet. As on most ships, the *Vance*'s enginemen customarily came up to the main deck after a four-hour shift in the 105-degree heat of the vessel's bowels for a smoke in the sea breeze before eating their meal. Every time Arnheiter spotted one he would shout for Hardy or Mason and angrily recount the same tale: a snipe had once appeared in greasy regalia on the main deck of a destroyer while she was berthed alongside a flagship and had annoyed an admiral.

"That's not going to happen on my ship," Arnheiter would repeat.

"Captain," Hardy tried to explain, "our enginemen never come up on deck in port. They only do it out here at sea where there's no one to see them. The man's been doing a filthy job down in the engine room. He's worked hard. The first thing he wants to do is to come topside and have a cigarette and relax."

"I don't care," the captain would reply. "They have to get cleaned up first. We must present a good appearance topside."

On one occasion the captain caught an engineman not only begrimed but reading *Playboy* magazine as well. He sent for Mason instantly.

"Do you realize what I've seen?" he asked.

"No, Captain, I don't," Mason said, surprised.

"I found one of your enginemen reading one of those magazines." Mason understood from the inflection in the captain's voice exactly what he meant. The sexual reveries that the unclothed female form stimulates are a sailor's cherished pastime. "I won't have that disgusting trash on my ship," Arnheiter said. "Do you understand, Mr. Mason?"

"Aye, aye, Captain," Mason replied. He ordered his enginemen to destroy their girlie magazines. The sailors hid them.

Early-morning coffee stains and cigarette ashes on the ladder leading to the bridge and on the bridge itself also annoyed the captain. He interdicted all smoking and coffee drinking on the bridge by enlisted men. The officers were still permitted to smoke there, "because they have more privileges," as he told Hardy. The officers could also continue to drink coffee on the bridge. "But they must drink their coffee in gentlemanly fashion, with a cup and saucer. No mugs," Arnheiter said.

"Captain," Hardy protested, "it's dark on the bridge at night and the ship rolls and the coffee's bound to spill. It's also windy, and the cigarette ashes get blown around. That's why we clean up the bridge every morning. Smoking is one of the small things a man can do to make his watch easier, and coffee drinking makes him more alert. We're not doing the men a favor by letting them smoke and drink coffee. Both are very definite factors in increasing their alertness and vigilance."

Arnheiter was not persuaded. He listened to Hardy with a blank expression and then countered with several illustrations of why Hardy was wrong. All were anecdotes involving the displeasure coffee stains and cigarette ashes had caused an admiral on a flagship and bore no relation to the U.S.S. *Vance* en route to Viet Nam. Hardy sensed that his protests were worse than useless; they vexed the new captain. Hardy got the impression that Arnheiter had somehow stored up these ideas during the thirteen and a half years of service that had preceded his captaincy of the *Vance*. Now that he was master of his own ship, he was determined to enforce them.

One afternoon the officers were instructed to wear tropical dress whites to that evening's meal. The order puzzled them, since dress whites are virtually unheard of at sea in a working-class ship. "All officers are invited to join the captain on the bridge," the loudspeaker announced shortly before dinner. They arrived to find Arnheiter leaning on a gyro compass on one of the exposed wings. He spoke poetically of the sunset and told the officers they must learn to be good navigators by recognizing the stars. Generous felt distinctly uncomfortable. Some of the sailors were snickering and grinning at the sight. "Christ," Generous said to himself, "we look like fourteen Good Humor men or the Bobbsey twins in these dress whites. What the hell is he doing this for?" He and the other officers would shortly learn why. Hardy was in the wardroom hiding a little slip of paper under each plate. During the meal the captain praised the merits of public speaking and the benefits he had derived from the Annapolis debating team and membership in Toastmasters' International while a staff officer at the Pentagon. Dessert over, he informed the officers that as he called their names in turn, they were to reach under their plates and take out a slip of paper. A speech topic was written on the slip. They would have one minute to think about the topic and would then rise and deliver a three-minute speech. Afterward the captain would give a critique of each speech. "We'll be visiting Bangkok for a week of shore leave," he had earlier explained to Hardy, "and my officers may be called upon to serve in a diplomatic capacity. I want to make certain they know how to speak in public."

Ensign Bernard O. Black III, twenty-two years old, the youngest and greenest officer on board, drew "The Proper Use of a Finger Bowl." Black had joined the *Vance*, still soft-skinned from college and cadet school, a month before Arnheiter. His bride had bought his uniforms for him and they were too large and baggy. Black could never seem to keep his shirt tucked in at the back. He had been nicknamed "Tuck" by Lieutenant (j.g.) Edward G. Fuehrer, twenty-five, an easygoing blond youth who was the main propulsion assistant, Mason's deputy. Black's face spoke fear as he read the slip of paper. "Stand up and speak, Mr. Black," the captain said.

Black got up awkwardly and mumbled for three minutes. The words "finger bowl" were barely intelligible.

In his critique, the captain ignored Black's incoherence and discoursed at length on the many elegant and hygienic uses to which the finger bowl can be put.

Merkel was no neophyte like Black. Yet Columbus, Ohio, was not a sophisticated city, and Merkel too was embarrassed. The words on his slip of paper read: "Etiquette in an Opera Box in Edinburgh." He stood and stammered while Generous, Belmonte and the others could not resist laughing at him. "I won't whistle," Merkel promised. "I'll be careful not to boo. I won't pick my nose and I'll dress good." At the end of Merkel's humiliation, the captain enlightened his officers on opera-box behavior. He seemed to take delight in the subject. Once seated in the box, they were to look about discreetly until they sighted a pretty and obviously unwed girl in a nearby box. During the first scene of the first act, they were to smile at her. If she responded, they were to smile at her again during the second scene. At the intermission after the first act, they were to wait until she had gone to the powder room, and then they were to walk over and leave a calling card on her chair. If the young lady had been sufficiently impressed, her servant would come over during the second or third act and make arrangements for the handsome young naval officer to call upon her at her parents' home.

"Jesus," Merkel said to Belmonte afterward, "how was I supposed to talk about that? I've never been to a goddamn opera." Merkel would not have had to worry in Edinburgh. The city has no opera house.

A few days out of Pearl Harbor one of the diesels over-heated critically. It exploded and ignited a minor fuel-oil fire. Mason sprang from his bunk at the detonation and the clangor of the general-quarters alarm and dashed shirtless and unshaven to the engine spaces. Bernie Black, who was the damage-control officer and one of Mason's assistants, managed to pull on a shirt but forgot, as ever, to tuck it in as he ran out the door of his compartment. Arnheiter did not venture below to inspect the damage. He mentioned the engineering officer's lack of proper attire when Mason hurried to the bridge to give him a preliminary report. And the captain ordered Black to tuck in his shirt.

Mason and the captain had differences over the engine casualty report, a radio message on the extent of the damage, which the *Vance* was required to send to several higher authorities. The Navy has a standing rule that all of its ships must report any mishap that impairs their capabilities. The rule is designed to provide accurate information on the physical status of every ship at sea in case a vessel has to be diverted from its normal duties for a rescue effort or some other emergency. One of the *Vance*'s four diesels was now useless until it could be repaired, and the ship consequently could not operate at her maximum speed. This kind of information is essential for a rescue coordinator, who must calculate how fast a given ship can reach the scene of a disaster.

Arnheiter first violated regulations by delaying the engine casualty report for twenty-four hours. He then haggled Mason down to an eight-hour repair-time estimate. Mason warned that eight hours was completely unrealistic, that several days would be needed to put the engine back into working order. "Oh, you can do it," the captain insisted. "I know you can do it." The eight-hour repair time stood. Mason sensed that the captain was somehow afraid of making a bad impression on his superiors by radioing the much longer, but honest, estimate. A rag left in a lubricating-oil line by the shipyard workers at Pearl Harbor, Mason found, had caused the overheating and the explosion. He told the captain of his discovery. Arnheiter did not seem to hear the words about the shipyard workers.

"Who did it?" he asked.

"What do you mean, Captain?" Mason said.

"Who did it?" Arnheiter repeated harshly. "Who doesn't want to go to Viet Nam?"

Mason's light features colored with indignation. "None of my men would ever do anything like that, Captain," he said. "I'm upset that you would even mention something like that."

There was an embarrassing silence. The captain had that billiard-ball expression on his face again.

The engine repairs were to use up a week at the Guam Naval Station after the *Vance* docked at the island on January 7 at the end of a tardy, nine-day voyage.

The night before the *Vance* departed on January 14 to resume the journey to Viet Nam, the captain staked a party for the sailors at the Guam enlisted men's club. He financed the festivities with the remains of the crew's recreation fund, sorely depleted by the purchase of the speedboat at Pearl Harbor. Arnheiter appointed Signalman Second Class Wayne Farnum, twenty-two, as chief shore patrolman for the evening. The appointment made Farnum the sheriff for the night. "Flash" is a Navy nickname for signalmen which is applied selectively. Farnum was called "Flash." He was, in his self-description, "a lone wolf." One reason for Farnum's unpopularity was that he was more intelligent than the majority of the sailors and he let them know it. While his education had been limited to high school and a summer college course, he aspired to become an officer and liked to assert the knowledge he had garnered from his reading and the minute authority he possessed as a junior petty officer. His intentions were usually good, but they had unfortunate consequences just the same. Farnum had a fine sense for the proper procedure in everything, a trait akin to the captain's pleasure in protocol. Since Arnheiter had come aboard, they had formed a friendship. The captain spoke kindly to Farnum whenever they met, and they met often because Farnum worked on the bridge as the assistant to Boson, the leading signalman. Arnheiter frequently invited Farnum to his cabin for long conversations.

By the end of the evening, the club's wine and beer stocks were as depleted as the crew's recreation fund. The traditional fistfight between Mason's snipes and Belmonte's deck apes, who were inveterate rivals, broke out on the bus back to the ship. Farnum immediately invoked his authority as chief shore patrolman and was told by the combatants on both sides that he committed indecent acts with his mother. The brawl flared again aboard ship. Farnum again intervened and was told more emphatically that he habitually dishonored his mother. He stalked up to the captain's cabin and reported the four principal offenders. One was a fireman's apprentice who worked for Mason, two others were seamen in Belmonte's gang, one a hefty plowman from South Dakota nicknamed "Moose," the other an equally earthy sailor with a tattoo on his chest of crossed American flags and a scantily clad female perched in between. The fourth offender was one of Belmonte's junior petty officers who had a reputation for quick fists.

The new captain seized the opportunity to demonstrate that under his reign no infringements of discipline would be tolerated. He held two public captain's masts.

A captain's mast is the lowest type of formal punishment in the Navy. It is called nonjudicial punishment. Although formal charges are drawn up and the accused is informed of his constitutional rights, the captain acts as sole judge and jury. Both the officer who is the sailor's immediate superior and the next ranking officer in charge of the sailor's department are usually present, to recommend leniency or strict punishment, whichever appears appropriate. A captain's mast is held in private, on the theory that the accused should not be subjected to the additional punishment of being degraded in front of his peers. The custom of public captain's masts died in the United States Navy with the nineteenth century. The custom had expired—that is, until Captain Arnheiter resurrected it. The crew of the *Vance* would learn to their discomfort that the new captain enjoyed reviving embalmed traditions.

The captain ordered the ship's senior clerk, the "chief yeoman," to type the charge sheets during the predawn hours. He did not notify Belmonte (who happened to be the *Vance*'s legal officer, as well as the immediate superior of three of the men), or any of the other officers. The accused were not awakened and informed of their constitutional rights.

After breakfast in the morning, the captain had a microphone and a lectern, draped with a large flag, set up on the O-1 deck just aft of the smokestack. He instructed Hardy to form the crew in ranks on the dock alongside the ship. The first three culprits, the fireman's apprentice and the two seamen, were suddenly informed of the charges—willful disobedience of an order and interference with a petty officer—and marched before the captain. While the three sailors stood at attention in front of Arnheiter, transfixed with the multiple pain of shame, hangovers and bruises, the captain delivered a sermon as fiery as his speech at the change-of-command ceremony. Proper respect for petty officers was an absolute necessity on his ship. He would brook nothing less at all times. The captain read the charges and held the microphone toward each of the sailors in turn.

"Do you have anything to say in your defense?" he asked in a resonant voice.

None of the sailors said anything. They wished they could miraculously fall through the sun-seared deck into the harbor below. They looked down at their shoes. A crowd of Guamanian shipyard workers had gathered on the pier beside the crew to watch the curious spectacle.

"What would your mother and father think of you if they could see you like this?" the captain asked. "Is this the way you serve your country?" The flag draped over the lectern rebuked the seamen with a loud silence. The knees of the fireman's apprentice were shaking.

"Think of how you have let down your shipmates by spreading disorder and indiscipline on a man-of-war," Arnheiter said. "How can we depend on men like you to do your duty in the violence and peril of battle?" His voice rising, he turned toward the rows of sailors on the dock. "I intend to take this ship into harm's way," he said. "If the enemy can be engaged, we shall engage him." One of the captain's heroes, John Paul Jones, had remarked during the American Revolution that he would decline command of "any ship that does not sail fast; for I intend to go in harm's way."

Boiler Tender First Class Richard A. MacSaveny, a tall twenty-five-year-old petty officer from eastern Long Island, shuddered. Danger was a risk of a sailor's trade and MacSaveny, like the other men, was prepared to face what danger came his way. But something in the tenor of the captain's voice, something about the words Arnheiter used and the look of a zealot on his face, spooked MacSaveny.

The captain meted out severe punishment to the three sailors: reduction two grades to the rank of seaman recruit for the plowman from South Dakota, who had allegedly given Farnum the most trouble, and $100 fines for all.

Judgment rendered on the ordinary seamen, Arnheiter had Hardy muster all the petty officers in the crew's mess compartment on the main deck. At the end of a second harangue on respect for petty officers, he turned to the fourth culprit, the junior petty officer who worked for Belmonte.

"Stand up," the captain said. "You're at mast."

The petty officer leaped to his feet, astonished, from one of the stools beside the tables.

Arnheiter read the charges of disorderly conduct and then asked the assembled petty officers to raise their hands in the gestures of the Roman arena: thumbs down if they wanted the accused punished, thumbs up if they thought him not guilty.

Radarman Second Class Robert V. Cheadle, twenty-four, a short, outspoken young man with red hair, from Billings, Montana, who worked in the combat information center, kept his hands folded on his lap. "This whole thing is really lousy," he muttered to another petty officer beside him. "Who in the hell does this guy think he is?"

Several of Cheadle's fellow petty officers also held their hands folded on their laps. Despite the paucity of thumbs down, Arnheiter found the petty officer guilty. He was fined $200.

The captain ordered the engines started. The *Vance* moved off for Viet Nam.

Prior to the week's stop at Guam, on the first Sunday morning at sea out of Pearl Harbor, Captain Arnheiter had also seen to the spiritual needs of his crew. He directed Hardy to delete from the Sunday plan of the day the scheduled Protestant lay-leader service. Under Captain Wright, voluntary Protestant and Catholic lay services had been held every Sunday on the *Vance*. Each service was led by an officer of the faith, who volunteered for the duty. "I'll print up something myself," the new captain informed Hardy. "Send Hannigan up to my cabin with one of the Protestant hymnals." Ensign Hannigan was the Protestant lay leader. Most of Saturday night, Arnheiter was busy writing at the small desk opposite his bunk. In the early-morning hours, Hardy saw the chief yeoman and one of his assistants frantically typing and mimeographing in the ship's office. A substitute plan of the day was soon posted, which ordered "all hands not actually on watch" to gather on the fantail at 10:20 to hear "the captain's remarks." Arnheiter also had Hardy strip the watches of half the men who were working, to make certain there would be maximum attendance. The seamen mustered in front of the same microphone and flag-draped lectern the captain would use as props to dramatize his public dispensation of justice. They waited, shuffling their feet, for ten minutes before Arnheiter appeared in natty tropical whites, with Hardy following right behind.

"Have the men uncover, Mr. Hardy," the captain said as he stepped behind the microphone.

"Uncover," Hardy commanded, and the officers and sailors doffed their hats, an act that is performed in the Navy only in church.

Arnheiter gazed intently for several moments at the rows of faces before him. His large, round dark eyes moved slowly along the ranks from man to man.

"General George S. Patton, 'old Blood and Guts,' . . . before his big offensive after the Battle of the Bulge, issued a general order to all his troops," the captain's voice rang out. "It was to be read by all his men.

"What was it?" Arnheiter asked, poking a stiff forefinger at his crew. "It was a prayer to Almighty God," he said, his voice louder now, "and it began, 'Sir, this is Patton talking.' General Patton wanted his men to know that their general was asking Our Father who art in heaven for help."

The *Vance* was headed for "a combat zone," the captain

reminded the assembly. And all the great American military leaders of the past, Admiral David G. Farragut, General Thomas J. "Stonewall" Jackson, General of the Army Douglas MacArthur, had known a deep faith in God. They had always prayed before battle.

"My friends, there is no atheism in a foxhole," the captain shouted. "There is no atheism on a sinking ship. We have a movie on board called *Titanic*. It shows how at the end of the *Titanic*'s life, after she had struck an iceberg and was sinking, the ship's band stopped playing ragtime and played 'Nearer, My God, to Thee.' For many, it may have been too late. For the Bible says: 'Remember thy Creator in the days of thy youth.' "

The captain led his congregation in two Protestant hymns, "Faith of Our Fathers" and "Oh God, Our Help in Ages Past." He ended the service with the singing of the Navy hymn, "Eternal Father! Strong to Save." Any sailor or officer who did not seem to be singing enthusiastically was spurred on with an angry scowl. To make certain the crew would know the verses of the hymns and would follow his sermon carefully, Arnheiter had arranged for mimeographed copies of both to be passed out in advance. The singing over, he urged the men to mail these mimeographed copies home to their wives and parents "to show your loved ones the upright life you are leading on this ship."

Hardy was frightened. "This really looks like a time bomb, this required church service thing, Captain," he said to Arnheiter as soon as they were alone.

The captain reacted with a condescending smile. "You know that at the Naval Academy all midshipmen are required to attend church services. In boot camp all sailors are required to go to church."

"Yes, Captain," Hardy said, "but they go to a service of their choice, and the regulations state explicitly that we are not supposed to force men to attend any type of service at sea."

The captain did not seem to hear Hardy's words. "As a

matter of fact, who used to hold services on the ship a hundred years ago?" he asked.

Hardy thought for a moment. "The captain," he said. "He would inspect the ship on Sunday morning, give out punishment and hold divine services."

Arnheiter beamed at Hardy's knowledge of naval history. "That's it," he said. "Look, Ray," he continued in a friendly tone, "there are a lot of young sailors on this ship, minors who have not yet matured to manhood. They're fresh-caught lads and they need some spiritual guidance and uplifting. If they were given their choice they wouldn't attend, because they don't really know what's good for them yet. Therefore, we will see that they have this experience. It's our responsibility. We are their parents now."

"But, Captain," Hardy argued, "this could be against freedom of religion. You're not supposed to have to go to church."

"You just don't understand, Ray. I've thought about this a long time and I know this is what has to be done," the captain said impatiently. Hardy insisted that in conversations with the officers or enlisted men Arnheiter at least not admit that the gatherings were church services.

"Well, what do you suggest I call them?" the captain asked.

"I recommend you call them moral-guidance lectures," Hardy said. Henceforth the captain's compulsory Sunday services were announced in the plan of the day under the ambiguous title "All Hands Aft."

The Roman Catholics among the crew were outraged. Belmonte, who was the Catholic lay leader, and Chief Petty Officer Cornejo, the senior medical corpsman, a quick-witted man with a brambly sense of self-respect, felt their constitutional rights were being violated. Some of their more unsophisticated coreligionists, the Filipino stewards and the Puerto Rican and Mexican-American sailors, told Belmonte they were committing a sin by attending a Protestant service. Belmonte protested to Hardy, but the executive officer, to protect the captain, took the line that the fantail services were the kind of routine moral-guidance lectures a captain is supposed to give his crew. He warned Belmonte that all Catholics would have to attend in the future. Belmonte called the Catholic sailors together and assured them that since their presence was forced, they were not expressing approval of another faith and thus were not committing a sin.

Generous also happened to be a Roman Catholic. He had escaped the first "All Hands Aft" by the accident of being officer of the deck on the bridge that morning. The sounds of the hymn singing wafted forward, however, and the other officers later gave him a vivid account. Generous' parents had separated when he was in the sixth grade. His adolescence had been a trying one and he was an intense man, given to occasional moods of exhilaration or depression. "God," he thought, lying on his bunk that afternoon, "I can't go to one of those things. I just can't do it." He had not been attending services regularly in his own faith because he was having difficulty, in his mind, in living up to the rigorous ideals of Roman Catholicism. With his conscience troubling him he felt uncomfortable going to mass, and so he had been avoiding it. His failure to fulfill the ideals of his church had not, however, weakened his faith. He was a convinced Roman Catholic. He had no wish to turn his back on the church of his faith for one in which he did not believe. And he rebelled instinctively against being forced to attend any religious service, particularly a Protestant one. With the exception of a baccalaureate service at graduation from Brown University, he had never been to Protestant worship.

That Sunday night, Generous was again OOD on the eight-to-midnight watch. Arnheiter came up for a look at the stars, and Generous decided to confess his dilemma.

"Can I speak to you about something, Captain?" he asked.

"Certainly, Tom," Arnheiter said. "Go ahead."

Generous had no other grievances against the new captain. Some of Arnheiter's actions had seemed bizarre, but Generous had pigeonholed these as the idiosyncrasies any skipper might display. He admired the way the captain had been burnishing the *Vance* with spit and polish, and began by telling Arnheiter this.

"Captain," he said, "you know, my morale is really outstanding. I've really enjoyed your spit-and-polish program. I think it's just what this ship needs to go along with an outstanding record operationally. I like the new emphasis we're placing on military protocol and the chain of command and all that. There's just one thing that bothers me."

"What's that, Tom?" Arnheiter said.

"It's this business about the church service this morning. I think spiritual guidance is wonderful, but it's pretty dangerous to require people to go to these things, to force them to go."

Despite Hardy's advice of the morning, the captain made no attempt to equivocate over the nature of his fantail exercise. Instead he gave Generous, as he had Hardy, his pep talk about "all the fresh-caught lads aboard who need a spiritual awakening."

"I can understand your intentions, Captain," Generous said, "but the Constitution of the United States is pretty clear on this. You can't force people to go to religious services."

"Well, you're a good department head and you'll back up the program and go," Arnheiter answered with a tolerant smile.

Generous tried the tack that some military orders were "superseded by higher moral demands" and told the captain of his own disturbed conscience. Whatever his difficulties in meeting the ideals of his own faith, he explained, "I'm not going to compound my problem by going to someone else's church."

"You're a department head and you'll go," the captain said, turning away and walking off the bridge to his cabin.

5

ON THE EVE OF BATTLE

Tom, I've wanted a ship all my life, and
I've known how I was going to run it when
I got it.

—Captain Arnheiter to Lieutenant Generous

As the *Vance* sailed toward the war in Viet Nam, the 14 officers and 135 men aboard her sought to adjust to life under Captain Arnheiter. Accommodation was difficult within the confines of a steel hull that measured 306 feet long by 37 feet wide at the beam.

To avoid the offense their begrimed appearance caused the captain's eyes, the enginemen denied themselves the pleasure of a cigarette and a whiff of sea air after a four-hour shift in the heat and humidity of their habitat. In fact, some took to sleeping in the engine compartments when they were not working. The captain never ventured down there and they ran no risk of being spotted during one of his occasional inspections of the crew's mess and bunking quarters.

The officers abstained from smoking on the bridge because the sailors were forbidden the privilege. They adopted the habit of sending the men below in turns to fetch coffee for them. The errand gave the sailor a few minutes to swallow some coffee himself and to have a quick smoke. Drinking from a cup and saucer diminished the enjoyment of the coffee for the officers, however. The rolling of the ship in the trough forced them to hold the cup and saucer with both hands. An ungentlemanly mug required only one hand and left the other free to take notes, to raise binoculars, or to balance oneself in a heavy sea.

Whenever an officer was not about, the sailors stuffed the ship's loudspeaker extensions with rags to dim a bedlam that whiz-banged on their nerves with the regularity of a grand-father clock sounding the hours. For the boatswain's whistle that had formerly piped the coming of the day at 6:30 A.M., the new captain had substituted an innovation called "Hell-cats Reveille." This was a turned-on version of the Army's traditional reveille call, which Arnheiter had heard the West Point band play during his year as a plebe there. It now rat-tled souls for four minutes and ten seconds every morning on the *Vance,* a pandemonium of fifes, drums and bugle blasts played at peak decibels over the ship's loudspeaker system. The captain had brought a record aboard with him at Pearl Harbor, and Generous, on his instructions, had transcribed this ballyhoo onto a tape for the loudspeaker system. Bel-monte bet Merkel the racket could be heard a mile away.

Another musical innovation of the captain's was "Roast Beef of Olde Englande," a fife-and-drum march also played at top volume, for five minutes, before every lunch and dinner. "This is a very stirring thing," Arnheiter assured Hardy when he ordered him to have Generous tape this march too. "It gets the digestive juices going." The captain apparently did not need such tonics to wake up in the morning or to whet his appetite. He had the loudspeaker extension in his cabin dis-connected. When "Hellcats Reveille" or "Roast Beef of Olde Englande" was not warping the bulkheads, the captain's me-tallic voice always seemed to be scratching from the loud-speaker with some lecture on how the Viet Cong would rue the day the *Vance* appeared off Viet Nam. "Jesus Christ, this guy never stops talking," Radarman Sides said to a shipmate. "He goes on and on and on."

The officers were trying, unsuccessfully, to escape meals with the captain. Under Ross Wright, meals had been half-hour affairs, leaving everyone as much time as possible for work or relaxation. Now they became "leisurely conversation sessions," in the captain's phrase, at which Arnheiter did most of the talking. Lunch lasted an hour and a half to two hours and dinner two and a half to three hours, depending on how the spirit of rhetoric moved the captain. "We're spending more goddamn time at the table than we are in bed," Merkel complained to Gwynn. These marathon meals were depriving the officers of sleep by making it difficult for them to accomplish their work in the hours in between. The majority of the captain's monologues were harangues on how he was "tautening this ship into a man-of-war." He frequently mocked Captain Wright. The *Vance* was no longer going to be run "like the merchant marine or McHale's Navy," an allusion to the bumbling mariners of the television series. The officers must learn to set a good example for the enlisted men, to be "imaginative and audacious" and always "to bring home the bacon." The sight of a sweat stain under an armpit, an oil spot or a frayed collar invariably set off a lecture that they were not leading sufficiently upright lives. (Ship's Serviceman First Class Willie E. Johnson, a black sailor from Arkansas who lived in the steam bath of the un-air-conditioned laundry belowdecks, grumbled to Generous one day, "You goddamn officers send down five sets of khaki shirts and pants and two sets of underwear.")

On other occasions, Arnheiter impressed his juniors by dropping the names of all the admirals he knew. Rear Admiral Walter H. Baumberger, the Commander, Cruiser-Destroyer Force Pacific, a distant god to the ensigns and lieutenants junior grade, was "Bombo" in the captain's table talk. Or the captain praised the wisdom of the solution his professional mentor, Vice Admiral Settle, proposed for the China problem—an invasion of the mainland by Chiang Kai-shek. Arnheiter enjoyed caricaturing the speech habit of his most recent senior, Rear Admiral Raymond F. DuBois, commander of the cruiser-destroyer group that conducted shore bombardment of the Viet Nam coast. Admiral DuBois comes down hard on his consonants and speaks with a slight hesitancy.

In Arnheiter's burlesque, the admiral, who was born and grew up in Connecticut, acquired a Bronx accent. The captain would screw up his face like a chimpanzee and mispronounce the *th*'s as *d*'s. Arnheiter caricatured brilliantly, and as soon as their astonishment at the act had passed, his subordinates were in stitches. DuBois was one of the few admirals for whom Arnheiter had worked directly without seeking to ingratiate himself in the process. In the verbal jousting with the admiral that the captain recounted to his officers, he, Arnheiter, always came off best.

When it was possible to converse with the captain, Generous and Belmonte were the only officers, besides Hardy, who dared to do so. Generous became Arnheiter's resident "Ivy League intellectual" because he was able correctly to identify October 21, 1805, as the day the Battle of Trafalgar was fought. Arnheiter enlightened his officers with a snippet of Nelson lore at dinner one evening by describing how the fallen hero's corpse had been pickled in a barrel of rum after the battle to preserve it during the voyage back to England for the state funeral.

Lunch itself was no longer the solid meal of hamburgers or the like to which the officers had been accustomed. They began to subsist on a diet of cottage cheese and fruit or peanut-butter-and-jelly sandwiches. The captain told Hardy that light lunches were part of "a gentlemanly code" he wanted his officers to observe and that some who were plump, like Merkel and Ensign Gerald J. Prescott, twenty-five, the communications officer, ought to lose weight. "If it weren't for that peanut butter, we'd die," Belmonte said to Generous. Hannigan, 205 pounds of muscle and bone, was irascible all day because he was perpetually hungry. Fuehrer was not quite as irascible, but just as hungry. "Sometimes you just want to stand up and shout, 'I'd like to have something to eat,'" he said to Hannigan. No one dared. Several of the ensigns, who had the least dignity to lose, resorted to cadging food from the first class petty officers' mess.

For dessert in the evening the officers were served what the captain called his "epicurean delights." Some of the juniors were "from rustic backgrounds," Arnheiter told Hardy, and he intended to educate their palates "with gourmet dishes." These sophisticated treats were baked apples, or canned peaches or pears doused in Cherry Heering liqueur or medicinal brandy from Cornejo's drug chest. Prescott, who was the mess treasurer, had bought the Cherry Heering on the captain's order during a day's stop to refuel at Subic Bay, in the Philippines. "Ray, break out the Guamanian guava-berry juice," the captain would say to Hardy with a chuckle of anticipation at the end of the main course. Hardy would go to the safe in his compartment, where he now kept Cherry Heering and medicinal brandy locked up alongside secret documents, and pour some into a small cream pitcher. Arnheiter would spread a helping on his own dessert and then insist that his subordinates take some too. One of the captain's favorite desserts, canned pears and medicinal brandy, he referred to as "pears Napoleon."

"Napoleon had better taste," Belmonte quipped to Generous.

Besides interfering with their work, the tedium of these meals became an almost physical sensation. Some of the officers contrived for a few days to stay away and to hustle a sandwich between regular mealtimes. But the captain abhorred an empty chair. He would not permit absenteeism. He sent Hardy round the ship to collar the delinquents.

On the way from Guam to Subic Bay, the captain relived his youthful role as an Army rifle instructor, and the *Vance's* diesels began to feel the strain. Ross Wright and the other ship captains on Operation Market Time had been content to leave the land war to the Marines and the Army. Captain Arnheiter was not. Shortly after the *Vance* left Pearl Harbor, he had organized a thirty-man Special Fire Team from among the crew. He armed the sailors with the fifteen extra M-1 rifles Belmonte had cumshawed and with other M-1's and Browning automatic rifles from the ship's authorized small-arms inventory.

Arnheiter had been forming landing parties of sailors on every ship he had served on since his days as a lieutenant junior grade aboard the *Coolbaugh*. These phalanxes had never done more than parade in port, but the captain had vowed to Hardy that if the opportunity arose to send a landing party ashore in Viet Nam for a genuine, bloody infantry battle with the Viet Cong, he would not let it pass. He might find an opening for action, he noted, in the relief of some beleaguered outpost along the coast. The practice of dispatching groups of sailors ashore to fight as impromptu infantrymen is a centuries-old naval tradition that has, during the last fifty years, been mostly honored in the breach. The Special Fire Team would also come in handy to shoot up Viet Cong and North Vietnamese junks, the captain said, and to repel the guerrillas if they were foolish enough to try to board the *Vance*. First, the seagoing infantrymen had to be taught to hit what they aimed at.

While the *Vance* was docked in Guam, the captain had ordered Belmonte and his deck gang to put empty oil drums and heavy sandbags on board ship, with just such target practice in mind. Now the captain mustered the thirty sailors onto the O-1 deck (the open-air center deck one tier above the main level) and instructed them to stretch out behind the protective sandbags, which were placed along the railing on both sides of the ship. Belmonte and his crew conjured up enemy junks by tossing the empty 55-gallon oil drums overboard. The barrels had been painted yellow, at Arnheiter's order, for easier aiming. The captain directed the proceedings from the small O-3 deck two tiers farther up, like the master of a puppet show. He had thoughtfully arranged for the electricians to attach a long extension cord to a microphone piped into the ship's loudspeaker system. Whipping the extension cord behind him, he strode back and forth across the exposed O-3 deck, calling out the firing orders. "One round, ball ammunition, lock and load," he shouted in the best Army parlance. "Unlock your pieces. Ready on the right. Ready on the left. Ready on the firing line. Take aim. Fire!" A ragged volley splattered out against the oil drums jouncing on the waves. Most of the bullets went wild because the ship was rolling and the sailors could not steady their aim.

The captain encouraged them with a few spirited sentences and shouted to reload.

Watching from below, Generous could see the captain's step had that special bounce he displayed only when he was truly excited. "Look at him up there," he said to Belmonte. "He's buoyant. He's having a fabulous time."

The engines were not enjoying themselves. For the target-practice sessions the captain had ordered a speed of 17.5 knots, a knot and a half below the *Vance*'s top speed of 19, and continuous performance of a maneuver called a Williamson turn. (The day before, Mason had experienced great difficulty explaining to Arnheiter that the *Vance* could no longer attain her World War II speed of 21 knots.) To accomplish a Williamson turn, a ship steams down a straight track through the water for a short time and then swings off to one side into a sort of closed U-turn that swivels the vessel right back down the same track. Arnheiter was employing the maneuver to drive the ship back and forth between the oil drums that Belmonte's deck gang had thrown into the sea. Speed strains engines. Speed and turns increase the strain geometrically. Each time the ship turns, the screws bite deeper into the water and transmit their tension into the engines in the form of heat. As Arnheiter ran the *Vance* through one Williamson turn after another, the needles on the temperature gauges moved upward alarmingly. Mason and Fuehrer climbed to the O-3 deck several times to protest to the captain that he was endangering the engines unnecessarily. They pleaded with him to slow down. He refused. "You're babying your engines," he retorted. "Either the bridge runs the engines or the engine room does, and the bridge will run the engines on this ship."

After eighteen Williamson turns, the needle on the temperature gauge on one diesel rose past the red danger line. Mason had to shut the engine down before it exploded and caught fire. Later, after it had been cooled and restarted, the engine had to be shut down again because a timing chain broke. With the same fear of creating a bad impression on his superiors that he had displayed during the trip to Guam, the captain again violated regulations and refused to allow Mason to radio an engine casualty report. The enginemen saved the captain from eventually being forced to submit a report by repairing the diesel in six hours. Fuehrer was appalled. "This ship is just a big toy to this guy," he said to Generous. "He doesn't give a damn about anything except getting her to do the tricks he wants her to do. You're up there explaining some serious engineering problem to him and he looks at you all of a sudden and asks if you want peaches or pears for dessert after dinner."

The loss of an engine for six hours made the *Vance* arrive late at Subic Bay. The captain would not permit Generous to radio a warning ahead. Several officers from the squadron staff there, who had driven to the dock to greet the *Vance* and to bring the ship's mail, were kept waiting for three and a half hours.

Four days later, on Friday, January 21, the day after the *Vance* reached the port of Qui Nhon on the central Vietnamese coast, Generous attempted to warn Captain Arnheiter that he was destroying the morale of his officers and men.

The previous week Generous had come within a gnat's breath of a personal confrontation with the captain over the compulsory Protestant Sunday services. The crisis had dissipated as quickly as it arose, and Generous now felt foolish about his determination to raise a fuss. The trouble had started after he sought to persuade the captain, who had reacted negatively to Generous' first request for exemption from the Sunday services, to let him escape the "All Hands Aft" for that Sunday morning, January 16, by standing a bridge watch as officer of the deck. Arnheiter refused. Generous marched down to his compartment and defiantly typed out a formal memorandum from himself to the captain, via Hardy, the intermediary in the chain of command. It read:

Subj: Meetings on Sunday, compulsory attendance at.
Ref: (A) Constitution of the United States, Article I in amendment thereof.
1. Your attention is respectfully invited to reference (A),

which, as interpreted by several recent significant court decisions, prohibits enforced attendance at religious services, however euphemistically disguised they may be.

2. Please accept this letter as a statement of my desire and intent to preserve this constitutional right.

"He'll never let me off the hook," Generous said to himself, "but I'll be damned if I'm going to accept an illegal order and a sin and go quietly. If I go, he's going to make me go in writing and on paper and not in some darkened little corner of the bridge. He's going to commit the crime, not me." So after he signed the memorandum, Generous typed an endorsement at the bottom of the page for the captain to sign if he wished:

From: Commanding Officer
To: Lieutenant Junior Grade Generous
1. Returned, receipt acknowledged. You are hereby ordered to present yourself on the fantail this morning at 10:25 to hear an address by the executive officer, in accordance with the plan of the day [Hardy had been ordered by the captain to conduct the service that Sunday].

Hardy did not forward the memorandum to the captain. He walked back to Generous' compartment with it, and his bland face was angry.

"You're just going to slit your own throat in any kind of open attack on a program like this," he said.

"I'm not going to submit like a sheep, XO," Generous replied. "He's going to have to make me go."

"Don't give me any of this legalistic crap, Tom," Hardy said irritably, tossing the memorandum onto Generous' bunk. "You don't have any choice. Just go. Understand. Just go." He whirled and slammed the door on his way out.

Generous had agonized over Hardy's advice and decided to accept it. His career and the future of his wife and a child to be born in a few months were at stake. He would make this compromise. When he had reached the fantail that Sunday morning, however, the sight of the sailors with their hats off, shuffling their feet and whispering to each other was too much for him.

"My God," he thought. "It's just like before mass. To hell with Arnheiter. I'm not going to stay." He had begun to sneak back down the main deck toward the bow of the ship, hoping no one would notice his absence. But he encountered Hardy on the way, and Hardy had a rare fit of temper.

"Where the hell are you going, Tom?" he asked.

"I can't hack it, XO," Generous said.

"Listen, Tom. Don't give me a bad time. It's too late. We're about to start. Don't make a big issue out of this. Just get your ass back there on the fantail."

Generous began to argue and the two men had to strain their self-control to keep their voices from rising to shouts. Finally Hardy said, "Look, if you go back there and you don't like it and you think it's religious, then go out and seek help from your religious adviser. But in the meantime military orders are to get your ass back there on the fantail. Now do it."

Just then Generous spied Arnheiter walking toward them down the deck. He quailed at the consequences of outright defiance of the captain and returned to the fantail with Hardy.

Generous stood sulking as the service opened. But Hardy's talk was a sunny day to the night of the captain's fire-and-brimstone sermons. In a composed voice the executive officer recounted how divine services were held at sea on all Navy ships during the nineteenth century. He concluded by describing some of the thoughts of God and of the majesty of the universe that passed through his mind while he was navigating by the stars. He asked the men to join him in singing "My Country, 'Tis of Thee," a hymn more patriotic than religious. He did not order the men to pray. Instead he said, "And now I would like to pray in your presence." Most of the sailors and officers prayed too. The onus of compulsion that so repulsed Generous in the service Arnheiter had led was nonexistent here. At the end, Generous apologized sheepishly to Hardy.

"Boy, was I stupid," he said to himself afterward. "I made

a big thing out of nothing. I'm not going to fight this any more. It's not worth it."

Now, nearly a week later on that Friday, January 21, at dinner in the wardroom, off Qui Nhon, the captain lectured the officers again about the necessity of setting a good example for the enlisted men. The petty officers had been complaining about them, he said. "You're considered to be very poor leaders. You're not supporting the petty officers properly. You're not squared away."

Belmonte and several other officers, who believed they had fine relationships with their enlisted chiefs, were incredulous. They argued with Arnheiter and challenged the veracity of the complaints. Belmonte took particular pride in working with his hands alongside his men and had been honored by invitations to poker in the chief petty officers' quarters. Although the other officers frowned on this sort of fraternization as unseemly, Belmonte had managed to retain the respect of the enlisted men and to run an efficient deck force.

"I've never heard of a command in the world where the petty officers are used against their officers," he muttered indignantly to Merkel. "It's something that's just not done."

The captain was not persuaded by the arguments. He cited several notations he had made at recent meals of frayed shirt collars, oil spots, and sweat stains under armpits. Belmonte had a five o'clock shadow and could never seem to shave often enough to satisfy Arnheiter, whose body was nearly hairless. The captain harped on Belmonte's dereliction and added, "The petty officers are the backbone of the Navy. You must remember that, gentlemen."

As always when he lectured the officers at meals, the captain harangued softly, quietly. His voice hardly ever rose. He did not have to shout and curse to humiliate the officers. The imperious timbre of his voice was enough, and he salted the cuts with his gestures. His tone of voice said, "See how stupid you are," and his hand flips and his finger wags and his frowns said, "See what idiots you are . . . Frayed shirts in front of the sailors. You ought to be ashamed of yourselves."

Generous looked around the table at the faces of his companions. He could taste the tension on the end of his tongue. Fuehrer's hands were gripping his chair. Belmonte was staring at the deck and clenching his teeth. The others seemed equally incensed.

"It's obvious what they're thinking," Generous said to himself. "They're thinking, 'Captain, what kind of an example have you been setting for us?' Practically everything this guy's done over the last month has been illegal, or irregular, or lacked common sense as far as they're concerned. I'm probably the only one left who thinks he's all right. They don't realize that this guy has some quirks and that he's basically sound. I know, because I made a mountain out of a molehill over that church service."

Generous screwed up his courage and decided to intervene. "Captain," he said aloud. "I'd like to talk to you later if it's all right with you." He immediately tasted a new sort of tension in the room.

After coffee, Generous, Hardy and Arnheiter went to the executive officer's compartment. They spent the next two hours there, and for once in the captain's presence, Generous did most of the talking. He commenced by reiterating, as he had that night on the bridge, that he liked the new regime of spit and polish Arnheiter was enforcing on the *Vance*. "But a lot of the other junior officers don't," he said. "They have some serious questions they can't answer for themselves. A whole lot of funny things have been happening, and I'm beginning to develop a few questions myself. We're starting to have a major morale problem on this ship." Generous then slowly ticked off in broad terms to Arnheiter the list of weird occurrences and petty and large annoyances that had driven his fellows to distraction.

Some of the queerest happenings had taken place during the week the *Vance* was docked at Guam for the engine repairs. The first morning in port the captain told Gwynn that he intended to transform the *Vance*'s cafeteria-like wardroom into "a gentlemen's club." Gwynn, who was known to his shipmates as "Porkchop," the Navy moniker for a supply officer, was to purchase the appurtenances of gracious living on the small island. The captain ordered him to buy two silver candelabras, a silver coffee server, two dozen demitasse cups and saucers, and a cigar humidor. Also out of government funds, he was instructed to purchase $285 worth of movie and still-camera film, in color and black-and-white (Gwynn had already spent $85 on film in Pearl Harbor, but the captain liked his picture taken and wanted more), to buy a special air conditioner for the captain's cabin, and to requisition weather balloons for antiaircraft gunnery practice. The weather balloons puzzled Gwynn the most, since the Viet Cong did not boast an air force. Arnheiter exhorted Gwynn "to search under every rock and shoal" for these sundries and "to bring home the bacon."

Belmonte and his deck hands had already brought home some bacon. At the captain's direction, they had taken the twenty-five 55-gallon oil drums off the pier, to simulate Viet Cong junks for the target practice he was planning.

"It's all right," the captain explained to Hardy with a wink. "We're transferring those drums from one part of the Navy to another."

The steel drums hustled aboard, the captain ordered Belmonte to procure two hundred sandbags and to stack them along both sides of the O-1 deck to protect the sailors in the Special Fire Team from the enemy bullets he expected.

"Captain, we can't put two hundred sandbags on the O-1 deck," Hardy protested. "That's fourteen thousand pounds of weight. We might tip the ship over in a gale. There's twenty thousand pounds of pig iron down in the bilges to keep the stability at a safe level as it is." Hardy sensed that the captain did not agree with him and thought he was seeking to excuse Belmonte and his deck gang from some extra work. Arnheiter settled for sixty sandbags, however. Belmonte haggled the bags from a Guamanian feed-and-grain-store clerk with a butane cigarette lighter. He and his men had filled them with sand from the beach.

"We've been hearing all these lectures about running a nice, smart, trim, taut ship," Belmonte said to Merkel, "and now look at those ugly goddamn burlap bags oozing sand all over my deck."

While his officers and men were caught in this whirlwind of activity—Generous reminded a silent Arnheiter—the captain had relaxed, playing tennis, swimming, fishing and enjoying the new speedboat. Belmonte and some of the sailors had been permitted to use the boat occasionally to train for their role as bait to draw Viet Cong fire so that the captain could circumvent the rules of engagement and bombard the Viet Nam coast. Arnheiter drove the runabout most of the time, however, and the sailors began to grumble about their $950.

The second morning in port the captain asked Hardy if all of the officers owned white mess jackets for formal dinners and other full-dress occasions. Mess jackets are short, tightly fitting affairs in Victorian style, worn with Navy dress-blue pants and a black bow tie. They make an officer look like an oversized penguin or perhaps a waiter in an expensive French restaurant. Naval officers of the rank of full lieutenant and above are required to own them. Hardy and Arnheiter were the only officers in this category aboard the *Vance*. Hardy had pointed this out. "In any case, Captain," he said in an attempt at a joke, "I doubt that anyone packed his formal dinner dress for Viet Nam."

"Well, I think you should start a vigorous program right away to see that everyone has dinner-dress uniforms," the captain had replied severely. "You never can tell when the ship might be invited to some formal function and therefore everyone would have to be dressed correctly. There's only one correct dress, you know."

The officers objected to Hardy about the $25 expense. He was firm, however, and off they went in search of mess jackets. The sales clerks at the Air Force and Navy post exchanges on Guam were surprised to find that they did have moth-balled mess jackets in stock. Unfortunately, the only sizes available were either very large or very small, but the captain was not swayed by this excuse. Engineman Second Class Billy Joe Nuckles, who did seamstress work and was appropriately nicknamed "Mother Knuckles," hurriedly altered the mess jackets to fit their new owners.

The purpose of the formal wear became evident several days later when the captain staged a mess night at the Guam officers' club with money from the *Vance*'s wardroom mess fund. Naval officers pay for their own food. Generous now made a point of emphasizing to Arnheiter that since the wardroom mess fund was a communal treasury, for which each officer was assessed a share every month, the captain might have consulted his juniors before spending their money.

The mess night is a custom that originated in the British navy and has occasionally been imitated in the United States Navy and Marine Corps. It is supposed to be an evening of drunken horseplay, made more hilarious by the pomp and ceremony of a very formal dinner. All of the officers were required to attend except Black, the fresh-caught ensign, who was left to guard the ship. The next morning the officers admitted to themselves that despite the compulsory nature of the fun, and despite several embarrassing incidents, most had enjoyed themselves. The captain had ordered Prescott to mount a table, roll his trouser legs up to his chubby thighs and dance like a pompon girl. The worst moment of the evening occurred when Mason, the Georgian who was married to a graceful blonde from Alabama, was ordered to give an impromptu speech on "the decadence and degeneration of the Old South." Belmonte, looking at the captain through a fog of alcohol, got the impression from the way Arnheiter was leering at Mason that the speech was supposed to include some disparaging remarks on the virtue of Southern womanhood. Hardy, who was relatively sober, had also been embarrassed at the captain's sense of humor. Belmonte rescued Mason by staggering to his feet and shouting a toast. And the memory of that $25 spent for an unwanted mess jacket had also dimmed the fun a bit.

Gwynn bought the $285 worth of additional movie and still film as the captain had ordered, but he was unable to find weather balloons for antiaircraft gunnery practice, the special air conditioner for the captain's cabin, or the gentlemanly trappings for the wardroom—the silver candelabras and coffee server, the demitasse cups and the cigar humidor—under the rocks, shoals and store counters of Guam. Arnheiter had acquired one bit of frippery, however, at a buffet dinner he staged at the officers' club, three nights after the ship docked, for the wives of two officers whose home port was Guam. One of the officers was a friend and fellow DER captain. The wardroom mess fund had also paid for these festivities.

Generous looked at the captain, still sitting quietly on Hardy's bunk, and continued his recital:

Fairly early into the evening of the buffet dinner, Arnheiter had remarked to Generous how "great" that silver coffee server on their table would look in the *Vance*'s wardroom. Nodding toward a side table nearby, where four similar coffee servers were arrayed, he whispered, "They won't miss one, Tom. Why don't you see if you can take it?"

Generous glanced around and saw that he was closest to the door. He wrapped the coffee server in his raincoat, smuggled it outside and hid it behind a bush.

Much later, after considerable drinking had been done and the ladies had departed in a staff car, the captain's attention turned to two of the club's large silver candelabras. "I see some excellent candelabras over there that would look fine in the wardroom. In fact, I'm surprised the wardroom doesn't have candelabras," he said to Hardy, poking the executive officer in the shoulder and pointing toward another side table, where the candelabras stood. They were elegant, tiered models.

"I don't think those would be very tasteful in the wardroom, Captain," Hardy replied.

Arnheiter ignored him. "As a matter of fact," he continued, "I think an audacious officer would bring it about so that we might get those candelabras. Besides, the club probably has two sets, and they use only one set at a time. We certainly have a need for them. There's no question about that."

"Jesus," Hardy thought, "he really wants us to steal them."

The captain rattled on for ten more audacious sentences before Hardy could force himself to get up and walk over to the table where Belmonte and Ensign Michael R. McWhirter, a rugged, outgoing youth of twenty-four who was the *Vance*'s electronics material officer, were sitting.

"Do you think you could get those candelabras out, Luis?" Hardy asked.

"You really want them, XO?" Belmonte said in a voice slurred by too much gin and Chianti.

"They're wanted, Luis," Hardy replied.

McWhirter was caught in the act by a waiter, but Belmonte managed to get his candelabra out of the club. The captain carried it to the ship in the trunk of a staff car.

The next morning Hardy told Arnheiter that the candelabra would have to be returned. McWhirter's unartful dodgery had made it obvious that an officer from the *Vance* was the thief.

"I think the best thing would be for you to drop it off and give an explanation that your officers had been drinking and were in a playful mood and jokingly took it out and you're bringing it back," he suggested to the captain.

Arnheiter asked Hardy to take the candelabra back.

The executive officer recoiled. "No, sir," he said, "I don't want any part of it."

The silver coffee server remained aboard, and Arnheiter would beam when coffee was poured from it after dinner.

Generous glanced at the captain, screwed up his courage again, and went on to the Boner Box:

Back at sea after Guam, Arnheiter demonstrated to the officers, as he had to the sailors at the public captain's mast on the fantail the morning of departure, that he would tolerate no lapses from his standard of conduct for others. He produced the Boner Box. This was a small wooden file-card box, padlocked, with crossbones painted in white on the front. The captain instructed Mason's shipfitters to erect a little shelf for the box on one of the wardroom bulkheads. He appropriated five cards from the bridge deck Belmonte had purchased for the wardroom, and had pasted above the box the "Death Hand" of aces and eights that Wild Bill Hickok supposedly held when he was shot in the back of the head during a poker game in Deadwood, Dakota Territory, in 1876.

Arnheiter began a daily ritual of levying twenty-five-cent fines on the officers for any offense against etiquette, dress, or behavior by themselves or the sailors in their departments or divisions. Most of the fines were for unshined belt buckles and shoes, for the perpetually frayed and stained shirts, or for some landlubberly sailor's answering "Yes, sir," instead of "Aye, aye, sir," when he was given an order by the captain. Other fines were for breaches of the captain's notion of table manners. Lieutenant (j.g.) Julian R. Meisner, a proud, witty twenty-six-year-old Annapolis graduate who was to join the *Vance* in early February as assistant weapons officer, would lose quarters on five occasions for laying down his knife on the table or on his plate with the edge turned outward. Merkel paid a quarter for neglecting to cut his bread into squares. Every officer was required to bring four quarters to lunch. Hardy would read off the offenses the captain had meticulously noted on a clipboard, and Arnheiter would stand by and watch each culprit drop his quarter or quarters into the slit cut in the top of the box. "Look at him smiling that sly little smile," Belmonte whispered to Merkel at one lunch. "He's enjoying this."

The captain was using the accumulated fines to purchase Dutch Masters panetelas for the wardroom. The majority of the officers were not fond of cigars. The captain, who was, did most of the smoking and kept the cigar supply in his cabin between meals so that he could partake of a cigar there too. "Every night he puffs on a cigar and talks and talks until after eight or nine o'clock and we never even get to watch a movie any more," Fuehrer complained to Hardy. "Those movies were bad, but at least they were better than sitting around the wardroom choking on cigar smoke."

Fuehrer became so angry one day at forfeiting another quarter for some peccadillo that he warned Hardy he was going to tell the captain "to take his Boner Box and shove it up his ass" the next time he was fined. Hardy talked him out of a confrontation.

Generous was beginning to wonder at the captain's patience in listening to these complaints. He decided Arnheiter's tolerance would not last much longer. He hurried on to the predicaments in which Merkel and Lieutenant (j.g.) Kenton D. Hamaker had found themselves:

Arnheiter had told Merkel to forget about being the ship's antisubmarine-warfare officer and to concentrate on a collateral duty—as public information officer. This occupation meant that Merkel was the captain's personal photographer. Hardly a day passed without the loudspeaker erupting with "Mr. Merkel, bridge, provide"—nautical lingo for "Mr. Merkel, come to the bridge with your camera." Merkel would bound up the ladder with his camera and some of the $370 supply of film Gwynn had purchased for the captain. Merkel's principal project was making a color movie of the captain that Arnheiter intended to send to his son, Jeffrey, to encourage the boy to adopt a naval career. Merkel filmed the captain being saluted by his officers on the bridge. He filmed the captain giving orders. He filmed the captain gesturing and pointing excitedly at an imaginary enemy during gunnery practice while the 3-inch guns flashed and puffed out clouds of smoke. Another sequence showed Arnheiter staring off toward the horizon from the rail of the bridge, like an admiral contemplating tactics on the eve of a fateful battle. "He sure loves to be saluted," Merkel said to Belmonte after one hand-popping session. The job shamed Merkel. He had become the laughing-stock of the crew and the butt of a good many jokes by his fellow officers. "It's always funny when it's happening to someone else," he complained bitterly to Generous one day.

Hamaker, a dark-haired, unobtrusive young man of twenty-five who was the ship's navigator, had, through no doing of his own, gotten into trouble with the captain and possibly with the United States Post Office. One of Hamaker's additional duties was to oversee the ship's post office. At Pearl Harbor the captain had helped himself to stamps worth

$11.57 to mail brochures commemorating the change-of-command ceremony to admirals of his acquaintance and to other friends. He refused to pay for them and ordered Hamaker to find a regulation that would justify charging off the stamps as a government expense. "I know it can be done, because I've seen it done in Washington," the captain assured Hamaker. Although Hamaker and Hardy scanned every manual even vaguely relevant, they were not able to discover any such regulation. Each time they attempted to convince Arnheiter that the regulation did not exist and that he would have to part with $11.57, he grew irritated and testily ordered Hamaker to search the manuals again. He would not permit Hamaker to submit the December postal audit with an $11.57 deficit in the stamp column, a discrepancy that would be certain to provoke an inquiry by the Post Office accountants. The Post Office was fastidious about receiving the monthly audits on time, however, and Hamaker feared that if the December report was not submitted soon, he would be blamed. He could not see any solution except to pay the Post Office himself for the captain's stamps, an indignity he was not yet ready to accept. Why should he have to pay the captain's debt? Hamaker asked himself.

One incident Generous did not dare mention to Arnheiter in his two-hour recital of complaints was the tale of the white toilet seat, a story that had strangely discomforted the other officers.

The episode had occurred at Pearl Harbor, two or three days before the *Vance* set off for Viet Nam. Arnheiter called Hardy to his cabin and instructed him to replace immediately with a white one the regulation black toilet seat in the private bathroom off the captain's cabin. The order nonplused Hardy, but he was anxious to please the new captain and sent for Gwynn.

"Bob, I want you to get us a white toilet seat for the captain's head," he said.

"Come on, you've got to be kidding, XO," Gwynn replied.

"I'm busy as hell getting stores and spare parts aboard so that we can shove off."

"I'm not kidding, Bob," Hardy said. "I want a white toilet seat for the captain's head. I think they're in the Navy supply center, and I want you to get one before we leave."

"Boy," Gwynn said, "I'll do the best I can."

"I don't care about the best you can do, just get one," Hardy concluded.

Later that day the captain spoke directly to Gwynn about the white toilet seat and told him to make certain it was aboard before the *Vance* left. The only way to comply in such a short time was to submit the toilet-seat request on a high priority, walk the paper work through the processing stages of the supply depot, and personally pick up the item. Gwynn was too embarrassed to ask the depot personnel to walk the request form through, and he felt rather foolish himself marching in with a Priority 5 requisition for a toilet seat. This priority was reserved for items, such as parts for radios, without which the ship's operational capability would be impaired. A toilet seat would normally have been ordered through channels on a Priority 17 and shipped to the *Vance* in a month or two. Gwynn had sheepishly obtained the seat, and Mason's shipfitters installed it during the voyage to Guam. Unfortunately, they scorched it with a brazing tool. *Whup, whup, whup,* Hardy's sound-powered phone extension had erupted in the middle of the night.

"Mr. Hardy, come up to my cabin instantly," the captain's voice crackled.

Arnheiter led Hardy into the bathroom. "Look at that," he said, pointing to the scorched spot on the white rim of the seat. "It's atrocious. Have those shipfitters clean that up right away." The captain was not satisfied until the shipfitters had thoroughly sanded the spot and painted it as white as the rest of the seat. Later Gwynn and the shipfitters talked about the episode, and the freakish tale spread throughout the ship, discomforting each man in an eerie sort of way. The incident was very much on Generous' mind as he spoke, but he did not dare confront Arnheiter with it.

The captain had listened to Generous' account with a unique tolerance. He puffed a cigar to pass the time and interrupted now and then to dispute some minor point—an incident Generous said had happened on a Tuesday had instead occurred on a Wednesday. By and large, he seemed attentive.

At the end, Hardy spoke up to buttress what Generous had said. "You really have to admire Mr. Generous' courage for saying these things, Captain. He's doing what he thinks is the right thing."

Generous sensed, however, that Arnheiter had conceded nothing. The captain's silence did not signify assent.

"Tom," Arnheiter said coldly, "I've wanted a ship all my life, and I've known how I was going to run it when I got it. Now I've got it, and I'm doing what I've wanted to. When you get a command, you'll do the same thing."

Although he realized there had been no agreement, Generous left the compartment convinced that he had succeeded in his purpose. "He knows now that he's got these officers completely discouraged," he thought. "He knows now what's been irritating them, and he'll just kind of taper off and cool it."

The others did not share his confidence. They had guessed at his presumptuousness and were waiting for him in the wardroom when he returned. "You got a lot of goddamn nerve," Fuehrer said. "Who in the hell do you think you are, going in there and blowing the whistle on us!"

"You guys have got it all wrong," Generous replied. "The way to handle something like this is to go in and face it. You'll see, things are going to be better now. The captain just hasn't understood. Now he understands, and everything is going to be fine."

The following noon the officers were standing around the wardroom table waiting for the captain to appear for Saturday lunch. Hardy stuck his head in the door. "The captain wants to see you, Tom," he said. The other faces, etched with hostility, turned toward Generous, and Generous was suddenly afraid.

Arnheiter was sitting at his desk, facing Hardy and Generous when they walked into the cabin. "Tom," he said, "I want the names of the officers who were complaining about the mess night." Generous was numbed. He could not speak for several moments, and the captain repeated the order. In his recital the night before, Generous had been careful, except for mentioning the personal predicaments of Merkel and Hamaker, not to specify the names of any of the officers who had actually complained. And where Merkel and Hamaker were concerned, he had tried to give the captain the impression that he and not they, was complaining about their plight.

"Come on, Captain, I didn't come in here last night to blow the whistle on anybody," Generous said as soon as he had retrieved his voice. "I came in here to hash out what I thought was a mutual problem. If you make me give you those names, I'm going to be on everybody's shit list."

"Never mind, Tom. Just give me the names," the captain said.

"Wait a minute, wait a minute," Generous protested. "I'm never going to be confident talking to you again. How can I ever have any faith in a conversation I might have with you if you make me give you those names? What the hell good are the names, anyway? It's a problem of general low morale on the ship, especially among the officers because we have the most contact with you."

"Come on, come on, Tom, give me the names," Arnheiter said testily.

"Is that an order, Captain?" Generous asked.

"Yes, it's an order," the captain replied.

Cornered, Generous searched his mind for the least damaging admission he could conceive. The peccadillo he related did not diminish his sense of betrayal, however. He confessed that in a taxi on the way back to the ship he had heard Merkel and Gwynn griping about all the money spent on the mess night. The captain had ordered the mess treasurer to disburse $185 from the communal wardroom mess fund for the compulsory mess-night high jinks and the buffet for the two officers' wives. Arnheiter seemed satisfied. He did not ask

Generous for the names of the officers who had criticized his other "programs."

The captain and Hardy stayed behind for a few minutes while Generous returned to the wardroom alone. The protective psychic mechanisms with which nature has thoughtfully provided man buffered Generous' agony. Numbness flowed through his body like an anesthetic. As best he could, he related to the other officers what had occurred in the captain's cabin.

"I told you so," Fuehrer said.

"Goddamn it, Tom, when we want you to speak for us, we'll let you know!" Mason said.

"I'm sorry, I'm sorry," Generous said. "I was Joe Naïve . . . wet behind the ears. I thought I had everything under control."

Lunch that Saturday turned out to be another rarity for the *Vance,* like the captain's patience in hearing out Generous. It was brief, and almost nothing was said.

Arnheiter did not take any disciplinary action against Merkel and Gwynn for grumbling about the mess night. He simply summoned them to his cabin after lunch and they had a relatively pleasant chat about their differences. The captain never mentioned the matter again.

On Sunday morning at "All Hands Aft" the captain stood behind the flag-draped lectern and preached another of his sermons, zealous for God and country. Generous was not on bridge watch and had to attend.

"Yes, Master, we're all here," Generous said to himself as the captain's fervid voice arched over the heads of the congregation. "We're all here to listen to your demagogy. You're dressed as your most wonderful, overwhelmingly beautiful self. You're crackling, you're so beautiful in your tailored whites. You're invoking all the major saints in the Arnheiter canon, MacArthur and all the rest of them. You're the worst kind of demagogue. You're the religious and the patriotic demagogue all wrapped into one."

Generous did not join in the prayer after the sermon, and the captain scowled at him. He did not sing the hymn and was glared at for this. At the end of the service the other officers and men sang the National Anthem, facing the ensign on the mast as they would in church, hats in their hands. Generous put on his cap, came to attention and defiantly saluted the flag. He walked back to his compartment as soon as the crew was dismissed and wrote a letter to Father Richard L. Osterman, a Roman Catholic chaplain at Pearl Harbor who had visited the *Vance* for a month during the previous Viet Nam patrol. He and Generous had spent several evenings discussing their faith and had become friends.

I wish I could spend some time in passing generalities [the letter began], but my rage forces me to use my limited time particularly. The enclosed mimeos [copies of the three "All Hands Aft" services that had been held thus far] should speak for themselves. Three times now the crew has been ordered aft . . . for these euphemistic church calls. The first one I missed by virtue of having the Deck, and the second, thanks to the good taste of the executive officer, who presided, was innocuous. But today's gem was no more nor less than a Protestant service . . . flat religion, led and directed by the Commanding Officer.

I have complained previously, both to the CO orally, and in a letter to the CO which was held up by the XO who advised me, "not to jeopardize myself, but to seek outside help anonymously." I do have the courage of my convictions, and I would refuse the order to lay aft on the basis of its constitutionality were it not for my responsibility to my wife and child-to-be.

The Nuremberg Trials settled for all time the loyalty a military man must show his superior. I cannot be openly disloyal to him, but I cannot accept illegality and infringement of my constitutional rights. I seek relief from this burden, but I do so anonymously, once again for the sake of my family. Is there something that you could do?

Generous was ashamed of the letter the instant he mailed it. A naval officer who writes a complaining letter to a chaplain is behaving like a milk-livered sneak, and Generous did not care to think himself craven. Whatever he might say to Father Osterman, he knew he did not have the courage of his convictions. If he had, he would have sent the captain

another memorandum and then forced the issue to the ultimate confrontation of a court-martial for refusing to obey
Arnheiter's order to attend. This would have been the courageous and honorable course to take. He was writing to Father
Osterman precisely because he wanted to avoid the perils of
an overt challenge. He was interpreting Hardy's advice to
"seek help from your religious adviser" to mean that he should
do so surreptitiously. He sought to escape the Protestant services and yet not have Arnheiter know how he had escaped.
For Generous was afraid of the captain now, very much
afraid. He had gambled and lost, and had been terribly humiliated. The magnitude of his stupidity and misjudgment
loomed in his mind. He wanted to spend his life in the Navy,
to rise to a command of his own someday. The captain could
destroy his career with one letter to the Bureau of Naval
Personnel. And so Generous had rationalized this fear for his
career into a concern for his wife, Diane, and the child she
was expecting. He realized all of this, even though he could
not yet admit it to himself in its entirety. An awareness of it
was there, nevertheless, and made him loathe the man who
had bullied him into this moral cowardice. His loathing
was a complicated, many-faceted and abiding emotion, made
that much more potent by the same stiff-necked will that had
led him obstinately to defend the captain to his fellow officers
for the past month.

Generous' hate, if it had been revealed, would not have
tempered the captain's joy. Arnheiter thought he had at last
found the war.

6

CAPTAIN ARNHEITER GOES TO WAR

Where the hell are the chickens?

—Chief Petty Officer Cornejo

The captain was standing on a wing of the bridge, sweeping with his binoculars a stretch of beach about eight miles north of the central Vietnamese port of Qui Nhon. For most of the past week he had been taking the *Vance* as close to shore as he dared, seeking trouble with impatience, poking so far into shallow bays and inlets that Hardy feared he might ground the ship.

"Look," Arnheiter suddenly said to Mason, who was standing beside him. "Look over toward that hamlet. Something suspicious is going on." Mason lifted his glasses and swung them in the direction the captain had indicated. He saw about a hundred and fifty Vietnamese walking down the beach in a scraggy line, carrying bundles. A short distance behind the last figure in the line, several poles with flags on top were sticking up out of the surf. Arnheiter ordered the helmsman to turn closer to shore. When the *Vance*'s bow angled toward them, some of the Vietnamese began running away across the dunes behind the beach.

"We've caught them," the captain yelled gleefully.

"Caught what, Captain?" Mason asked.

"I'll bet those poles are beach markers for a submarine

that's smuggled in arms and supplies. We've caught the porters before they could carry all of the stuff off the beach."

Mason raised his binoculars again. The figures on the beach seemed to him to be just some more scruffy fisher folk.

"Away the motor whaleboat," the captain commanded over the loudspeaker. "Hoppy," he said, his dark eyes rounder than usual with expectation, "take a landing party and go ashore and investigate." While Mason, Belmonte, Signalman Farnum, a Vietnamese navy ensign who was assigned to the *Vance* as a liaison officer, and a crew of four sailors armed with rifles and submachine guns clambered into the whaleboat, Arnheiter radioed the Navy's coastal surveillance center at Qui Nhon for fighter planes to circle overhead and strafe and bomb the Vietnamese on the beach if there was any resistance. Qui Nhon replied indifferently, saying there were no planes available. The captain's anticipation was undiminished. "Porters running wildly under heavy loads and dispersing over sand dunes," he radioed back. "An alert for hostile fire."

In between messages to Qui Nhon, he shot off a spate of orders over the radio to Mason in the whaleboat. From the wing of the bridge the captain could see more of the Vietnamese fleeing across the dunes. "Fire a few bursts over their heads with the thirty-caliber to make them halt," he ordered Mason. A .30-caliber machine gun had been mounted on a swivel in the whaleboat.

Mason is a deliberate and self-possessed man. Instead of loosing the machine gun, he took an M-1 rifle from one of the sailors and cautiously put two or three bullets into the sand about fifty yards in front of the lead figures. A few more Vietnamese ran away, and the rest threw themselves down on the sand. "Captain," he said, "I recommend we hold further fire until we have really determined these are enemy troops."

Arnheiter was insistent. "I told you to stop those VC porters. Don't let any of them get away. Shoot bursts over their heads. Fire, I said. Fire!" he yelled.

Mason ignored the order. The sun was lively on the red-tile roofs of the fishing hamlet down the beach, and he was worried that there might be more dwellings behind the dunes. "I'm not going to start incoherently firing a damn machine gun around," he said to himself. "We're not supposed to take any action against these people, anyway, unless we're fired upon." A more ominous thought occurred to him. If he loosed the machine gun, the captain might mistake the tracers streaking toward the beach for enemy fire directed at the whaleboat and blast away with the ship's 3-inch guns. "If there aren't any VC over there, a lot of people could get killed that shouldn't be," Mason thought. "He might even hit us. You never know what's going to go through his mind if there's a lot of shooting." Mason decided to keep the situation as tidy as possible. By now he was close enough to see women and children among the figures huddling on the sand. "They don't look like the enemy, Captain. There's women and children," he reported.

"Go ashore and investigate," Arnheiter ordered.

The Vietnamese liaison officer suspected that there were guerrillas in the area and thought it foolhardy to venture ashore with only a few men. "Many VC around here," he told Mason with a sweep of his arm. "Better stay in boat."

"No, we've got to go ashore," Mason said.

"I stay here," the Vietnamese replied.

"The hell you aren't going," Mason said and grabbed him by the shirt.

"Okay, okay," the Vietnamese said, borrowing a rifle from a sailor and wading through the surf with Mason and two seamen armed with Tommy guns.

The surf put Mason's radio out of commission. To avoid any more orders from the captain, he did not attempt to dry it. The Vietnamese lying on the sand turned out to be the surviving inhabitants of another fishing hamlet, which had been bombed and incinerated with napalm earlier that day in a raid by American or South Vietnamese planes. They were fleeing to a hamlet farther down the beach with what possessions they had managed to salvage. They explained to the liaison officer, who acted as interpreter, that their companions had run away because they were afraid that the ship might shell them or bring more planes and bombs and "fire from the sky." Mason and the sailors searched their bundles and found nothing beyond such unwarlike sundries as soap, rice and woven-straw sleeping mats.

Belmonte, who was watching from the whaleboat pitching in the surf just offshore, had lost sight of Mason and the others in the midst of about fifty Vietnamese men, women and children, dressed in a motley of black, blue and maroon pajamas, with checkered bandannas for hats, who had crowded around during the questioning and the searching of the bundles. What if the refugees were unfriendly or the liaison officer had been correct about the presence of Viet Cong? "Jesus Christ, those people could be disarming them and cracking them over the head in the middle of that crowd this minute for all I know," he muttered. He had visions of Mason, the liaison officer and the two sailors being dragged off and dismembered in some palm grove. Also, the captain was driving him to distraction with a fusillade of orders relayed through Farnum, who was the radioman in the whaleboat. If a fight broke out, Belmonte was supposed to launch a red flare into the air to alert the captain and then spray the beach with the whaleboat's machine gun until Arnheiter had annihilated the guerrillas with the *Vance*'s guns. Belmonte could not imagine how Mason and the other three men ashore would survive this help. Also, the whaleboat was tossing so badly in the surf that "you couldn't hit the broadside of your ass at five paces," he thought. Farnum was increasing the irritation by becoming more assertive with each relayed instruction from Arnheiter. Actually, the signalman felt just as bedeviled by the captain's bing-bang orders as Belmonte did and was trying to help sort out the confusion, but Belmonte did not know that.

"Jesus, Flash," Belmonte bellowed, "you think you're the incarnation of the captain in this goddamn whaleboat. Turn that fucking radio off and shut up."

Belmonte had the sailors maneuver the whaleboat to a spot in front of the hamlet where the surf was not so turbulent, and leaped out with a submachine gun to help Mason. As he walked up the sand he could see Vietnamese faces peering suspiciously at him from the doorways of the stucco-and-thatched houses. The captain had instructed the landing party to don the brilliant orange life jackets the Navy issues. Belmonte peered through the rifle sights of his mind at what a splendid target he made. "Christ," he said, "I'm going to get it today. I'm going to buy it in this goddamn orange life jacket he's made me wear. What a stupid way to die. God and country and the thin red line of heroes and all that crap is fine, but this is idiocy." Fortunately, there were no guerrillas in the vicinity. A few minutes later an old man came out of the hamlet, and coaxed by the gift of Mason's cigarette lighter, said that a platoon of about thirty well-armed Viet Cong visited regularly to give propaganda lectures. They had been there seven days earlier, the old man said.

Back at the ship Mason went directly to his compartment to shed his cold, wet clothing. Just after he had taken off his shoes, the loudspeaker summoned him to the bridge. Remembering the reprimand for dashing out shirtless when the engine exploded, he called the captain on the sound-powered phone. "I'm soaking wet and I don't have any shoes on, Captain. Do you want me to come up to the bridge just like I am?" he asked.

"Yes, I want to get some pictures," Arnheiter said.

Mason posed beside the captain while Merkel performed his public relations duties. Oddly, since he had gone to war the captain was no longer his dapper self. His clothes were always hospital-clean, but now he wore pleated khaki shorts, cut long and baggy, often without the benefit of knee socks to sheathe his calves, a loose-fitting shirt, a khaki baseball cap, and a bone-handled .38-caliber revolver in a quick-draw holster strapped to his hip. He apparently thought this costume appropriate for action in the tropics. The junior officers felt it made him look a bit silly.

Arnheiter was very disappointed when Mason told him that the figures on the beach had not been Viet Cong porters toting off supplies smuggled in by a submarine. "Are you certain, Hoppy?" he asked.

"Yes, Captain, I am. They were refugees. They really didn't look like they were VC." Mason could tell from the skepticism on Arnheiter's face that the captain did not believe him.

In a teletype report to Navy headquarters in Saigon, Arnheiter noted that Mason's explanation

would appear satisfactory except for two inexplicable circumstances:
(a) dozens of porters were seen to flee over sand dunes on arrival of ship, taking large sacks and containers with them,
(b) markers observed on beach similar to U.S. Navy amphibious landing markers that are set up by beachmaster. By the time motor whaleboat arrived at site, the containers had been carried away.

Rear Admiral Norvell G. Ward, the naval commander for South Viet Nam, complimented Arnheiter on his enterprise. "Your alert and aggressive action in detecting and investigating suspected infiltration attempt 27 January," the admiral radioed from Saigon the next morning, "is a refreshing example of individual initiative. Well done." The captain was overjoyed at the message and passed it around the wardroom table at lunch for all the officers to read. Another message later that day, revealing that the poles sticking up out of the surf had been exactly what they looked like, United States Navy landing markers erected during a survey of the beach the previous week, did not taint the captain's pleasure at the admiral's praise.

"He really wants to pull off the one big move that will make Marcus Aurelius Arnheiter the national focus, like ambushing five hundred VC and capturing them all or something," Mason said to Generous. "It's on his mind all the time, and I'm beginning to wonder how far he'll go with it." That same morning, encouraged by Admiral Ward's message, the captain gave some indication.

He sighted the U.S.S. *Leonard F. Mason* steaming north up the coast. The *Mason* was a full-fledged destroyer. Her lethal 5-inch gun batteries were kept busy hurling shells inland to support the American and South Vietnamese ground forces. The captain knew the *Mason*'s silhouette well because he had been importuning the destroyer's skipper to help him find a shore-bombardment mission. He had Boson, the tall black sailor who was the *Vance*'s leading signalman, flash the *Mason* with a blinker light and ask in Morse code where she was going.

"They want me up north . . . in hurry. I do not know what for," the *Mason*'s captain flashed back. "If anything develops, will let you know."

Arnheiter surmised "what for." He knew from the coded fleet radio teletype traffic that the Army's First Air Cavalry Division was about to launch Operation Masher, a major offensive against the Viet Cong and North Vietnamese army units operating in the Bong Son district at the northern end of the *Vance*'s patrol zone. He set off after the *Mason* at 17.5 knots.

An hour or so later, another message clacked in over the radio teletype from Navy headquarters in Saigon. All Market Time vessels were ordered to stay out of an area off the coast from where the offensive was taking place, to give the *Mason* and the other gunfire destroyers uninhibited freedom of maneuver for the protection of the infantrymen. Generous marked off the prohibited zone on a chart, then carried the chart and a copy of the order up to Arnheiter on the bridge. The captain read the message, grunted and initialed it. He glanced at the chart and silently returned both to Generous. He did not change course. The helmsman steered straight for the forbidden zone.

The *Vance* was required to report her position to the coastal surveillance center at Qui Nhon every two hours. When the next reporting time came, at 2 P.M., the ship was inside the prohibited area. Nevertheless, Generous prepared the normal message, giving the *Vance*'s correct position, and sent it up to the bridge for routine approval before transmission. The message came back with the correct location crossed out and a different position penciled in which put the *Vance* farther out to sea and about fifteen miles from where she actually was. Generous phoned Hoppy Mason, who was the officer of the deck, and told him this position was incorrect.

"That's the way I was directed to send it," Mason said tersely.

"Well, it's not right," Generous said. "Let me speak to the captain." He told Arnheiter the ship's true location and repeated that the position penciled onto the message was inaccurate.

"Well, you can send it like that, can't you, Tom?" the captain said.

Generous had recovered slightly from the shock of his humiliation. He was still afraid of Arnheiter, but he had recouped some of his self-confidence and his fear was now educated by wariness. He immediately thought: "If I say, 'Yes, I can,' then that's my baby, and if we ever have to go to a court-martial or any kind of legal proceeding, he's going to say, 'I asked him if he could send it and he said yes; therefore it was his responsibility.'" So he answered, "If that's what you want me to do, sir."

The captain repeated the same rhetorical question. Generous reiterated his reply, and they went round two or three times more. The captain abruptly ended the contest of wills.

"I desire it," Arnheiter said, using an expression which he had informed his officers was tantamount to an order, and which he often emphasized with a flip of the hand to hurry the subordinate on the errand.

"Aye, aye, sir," Generous said, and radioed the message. He took the precaution, however, of noting the *Vance*'s correct position in the combat information center log, and instructed the CIC crew to be certain they logged the ship's true location every time the bridge ordered a false position sent.

What Generous did not know was that as soon as he had walked back down to the combat information center after showing the captain the order from Saigon, Arnheiter calculated a series of false positions that would give Qui Nhon and Navy headquarters the impression that the *Vance* was conscientiously patrolling her assigned area. The captain marked these fictitious locations on the bridge chart for the officer of the deck to transmit at the required two-hour intervals. The surveillance center at Qui Nhon was one of several such stations set up along the Viet Nam coast to monitor the activities of the Market Time ships for the Saigon headquarters. Except in certain specified circumstances, the ships reported to these coastal stations rather than directly to Saigon. The surveillance centers then relayed the information, and Navy headquarters kept track of ship movements in this indirect fashion.

The captain explained to Hardy that the subterfuge was necessary "to keep those dunderheads and rustics in Qui Nhon from interfering with us. They just want to sit on their duffs. They're not interested in vigorously prosecuting this war."

"But, Captain, what if an emergency develops and someone needs help in a hurry?" Hardy argued. "Qui Nhon will look up at their chart and see the position we've reported and think we're the closest ship. They'll order us to go and we won't be there. We'll be twenty miles away. What happens then?"

"You don't understand, Ray," the captain said.

He caught up with the *Mason* off the Tam Quan Peninsula; the destroyer's superstructure was heaving backward with the recoil of each salvo from her batteries. Now that he had reached his destination, the captain threw the general-quarters-alarm switch on the loudspeaker panel. At the clangor of impending action, the men of the *Vance* bustled into flak jackets and steel helmets and ran for their battle stations. They spent the rest of the afternoon there, shuffling their feet as the captain pestered the *Mason* and a naval gunfire spotter (who was over the battlefield, controlling the destroyer's batteries from an observation plane of the Piper Cub type) to give him a target. Arnheiter forgot his radio call sign and addressed the spotter as "circling aircraft," two gaffes of the first order in military etiquette.

"Circling aircraft, circling aircraft, this is *Vance*," he announced. "Hey, Ray, what's our call sign?" he asked, after the spotter warned him he was compromising the code by giving the *Vance*'s name in the clear.

"Silk Point, Captain," Hardy said.

"Circling aircraft, circling aircraft, this is Silk Point," the captain resumed. "Am able to assist in direct-fire mission."

The spotter asked Arnheiter for a "pepper report"—a list of the types of ammunition the ship carried for her 3-inch guns. The captain did not know pepper from salt, and the *Mason* had to interrupt her work to explain the term to him by flashing light. The spotter instructed Arnheiter to "stand by." But the captain could not bear idleness with the war so near. He paced back and forth across the bridge, grabbing the radio microphone and breaking into the network whenever his eagerness overcame him, to urge the spotter to find him something to shoot at. The radio circuits were very crowded. The fight was going badly for the Americans and the South Vietnamese. Several infantry companies were pinned down in the rice paddies by North Vietnamese troops well ensconced in bunkers built into the canal dikes around the peasant hamlets. The low-lying fog and rain of the monsoon were making it difficult for the planes and the guns of the artillery and the destroyers to smash the enemy automatic weapons that were killing the infantrymen. The spotter eventually lost his forbearance and asked the captain to please get the hell off the air.

Captain Arnheiter was not about to be discouraged. He was back the next morning with a cheerful greeting for the skipper of the *Mason*. "Good day, Captain," he had Boson signal by blinker light. "Ready to join you again." The gentlemanly tenor of his greeting notwithstanding, Arnheiter committed another gaffe in military etiquette by fouling the *Mason*'s gun range—maneuvering the *Vance* between the destroyer and her targets inland—and had to be peremptorily directed out of the way. The skipper of the *Mason* told his communications officer to turn on a tape recorder and make a record of Arnheiter's radio transmissions.

By midafternoon of this second day, Arnheiter could restrain himself no longer. "I hold some bunkers and trenches

. . . on top of a sand dune. It looks like a good mission for me," he radioed the spotter in the observation plane.

"Is there any activity?" the spotter asked.

"Negative," the captain first acknowledged. "I see no people. But there are trenches . . ." He apparently thought better of his candor and informed the spotter he could see a "machine gun in sand dune."

"Fire!" he shouted, without waiting for permission from the spotter. A seaman instantly relayed the command over the phone to Williams at the main gun-control apparatus on the O-3 deck above. Williams had sent two shells flying toward the dune before the spotter could stop Arnheiter with a "Cease fire! Cease fire!"

"I am unable to see gun emplacement," the spotter said. "Can you observe it?"

"We can observe," the captain assured him, and the spotter gave Arnheiter permission to fire six more shells.

"We sure scared the hell out of those sand crabs over there," Belmonte said to Williams.

The captain of the *Mason* had been scanning the dune through binoculars from his bridge, and he saw nothing but sand. He was afraid that several of the *Vance*'s shells that had overshot the dune might have landed among the American and South Vietnamese troops fighting two to four miles inland. There had been enough misses to arouse condescending remarks from his officers. Although the *Vance*'s 3-inchers were puny compared to the *Mason*'s 5-inch guns, they had a high velocity and a range of four miles.

At dinner that night the captain instructed Merkel to compose a combined after-action report and press release. After any action worthy of note, a ship transmitted such a report to Navy headquarters in Saigon. The reports were also routed to other Navy commands in the Pacific over the fleet radio teletype network, and were read by the officers of most ships at breakfast in lieu of a morning newspaper. The Navy Information Office in Saigon passed the reports along to the civilian newsmen there. Merkel wrote as unadorned an account as he could and sent it up to Arnheiter. "This isn't adequate at all," the captain said. "You don't understand how to write press releases. I'll write it myself."

Picket Destroyer Escort U.S.S. *Vance* delivered urgent naval gunfire support on 29 January, 1966, in the Tam Quan area of the coast of Viet Nam on the South China sea [Arnheiter's superiors and the rest of the Pacific Fleet learned over their morning coffee]. *Vance* directly supported the major push by the U.S. Army's First Cavalry Division in their assault of the Viet Cong stronghold in the Trung Phan [Bong Son] district. The urgent fire request was issued by the II Corps U.S. Navy gunfire support team, while the *Vance* was conducting a surveillance patrol of the Vietnamese coast as part of the Market Time coastal surveillance task force. The ship, whose watchwords are, "Seek out, Engage, Destroy" [a traditional battle order in the Royal Navy], responded to the call by proceeding at full speed to a position within 1,200 yards of the Viet Cong controlled coast line. In this position she delivered highly accurate bombardment against known Viet Cong machine gun bunkers and an entrenchment area approximately 2½ miles away. The very first round was observed to hit one of the bunkers. Upon destruction of the target area, after firing seventeen rounds of high explosive ammunition, *Vance* remained in shallow off-shore waters to provide further support when and where needed, until the spotting aircraft was compelled to leave the area due to refueling requirements. Lieutenant Commander Marcus A. Arnheiter, USN, a 1952 Naval Academy graduate, of New York and Kezar Lake, Maine, is the commanding officer. He is the son of Dr. D. B. Arnheiter of New York and is a grandson of the late Baron Louis Von Arnheiter, an early pioneer in manned flight.

After reading Arnheiter's press report, the captain of the *Mason*, whose ship was still on station, scanned the dune once more. Again he could see nothing but sand. He remembered that "the very first round" had missed, not hit, the dune. None the wiser, the Navy Information Office in Saigon distributed the account to the reporters there, and the U.S.S. *Vance* and her intrepid skipper rated a sentence or two in some of the news dispatches that day.

By attributing his exploit to an "urgent fire request" from the spotter, Arnheiter fulfilled the rules of engagement in his operations order, which permitted him to respond to emergencies. An emergency also made it legitimate for him to sail into the prohibited zone. The captain gave no indication that he was worried that the spotter or the skipper of the *Mason* might contradict him. He apparently assumed that any reports they might file would get lost in the labyrinth of the military bureaucracy and that if the reports did not, he could explain them away afterward.

Arnheiter sailed south the next day, January 30, to renew battle. He found another destroyer, the U.S.S. *Bache,* bombarding a group of huts located several miles inland. They supposedly comprised a guerrilla training camp. Arnheiter harried the *Bache* and her airborne spotter for a target, just as he had the *Mason* and her controller, and with the same outcome—Arnheiter had to find his own.

Standing atop the O-3 deck above the bridge, accoutered in helmet and flak jacket, the bone-handled .38-caliber revolver strapped to his hip, the captain had the helmsman swing the ship in front of the rock-and-foliage face of a mountain that plunged sharply to the sea about eight hundred yards from where the *Bache* was anchored. "There's something moving up there," he said, pointing at a clump of trees and brush among the rocks. He picked up an M-1 rifle and fired several bullets. They glanced off the rocks with the slight sparks of steel on flint.

"See, Ray, see," he said excitedly to Hardy, who was standing beside him. "They're shooting at us. Look at those muzzle flashes from their automatic weapons."

"I don't see anybody, Captain," Hardy said.

"Can't you see them moving around up there?" the captain asked.

"No, I can't," Hardy persisted.

Arnheiter turned toward Williams at the main gun-control apparatus. "Spray that place with a few bursts from the fifty-calibers," he said. "That'll flush them out."

The armor-piercing bullets of the heavy machine guns ricocheted off the rocks in a string of bright white flashes.

"I saw them, I saw them! There are the muzzle flashes. They're shooting at us!" the captain yelled in a voice of genuine fright. He dove behind the thin metal shielding that ringed the gun-control equipment. "Fire! Fire!" he screamed at Williams. "Get those three-inchers going. Shoot! Shoot!" The twin 3-inch guns in the fore and aft turrets joined the .50-calibers in an immense racket.

Cornejo, the ship's chief medical corpsman, was sitting at the wardroom table below, his general-quarters station, in helmet and flak jacket. In actual battle the wardroom would be converted into a rudimentary hospital. He could hear the detonations of the *Vance*'s guns, but no return fire. His curiosity forced him out onto the main deck. He found Chief Radioman Everett R. Grissom leaning on the rail, watching the mountainside through binoculars.

"Hey, Chief Grissom," Cornejo asked, "what are we shooting at?"

"Two chickens," Grissom said, handing Cornejo the glasses.

Cornejo could see only patches of dense brush and trees and the ricochets of the *Vance*'s shells on the rocks.

"Where the hell are the chickens?" he asked.

"Look to the right," Grissom said.

Cornejo swung the binoculars and saw a Vietnamese peasant's thatched hovel perched on a kind of ledge that jutted out about eighty to a hundred yards off to the right. Each time the 3-inchers cracked out another shell, the chickens would flap their wings and run around the dirt yard in front of the hut as if a dog were chasing them.

Hardy looked down at Arnheiter, crouched behind the gun-control shielding, his boyish features hard with fright. "You really do think they're shooting at you, don't you?" Hardy said to himself. Earlier that morning the captain had told Hardy that he intended to make believe the guerrillas were firing at the ship in order to bombard the coast once more. He tried to rehearse the executive officer in a Mutt-and-Jeff sequence for the charade. "I'll fire an M-1 at some spot on the beach and say I can see the muzzle flashes of their weapons and you'll agree with me. Then we'll fire back in self-defense. That'll take care of the rules of engagement."

"I can't pretend something like that, Captain," Hardy had said. "What do you want to do that for, anyway?"

"We've got to keep up the morale of the crew by making them believe they're engaging the enemy," the captain replied.

Hardy now realized that Arnheiter had ended by deceiving himself with the ricochets of the heavy-machine-gun bullets. He felt instinctive contempt for his captain's behavior. "You were standing out there just as brave as a peacock until you saw those flashes and thought it was real live combat," Hardy thought.

"Captain," he shouted at Arnheiter, to halt the firing, "those are just our own armor-piercing shells striking on the rocks over there."

Arnheiter stared up at him in surprise. "Oh yeah," the captain replied. "Well, keep shooting. Get those three-inchers back on up there." He rose slowly from behind the gun-control shielding.

Belmonte climbed up to the O-3 deck from his battle station at the aft turret a few minutes after Hardy finally managed to stop the fusillade. The guns had punished the rocks and jungle with six hundred rounds of .50-caliber and sixty-two 3-inch cannon shells. The skipper of the *Bache* had been watching through long-range glasses and had seen only ricochets. He had considered ordering Arnheiter to cease fire, but had decided this would be too discourteous to another ship captain.

"I volunteer to go ashore and make a body count," Belmonte said with a sneer in the captain's presence.

"Pipe down, Luis," Hardy said.

"I'd have been happy to go over there," Belmonte said to Merkel afterward. "I'd have reported that we'd killed three Vietnamese peasants, unarmed, and two Marines."

Williams and some of the enlisted men had also noticed Arnheiter's uncaptainly behavior in ducking behind the gun-control shielding. Soon everyone on the ship had heard the story. Belmonte and the others remembered that when the captain had gone into Qui Nhon for a briefing at the coastal surveillance center, he wore his flak jacket and two pistols, the .38 on one hip and a .22-caliber revolver on the other, and had taken along a bodyguard of several sailors armed with Tommy guns. Arnheiter had told his subordinates that Qui Nhon was a very dangerous place and that once, while a staff officer with Admiral DuBois' gunfire flotilla, he had seen the body of an American soldier captured by the Viet Cong hung up in the outskirts of the town. The *Vance*'s officers thought this attitude curious because they had been to Qui Nhon several times during the previous Viet Nam patrol and knew it was a relatively secure place, filled with brothels, bars and tailor shops that catered to the United States and South Korean troops stationed there. Americans did not customarily carry weapons in town. The officers and sailors at the surveillance center had laughed at the appearance of the captain and his mini-phalanx. Arnheiter was forced to check his pistols at the door of the officers' club before the bar would serve him a drink.

In the captain's after-action report and press release that night, there was no hint to the admirals of the fleet that Marcus Aurelius Arnheiter had behaved in anything less than the tradition they expected of their ship captains. The Viet Cong had been impudent enough to fire at the *Vance* and the guerrillas had been exterminated for their temerity. The captain ended the tale with some I-was-there grist for the newsmen in Saigon, a quotation he composed and attributed to Seaman Walter L. Cochran, of Greenville, South Carolina, who manned the telephone at the main gun-control station. "That mountain was full of 'em. You could see the tracers coming from the rocky crevices," Cochran told the world.

Content, Captain Arnheiter rested his crew the next day. They refueled at sea from an oiler and refreshed their spirits at another "All Hands Aft" service on the fantail. January 31 was a Monday, but before preaching his sermon, the captain explained that Monday was as appropriate as Sunday for divine worship in the Pacific because the time difference put the

Vance a day ahead of Pearl Harbor time "and your loved ones at home are going to church right now." The following morning he returned to the Tam Quan Peninsula to help the destroyer *Mason* and the First Air Cavalry Division fight the North Vietnamese. Hardy and Generous pleaded with him not to go.

"Don't you realize that order from Saigon is still in effect, Captain? We're not supposed to be in that area," Generous said.

The captain did not reply.

"We haven't patrolled our area for days and days," Hardy intervened. "Now we're not going to patrol it for another day and we're going right back into that prohibited zone. Captain, we've got to stay out of there and start doing our job." (Although boring, the *Vance*'s appointed mission in Operation Market Time was not meaningless. The presence of the ship guarding the coast theoretically deterred the smuggling of arms and infiltrators from North Viet Nam into the South. And the alert might apprehend a smuggler. Later that year, two 125-foot steel-hulled trawlers from North Viet Nam were seized with thousands of weapons and tons of ammunition aboard. One of the trawlers slipped by a picket ship like the *Vance* before it was intercepted by a Coast Guard cutter as it was about to enter a river mouth to unload its cargo of munitions. A captured North Vietnamese crewman said the trawler had been running the American blockade on a regular schedule every month on a moonless night and was on its eleventh trip when caught.)

"Back there is where the action is, and that's where we're going," the captain said, ending the discussion.

Arnheiter had already taken care to give Navy headquarters in Saigon the impression that he was conscientiously patrolling the 105 miles of coastline assigned to the *Vance*. He was accomplishing this in the same fashion that he had pretended to stay out of the prohibited zone until he was called in by the airborne spotter for "urgent naval gunfire support." He was simply faking the daily reports the *Vance* submitted on the number of Vietnamese junks and sampans sighted and boarded for inspection. The captain invented his own arithmetic. A junk perceived on the horizon became a junk boarded and inspected. At the end of the day, liberal additions were made to both columns to compensate for junks that Arnheiter said his subordinate officers had "forgotten."

The North Vietnamese battalions in the Bong Son district were still, if sporadically, resisting the First Air Cavalry Division and the South Vietnamese paratroopers engaged in Operation Masher. When the *Vance* neared the *Mason*'s bombardment station, the captain was up on the O-3 deck again with his microphone on the long extension cord. The sight of the jet fighters and the helicopters strafing and dive-bombing the enemy-held hamlets inland enthralled him, and he became so mesmerized narrating the scene to the crew that he forgot he had command of the bridge—the "conn" in nauticalese. The latest command he had given the helmsman placed the *Vance* on a collision course with the rocks of the Tam Quan Peninsula. The captain talked on and on about the orange flare of the napalm and the grayish-black balls of smoke from the bursting bombs. The peninsula got nearer and nearer. Hardy, who had remained on the bridge one level below, was in the pilothouse glancing back and forth apprehensively at the depth reading on the fathometer and at the peninsula looming across the bow. When the depth and the distance became too slight for his nerves, he ran out onto a wing of the bridge and climbed the ladder until his head was level with the O-3 deck.

"Captain, we're on a collision course with that peninsula. We've got to turn," he shouted.

"It's beautiful. It's beautiful," the captain told the crew. "I see a splendid panorama of combat," he said, whipping the extension cord behind him and turning away from Hardy. Although several seamen on the O-3 deck with the captain looked at Hardy in consternation, none ventured to interrupt Arnheiter.

Hardy ran back into the pilothouse and took another look at the fathometer and the peninsula. He dashed out again and bounded onto the ladder.

"Captain, Captain," he screamed, "you've got to turn or we're going to slam right into those rocks!" Arnheiter saw more blossoming napalm. He heard nothing.

Hardy fled into the pilothouse. He could see the surf breaking on the peninsula so clearly now that its thunder reverberated in his mind's ear. In moments the ship would rip out her bottom on the jagged granite and the impact would crush to death or mutilate some of the sailors down in the hold.

"This is the exec," he shouted to the helmsman. "I have the conn. Right hard rudder. Starboard engines back full!" This emergency maneuver had the effect of turning the ship sharply, at the same time abruptly slowing its forward momentum. The old hull shuddered, but Mason's enginemen managed to force enough air through the wheezy clutches to reverse the starboard diesels. The *Vance* edged away from the rocks.

When the captain came down to the bridge a few minutes later in a jovial mood, his executive officer—calm, deliberate, polite, obedient Hardy—was trembling. The ship had almost been driven aground and men killed in the most absurd of circumstances, and the symbolism of Hardy's seizure of the conn was not lost on himself or the other officers and seamen on the bridge. Hardy had, if only momentarily, taken command of the ship away from the captain. His face ashen, Hardy beckoned Arnheiter out onto a wing of the bridge.

"What's going on, Ray?" the captain asked.

"Do you realize, Captain, that I couldn't get through to you to advise you that you were running the ship aground on those rocks over there, and all the bridge personnel know that you forgot you had the conn and I had to take the ship out of a situation in extremis?"

"That's all right, Ray, you brought the ship around fine, didn't you?" Arnheiter said cheerfully.

"The motto of this ship," Belmonte said to Merkel in a wry play on the captain's first press release, "shouldn't be 'Seek out, Engage, Destroy.' It ought to be 'Seek out and Collide with.'"

The captain was soon on the radio speaking to the *Mason*'s

spotter. "Circling aircraft, circling aircraft, this is Silk Point. Be advised I am available for an urgent mission." Hours later the *Vance* was still available and the spotter still unimpressed. So the captain punished the peninsula by demolishing the one relic of man on its barren end—a deserted masonry structure sitting on a slope about five yards below the peninsula's crest. The small gray building looked like "a brick outhouse" through Hoppy Mason's binoculars. It might have been one of the many Buddhist and Taoist shrines that dot the Vietnamese countryside, Belmonte subsequently decided. The captain of the *Mason,* who had his tape recorder on this time and his long-range glasses focused on the spot, had no idea what purpose the building served. He knew he had not seen a human being within nearly a mile of it during the four days his destroyer had been on station. To obtain the spotter's permission to destroy the structure, Arnheiter radioed that he had found "a VC stone machine-gun emplacement." Hardy tried to persuade the captain not to open fire because he was afraid there might be a fishing hamlet or American or South Vietnamese troops along the beach on the other side of the peninsula. Any shells that missed the building would obviously sail over the crest.

"It's okay, Ray. This is all Viet Cong territory around here," the captain said with a sweep of his arm.

Hardy's stomach wrenched several times as the first few shells did miss the target and overshoot the crest. Belmonte, who also happened to be on the bridge, lost his temper. "What a stupid goddamn stunt this is," he said loudly. "We're liable to kill somebody."

"I know what I'm doing, Mr. Belmonte," the captain said irritably. "Your objections have been taken note of and I'll thank you to keep quiet."

After the initial misses, Williams and his gunner's mates rapidly tore the building to pieces with forty high-explosive shells. The spotter in the plane swooped low for a look and reported that the *Vance* had "knocked the hell out of it." The captain was elated.

The captain of the *Mason* was aghast. He flashed the

Vance to "clear the area immediately" after Arnheiter fouled the destroyer's gun range once more by steering between the *Mason* and her targets inland. The crew of the *Vance* were also sickened by the farcical heroics and ashamed for their ship. "This guy is making us the laughingstock of the fleet," Cornejo said to one of his fellow petty officers.

The sorry building sea-changed into "a hot Viet Cong target . . . a machine-gun . . . fortified emplacement" in the captain's press release that night, and he had, of course, responded with another "urgent direct fire mission at the request of a U.S. airborne spotter."

Arnheiter heaped rancor on shame by mailing copies of the press releases about each of his shore-bombardment stunts to the Fleet Hometown News Center at the Great Lakes Naval Training Center in Illinois, over the names of every officer and sailor on the ship. The center automatically forwards such releases to newspapers near the hometowns of the men whose names and addresses are attached. The papers are usually parochial enough to print the stories because their subscribers want to know what their sons and husbands are doing in the United States Navy. In this fashion, the news of how Boiler Tender Jones, his ship the U.S.S. *Vance,* and her courageous skipper, Lieutenant Commander Marcus A. Arnheiter, were lambasting the Communists in Viet Nam, could be printed in local journals around the country. Many of the sailors submitted written requests to the captain asking that the press releases not be sent out over their names. They were embarrassed at the thought of Arnheiter's fantasies appearing in their hometown papers. Also, they did not want to worry their parents and wives by giving them the impression that they were working, eating and sleeping under enemy bullets, when actually life would have been fairly dull except for Captain Arnheiter. One sailor wrote the captain that his mother had a weak heart and he did not want to endanger her. Arnheiter disapproved all of the requests and ordered the press releases copied on the Xerox machine and dispatched to the Hometown News Center. "They have to go out," he explained to Hardy. "This is not for the man himself. It's for the Navy.

It's done so that the Navy's image will be brought to his hometown and young men there will see what the Navy is doing and enlist."

Captain Arnheiter gave no indication that he sensed any of what his officers and sailors, and the captains of the *Mason* and the *Bache,* thought of his exploits. He was, in fact, very pleased with himself. He had command of a ship, he had found a war and he was winning acclaim. Promotion would surely follow. He was at last living one of those adventure stories of military heroism that he had filled his youth with reading. Cornejo might feel scorn and shame, and the sailors might protest the hometown news releases, but it was the captain's press accounts that went out over the teletype to the rest of the fleet and to local newspapers. And Captain Arnheiter was not very concerned with the opinion of small or middling men. He cultivated important individuals—admirals. Xeroxed copies of each of his press releases, accompanied by friendly covering letters, were mailed off to the admirals he knew, just in case they might have missed reading his stirring prose on the fleet teletype network. The night before the deserted masonry structure on the Tam Quan Peninsula became "a hot Viet Cong target" for the *Vance*'s guns, the captain had sat down at the desk in his cabin and composed a "Dear Admiral" to Admiral Baumberger, the Commander, Cruiser-Destroyer Force Pacific, in San Diego—the "Bombo" of Arnheiter's table talk.

The captain began the letter by reminding the admiral of a pleasant luncheon and a last talk aboard Baumberger's flagship just before Arnheiter flew to Pearl Harbor in December to take command of the *Vance.* He had, he said, been deeply impressed then with Baumberger's philosophy of aggressiveness and quick response to challenge in a hostile environment. The admiral could rest assured that Arnheiter was living up to this philosophy, not only by keeping a weather eye for smugglers, but also by vigorously searching out the Viet Cong, wherever the enemy might be, ashore or afloat. In the ten days the *Vance* had been "on the line" in Operation Market Time, Arnheiter wrote that he had fired an "urgent naval gunfire support mission" for the First Air Cavalry Division, discovered a suspected submarine supply landing point on the beach north of Qui Nhon (he was enclosing a copy of Admiral Ward's congratulatory message on this exploit for Baumberger's edification), and yesterday he had pasted the Viet Cong with a sterilizing barrage after the guerrillas had been foolish enough to fire upon his ship (he was also enclosing his press release on this feat in case the details might interest Baumberger).

In conclusion, he relished his work and appreciated the opportunity to command one of Baumberger's ships. He was,

"Very respectfully yours,

"Marc Arnheiter"

7

MARCUS TIME

Oh Jesus, it's just sick . . . It's
more than unhappy, it's a way of life.

—Lieutenant Generous

"You wake up every morning on this ship with a little bit of
fear in your breath," Merkel said to Mike McWhirter, the
electronics material officer, a couple of days after the near-
collision with the Tam Quan Peninsula. McWhirter nodded.
Merkel had aptly summarized the sense of apprehension that
had become a permanent element of life under Captain Arnheiter. And that night Ensign McWhirter, an uncomplicated,
cheerful youth, learned how very real the fear for survival
could be.

Besides dispatching the speedboat to skip along the surf
waving its three-by-five-foot American flag at the enemy in the
hope of stirring up his wrath, the captain had also been employing the larger whaleboat as a decoy. He would send the
whaleboat off with an armed crew to prowl some bay and
make as much noise as possible, while the *Vance* lurked outside the entrance to the bay, ready to rush in and decimate
the Viet Cong or the North Vietnamese as soon as they took
the bait. Although the enemy had never responded, the captain was not discouraged. After dark he ordered McWhirter
and a crew of sailors to scout another bay in the whaleboat.

When they returned to the ship a few hours later, the captain decided not to hoist the whaleboat aboard again. "I want them to search some junks later on," he told Hardy. "So we'll tow the whaleboat behind us. That'll make things easier."

"We'd better evacuate the crew first, Captain," Hardy said. "The sea's choppy and we might swamp that boat."

"No," Arnheiter said, "I want to tow the boat with the crew in it, so all I'll have to do is slip the towline and they can go off and investigate a junk. Tell them to stay where they are."

"You don't mean it, do you?" McWhirter yelled at Hardy when the executive officer walked back to the fantail to tell him what the captain intended.

"Yes, I do mean it, Mr. McWhirter, so stow it," Hardy shouted back. Tom Williams also protested the danger and Hardy silenced him too. "Just do what you're told and throw a towline out to McWhirter, Tom," he said, returning to the bridge.

The captain started off at 8 knots. The whaleboat yawed back and forth in the three-to-four-foot seas. Water surged over the bow, and McWhirter and the sailors cursed the captain and bailed for their lives.

Hardy had stationed Belmonte on the fantail with an ax to sever the towrope if the whaleboat foundered. "I'll never be able to chop through that rope in time," Belmonte said to Williams. "If this line goes taut at the same time that whaleboat noses into a wave, they'll be pulled right under." Belmonte grew so agitated that he wanted to defy the captain. "Fuck that flaming nut on the bridge," he shouted at Williams. "Let's cut Mike loose before somebody gets drowned."

Williams restrained him. "He's the captain, Luis, and we've got to follow his orders."

Hardy came back for another look and ran to the bridge. "That boat's not riding worth a damn, Captain," he said. "We're going to swamp it and lose those people. Let me bring them aboard."

"Maybe it'll ride easier if we go a little faster," Arnheiter said. He increased speed to 10 knots. The whaleboat took a worse buffeting.

"That whaleboat's not built like a speedboat, Captain," Hardy explained. "You can't get it up on the plane of the waves by going faster. It just won't work. Why don't you come to the fantail with me and have a look?"

The captain would not go. "You're wrong, Ray. I know what I'm doing," he said. "Let's try a bit more speed. That'll certainly make it ride better." He ordered the engine room to move up to 12 knots.

Hardy could see that the whaleboat was yawing very badly now, and that McWhirter and the sailors were bailing in a panic. Arnheiter had been towing the boat for an hour and ten minutes by this time. The quartermaster of the bridge watch had silently recorded the outline of the drama, jotting down in his notebook the changes in course and speed as the captain called them out. Hardy could stand the tension no longer. He pushed what authority his position gave him to the limit. "Goddamn it, Captain," he yelled at Arnheiter. "We have got to take those men aboard. You're going to drown them and you can't do this."

"Do you really think so?" Arnheiter asked mildly.

"Yes, I do," Hardy said. "And if you'd go back there with me and have a look at them, you'd see what I mean."

Arnheiter did, and glanced at the wildly pitching whaleboat. "All right, you can bring them aboard now," he said. Hardy stopped the ship.

A storm of four-letter words came over the deck railing with McWhirter and the whaleboat crew, loud enough for Hardy to hear them on the wing of the bridge. The captain stayed inside.

"Jesus Christ, what the hell was all that happy horseshit about?" McWhirter bellowed up at Hardy. "Were you trying to get us all killed?" Hardy shook his head and turned away.

The rest of the patrol ships off Viet Nam might be on Market Time. The crew of the *Vance* coined a new name for their existence—"Marcus Time." The sailors had nicknamed the captain "Mad Marcus," and with the exception of Hardy,

who would tolerate no derision of Arnheiter, they did not hesitate to make remarks like "He's crazy" and "When's he going
to get out the ball bearings?" in the presence of an officer. A
standing joke among the seamen was that someone should
write home for a copy of *The Caine Mutiny* so that they could
find out what was going to happen next. Generous, Belmonte,
Merkel and most of the other officers were, in turn, openly
cursing the captain in front of the sailors. They referred to
him as "Marcus," a nickname as mocking as the crew's, even if
it lacked the attribute of madness. Ross Wright had always
been called simply "the captain."

If the speedboat and the motor whaleboat were not being
dispatched on some fruitless expedition near the shore to
tempt enemy gunners, "Away the Special Fire Team" was
sounding over the loudspeaker system. The sailors who were
members would drop whatever they were doing, grab their
M-1 rifles and race to the sandbags on the O-1 deck so that
the captain could drill his ersatz infantry for the moment of
truth he was certain would come. "One round ball, lock and
load" became a sailor's greeting in the passageways. To distinguish their troop, the members of the fire team devised a
special flag. They drew the outline of a .30-caliber bullet in
black on a white pillowcase with a felt-tipped pen and crudely
lettered "Marcus' Marauders" underneath.

When the racket of the fire team was stilled, the captain
sat on one of the metal chairs he had had Mason's shipfitters
erect on the two open wings of the bridge and banged away
at sharks and sea snakes with a rifle, a Tommy gun or one
of his revolvers. He perpetually unnerved the officers by shooting at sea snakes and sharks swimming alongside junks they
had boarded to inspect. One afternoon Arnheiter almost frightened Belmonte into killing an old Vietnamese fisherman on a
junk he was inspecting. For some reason that Belmonte could
not put his finger on, this junk appeared suspicious and made
him uneasy. As he was climbing out of the small engine
compartment at the stern, the detonations of three quick shots
struck his ear and water splashed next to him. He instinctively
assumed that the junk crew were guerrillas who had opened

fire on the *Vance*. He leaped out onto the deck, jerked his
.45-caliber pistol from its holster and thrust it into the stomach
of the fisherman nearest him. The elderly Vietnamese started
trembling and babbling. "Why, you dumb son of a bitch,"
Belmonte thought as he suddenly realized what had happened. He looked up at a wing of the bridge. There was the
captain sitting on a chair with a rifle over his knee, like a
guard on a stagecoach, searching for another shark.

Arnheiter's habit of leaving loaded rifles and Tommy guns
haphazardly around the bridge was another nettle to the
nerves. The weapons would rattle about when the ship rolled
in a trough. The officers and seamen on bridge watch dreaded
that one might go off accidentally. Merkel developed a practice of unloading every rifle and Tommy gun on the bridge
as soon as he came on watch. This precaution also meant
that he would be alerted when the captain was about to start
shooting again, since he would hear Arnheiter chambering a
bullet. The captain had a way of nonchalantly opening fire
next to a man's ear or over his shoulder. If the officer or seaman jumped in surprise, Arnheiter would chuckle. Even the
laundrymen complained, for the captain absentmindedly left
bullets in the pockets of his dirty clothes; they were afraid that
the shells might explode in the dryer.

The Vietnamese fisher folk also learned who Captain Arnheiter was. He was always yelling at them and firing a revolver or rifle over their heads or in front of the bows of
their junks and sampans, to make them come alongside faster
for boarding. Cornejo watched in disgust one afternoon while
the captain snapped off shot after shot from his .38 revolver
over the heads of a fisherman, his wife and a small boy in a
sampan because they were not moving quickly enough to suit
him. The result was that the scared fishermen stove in the
gunwales of their boats or battered the hulls against the *Vance*
in the rush. "How they must hate us," Merkel said to Generous. "When you go aboard to search them, they're shaking
like a leaf."

The captain could not get along with the Vietnamese navy
liaison officers assigned to the *Vance* as interpreters and ad-

visers, and he angered them in numerous ways. One was his rough handling of the fisher folk. Another was his insistence on arresting fishermen and Vietnamese soldiers going home on furlough in passenger junks as draft dodgers, suspected guerrillas, or deserters, after the liaison officers had warned him that the men were innocent. Arnheiter, who did not read Vietnamese, would contend that they had no identification papers or that their papers were not in order. The prisoners would subsequently be released in Qui Nhon by the Vietnamese police, to whom the captain turned them over, but in the meantime he could relax a bit at the bar of the officers' club there, and he looked efficient in the daily reports to Navy headquarters in Saigon. The facts about the true identity of prisoners never caught up with the reports of all the malefactors Captain Arnheiter was apprehending.

The captain also embarrassed the Vietnamese liaison officers by correcting their lacerated English and by giving them unsolicited lessons in American table manners. "Now say it again, say it again. You'll get it right this time," he would coach the Vietnamese in his best boys' school Latin teacher's manner. When Vietnamese do not use chopsticks they normally eat in European fashion, with the fork in the left hand, because of their French colonial heritage. Arnheiter would reach across the table with a smile, take the fork out of the liaison officer's left hand and place it in his right hand. He insisted that the Vietnamese eat Western-style dishes they did not like and forced them to have second portions. "You're our guest," he would say, "and you have to eat heartily." He badgered one disconcerted liaison officer to the point where the Vietnamese took a bite of one of the captain's "gourmet dishes," shoved back his chair and walked out of the wardroom.

One morning the *Vance* stopped three large junks filled with refugees from the fighting, about half of them children. Among the passengers Arnheiter spied three Vietnamese soldiers, who were headed for Saigon on leave. He seized them as deserters over the protests of the liaison officer. The refugees seemed hungry. The captain gave them bread, milk and apples. As an afterthought he had Gwynn declare inedible $14 worth of candy from the ship's store and began passing it out to the children while his picture was taken. Fourteen dollars in candy at Navy prices was a lavish amount. Cornejo could see that the children were gorging themselves.

"You'd better not give them any more candy, Captain," he said. "They're not used to it and they'll get diarrhea."

"You don't understand, Chief," the captain replied. "The milk and bread and apples are for sustenance, and the candy is for quick energy because these people have a long way to row."

"Captain, these children won't be rowing, so they don't need any instant energy. But they will get diarrhea if you give them any more candy and then they'll crap all over those junks, and the grownups, who have to row, will get sick."

"Then I'll provide them with some toilet paper," the captain said and sent Gwynn for a dozen rolls. Cornejo watched the men in the junks roll cigarettes with the toilet paper. The captain had his picture taken distributing more candy. Cornejo retired to his dispensary.

The trouble with the Vietnamese liaison officers, Arnheiter told Hardy, was that they were all cowards and did not want "to vigorously prosecute their own war." He officially accused one Vietnamese ensign of cowardice in a report to Admiral Ward in Saigon. By mid-February the captain had worn out four liaison officers. The Vietnamese navy commander for the central coast refused to risk any more on Arnheiter's ship. In order to obtain another liaison officer, Navy headquarters in Saigon had to shift the *Vance* to the Gulf of Siam coast along the bottom of the Mekong Delta, the southernmost edge of Viet Nam, where the locals had not yet heard of Captain Arnheiter.

Men can live in an atmosphere of whimsical tyranny only so long before it starts to break down the veneer of restraint that society has imposed on their primitive emotions. The cycle of absurdity and pain disorients the mind, the senses and the emotions. A man finds himself laughing at another's pain one moment and weeping at his own the next. He loses his ability to discriminate, to judge and to balance, those qualities so important to civilized behavior. Laughter and fear and anger become the primordial forces they once were, before man, for self-protection, devised codes and traditions and laws to leash them in himself and others. Because the tyrant is unpredictable, life becomes unpredictable, and men grow equally so. By mid-February, Arnheiter was unknowingly beginning to work that strange and ominous disorientation on his crew.

The officers felt the captain's impact most tangibly, because they were physically closest to him and were not buffered, as were the sailors, by the ship's command structure. To the now commonplace aggravations like "Hellcats Reveille," "Roast Beef of Olde Englande," the racket of the Special Fire Team, the captain's war on the sharks and sea snakes, and his harangues at the wardroom table and over the loudspeaker system, Arnheiter was perpetually adding new exasperations. "You never knew when the big bird was going to come out of his cabin and shit on your head," Belmonte would say afterward.

Generous was gradually losing control over the workings of his fifty-man operations department because he was wasting a good part of his day acting the role of an admiral's staff officer. Besides using up four hours at meals, he spent the bulk of his morning giving the captain a comprehensive intelligence briefing similar to the detailed account of the Commander in Chief of the Pacific Fleet received after breakfast in Hawaii. Generous' briefing had to cover everything from military actions the length and breadth of South Viet Nam and the bombing campaign against the North, to political developments in Indonesia and the rest of Southeast Asia. The captain required elaborate, Pentagon-style charts to illustrate trends.

The forced neglect of his job led Generous to stumble one day. He sent an incorrect radio message to a shore station and embarrassed Arnheiter. The captain henceforth insisted on personally signing all messages before they were transmitted from the ship. The rule applied even to such banal traffic as sightings of merchantmen and large cargo junks, messages that had previously been transmitted by the CIC watch officer with the concurrence of the officer of the deck on the bridge. Unless the captain happened to be asleep, Generous also had to bring every message himself between the hours of 8 A.M. and 10 P.M. He could not send a sailor to Arnheiter for the signature. If the captain was sleeping, the message waited. The *Vance* received and answered about twenty-five to thirty radio messages on an average day, and fifty to seventy-five on a busy one. Generous would carry each one up to the captain on the bridge or in his cabin and explain its substance while Arnheiter asked question after question.

Generous had another problem. The captain seemed to have no concept of time, and of the inconvenience he caused others. The *Vance* was chronically late for her rendezvous with oilers and provisions ships when she had to refuel or to take on supplies at sea, because Arnheiter would become distracted by his Special Fire Team practice or would decide to visit a Vietnamese district chief to whom he had taken a fancy in a village along the Gulf of Siam coast. All day long he would pay no attention to Generous' warnings that they must depart for a refueling scheduled for that afternoon. Finally, a half-hour before the rendezvous fifty miles away, he would express surprise, order a dash at 18 knots, and instruct Generous to contact the oiler on the radio and inform her captain that the *Vance* had been unforeseeably delayed. If Generous was unable to do this, because of the frequent communications blackouts in the tropics, Arnheiter would castigate him for "another goof in the operations department."

"What's the matter?" he would ask impatiently. "Don't you people know how to use your radios?"

Belmonte and his deck force were in eternal trouble because they could never satisfy the captain's demand for instantaneous responses to his commands. Arnheiter issued orders like a child yelling for dessert in the middle of dinner. When a thought popped up in his mind, it had to be accomplished then and there. He would, in rapid cadence, order the whaleboat lowered over the side, the speedboat launched, and the anchor dropped. Each of these tasks required time and the majority of Belmonte's eight men. When they were not performed at once and chaos ensued because of the captain's lickety-split commands, Arnheiter berated Belmonte and Belmonte's senior petty officer, Boatswain's Mate First Class Johnnie Lee Smoot, a thin, nervous man. The deck apes were sometimes so enraged that their customary profanity choked into fits of silent fury. As fatigue from the long hours and hurry-scurry operations ground them down, they grew careless about leaving rifles and flak jackets in the boats. This aroused more of the captain's ire, which in turn provoked more resentment from the deck hands. The other sailors used Smoot as a kind of guinea pig to discover the captain's obsession for that particular day. The senior boatswain's mate had to inspect the bridge watch every morning, and Arnheiter inevitably found something wrong with Smoot's uniform and chewed him out in front of the bridge crew.

"What'd he ping on you for this morning, Johnnie?" the other sailors would ask as soon as Smoot returned from the bridge. "Scuffed shoes," Smoot would reply bitterly. The other sailors would hurriedly shine their own.

The captain was a night owl. He became most alert at the time everyone else wanted to sleep—between 10 P.M. and 2 or 3 A.M. He would launch the motor whaleboat or the speedboat to round up a flock of junks to be boarded and searched, or summon one of the officers to his cabin to listen to hours of monologue. His topics did not vary nearly enough to match his long-windedness. He spoke of the value of his "programs," the life and loves of Lord Nelson (Lady Emma Hamilton, Nelson's mistress, had been "a voluptuous wench," the captain would assure his listener with a smile of envy), and the exploits of his favorite Army heroes, Generals Douglas MacArthur and George Patton. He bragged about what a marvelous job he had done as executive officer of the *Ingersoll* and about all the admirals he knew, and commiserated with himself over the slack group of officers he had inherited on the *Vance*.

Hardy was his favorite captive audience. Arnheiter would lean back in the swivel chair in front of his desk, light a panetela from the wardroom supply, and douse Hardy in words and smoke. He told Hardy of his year at West Point and of all the hazing he had endured there. He was vague, however, about why he had left. Some of his remarks about General MacArthur seemed curiously uncomplimentary. "He won medals for just trivial little things," Arnheiter told Hardy, "because he put himself up for them and he wrote very eloquent citations. It's really all how you write it up and present it that gets you the medal—it isn't what you do, it's how you make it appear." Hardy got the impression that Arnheiter did not really care whether his executive officer agreed with him, only that he be present and seem to listen. Some nights the captain rarely looked at Hardy and stared off at the bulkhead, wrinkling his brow and frowning and smiling to himself as he talked.

Hardy had to struggle out of his bunk before dawn to plot the ship's exact position by the stars and to begin the day's work. The other officers also had to rise early, to supervise the sailors under them or to stand a watch. They would show the effects of the previous night's forced insomnia. The captain would sleep late and complain if they were inattentive at a briefing or at lunch. Arnheiter's helter-skelter style of operating made it impossible to maintain any schedule. An officer or sailor sometimes found himself standing two four-hour watches in a row on top of his normal duties because the man who was supposed to be on watch was off in the whaleboat or away on some other escapade. The cycle of fatigue spread beyond the deck gang and deepened. The performance of the crew deteriorated overall, and some of the captain's complaints were justified. His nagging grew worse.

As February wore on, boredom seemed to afflict the captain. He would lock himself in his cabin at night or in the predawn hours and sleep until noon. Hardy would assemble the officers in the wardroom at eleven-thirty for lunch and send a steward to wake Arnheiter. They would wait for twenty minutes to a half-hour before he appeared. The gunner's mates canceled their morning ritual of checking the temperature in the ammunition magazines because they could not get the keys from the captain's cabin. When Generous appeared with messages in the afternoon or in the evening, he often found Arnheiter lying on his bunk, his eyes unseeing, lost in some reverie. The officer of the deck on the bridge watch took to telephoning Hardy at night to report something unusual or to ask maneuvering instructions, because Arnheiter frequently gave incoherent replies. He kept a bottle of whiskey in his cabin, another violation of Navy regulations. Mason once called him on the sound-powered phone and said he could see the headlights of trucks moving in the darkness along a coastal road through guerrilla territory, a rare event. "Very well, signal them to close my port side," the captain said.

These periods of lassitude were interspersed with bursts of intense activity. An intelligence report that the Viet Cong were collecting fish in taxes from the fishermen provoked a three-hour afternoon "war council." His plan formulated, sketched, charted and explained at sufficient length to prepare an amphibious assault, the captain had Mason's shipfitters disguise the motor whaleboat as a junk by erecting a pole in the middle, to simulate a mast, and a false poop of plywood over the stern. Two crews were formed, of five sailors each, one headed by Mason and Williams and the other by Generous and Gwynn, and that night they took turns on alert in the whaleboat, floating amidst a group of fifteen to twenty fishing craft. The captain's scheme supposed that the Viet Cong would come sailing by to exact fish, mistake the whaleboat for a fishing junk and fall into the ambush. The two crews passed most of the night, however, answering Arnheiter's questions over the radio and flashing a light in response to his instructions to signal the whaleboat's position. It was a warm, hushed tropical night. The sea was placid. The sound of their voices talking into the radio carried far over the water, and the blinking light made it obvious that something unusual was going on in that group of fishing junks.

"If there's a Viet Cong within five hundred miles he'll know where we are," Mason complained aloud to Williams. "We're supposed to be on this big secret mission and here we are standing out like the Statue of Liberty. Thank God I'm way out here where nobody knows me."

During Generous' turn in the whaleboat he lost his temper at the captain's merry-go-round: "Whaleboat, this is Silk Point. Are there any junks around you?"

"Yeah, Silk Point," Generous replied, "there are a lot of junks around," and shut off the radio. The captain drove out of the mist in the *Vance* and illuminated the whaleboat with a searchlight. Generous stood up and smiled at Arnheiter peering down from a wing of the bridge.

A few days later a teletype message arrived from Navy headquarters in Saigon. It informed the *Vance* and other Market Time ships that Army intelligence agents along the coast had reported that some vessels were disguising their whaleboats as fishing junks. This practice was dangerous and was forbidden in the future, Saigon said.

Although most of the captain's expeditions were equally fatuous, the officers and men eagerly volunteered for them. The abortive ambushes and other stunts provided a fleeting escape from the captain, and for the sailors, who did not have to talk to Arnheiter on the radio, perhaps a few hours of sleep. The officers and seamen also lined up for familiarization patrols with the Coast Guard cutters and Navy Swift boats that guarded the Gulf of Siam with the *Vance*. A Swift boat is a fast, uncomfortable craft built like an oversized speedboat, with high-powered diesel engines that screech and whine and incessantly slam the bow into the waves. It is considered impossible to sleep on one, and the crews go to sea for only twenty-four hours at a time. The officers and men of the *Vance* found they could lose consciousness on a Swift boat for an entire night, without waking once. The captain assumed that all this volunteering meant morale was high, even if performance was not what it should be, and so he tightened discipline another notch.

Captain Arnheiter never sought to disguise his assumption

that there were two standards of behavior on the *Vance*—
one for him and one for the officers and seamen. He would
drink his coffee from a gentlemanly cup and saucer on the
bridge apparently unaware that the sailors, who had been
deprived of their coffee on his order, could taste each mouth-
ful he swallowed and cursed him under their breath. Taking
coffee away from a sailor is like telling a Frenchman he can
drink no more wine. When the captain caught a seaman assigned to the bridge watch swallowing a cup of coffee in the
crew's mess one day while the man was there fetching some
for Belmonte, Arnheiter upbraided both the sailor and Belmonte.

Restrictions were soon placed on an item more fundamental than coffee—fresh water. Sand stirred off the sea bottom by the ship's propellers during the captain's incursions
close to shore, and the heavy silt of the Gulf of Siam waters,
had fouled the *Vance*'s evaporators so badly that they could
no longer distill enough fresh water from the sea. What fresh
water the evaporators did produce was disappearing in unusual quantities into the washing machines in the laundry to
keep the crew's uniforms clean enough to satisfy Arnheiter,
who changed two or three times a day himself. Fuehrer
warned the captain that the fresh-water supply was being
drawn down dangerously, but he paid no attention. Hardy
eventually had to put the crew on strict water rations. Showers were permitted for only an hour and a half a day, between 7 and 8:30 P.M. The restriction meant that many of
the officers and men had to go about dirty and itchy much
of the time in the 90-degree temperature and equally high
tropical humidity. The rationing was particularly hard on the
enginemen, who worked in 105-degree heat and came off a
shift filthy with grease and oil. Those who were not sleeping
in the engine rooms to avoid the captain had to go to bed
still begrimed, foul their sheets and make the bunks uncomfortable as well.

The captain, however, had buckets of fresh water poured
every hour over blankets and a hemp deck matting which had

been hung around his cabin to cool it from the sun by evaporation. The sonarmen, whose compartment was next to his private bathroom, kept a log of the twenty-minute showers which he took several times a day. The record on one day was twenty-seven minutes. To pass the time and to stoke their anger, the enginemen below would watch the dials on the fresh-water line from the evaporators and calculate exactly how much water the captain used up with each shower. Hardy was mortified at Arnheiter's self-indulgence because it created a moral dilemma he could not explain to the crew. "What the hell am I going to tell them?" he asked himself. "The captain gets dirtier than the rest of you, so he gets to take twenty-minute showers whenever he wants?" Once a young engineman was apprehended at 2 A.M. trying to sneak a shower. Hardy suppressed his moral qualms, bawled out the sailor and sentenced him to an extra two-hour watch over the evaporators, where the temperature was slightly higher than the 105 degrees in the other engine spaces.

Besides simple measures like stuffing the loudspeakers with rags to stifle the captain's voice and his inspirational reveille and mealtime tunes, the officers and sailors devised other expedients in the attempt to preserve their sanity. Generous, who played the ukulele, composed several underground songs that were sung at barbershop-quartet concerts in the officers' compartments when the captain had locked himself in his cabin. The favorite song was called "Ave, Ave, Marcus A." It was sung to the tune of "There Is Nothing Like a Dame":

> "We got brasso, we got guns,
>> We got mess nights with our funds,
>> We got scratches on the keel plates from the shallow-water runs,
>> We got speeches after dinner, when the smoke gets very dense.
>> What ain't we got? We ain't got sense."

The officers would swing into the chorus while Generous plunked his ukulele harder:

"Ave, ave, Marcus A.,
    Ave, Caesar Rex,
    Ave, ave, Marcus A.,
    You're so funny we don't need sex."

"He's got a white toilet seat and the speedboat is neat
    Candelabras we steal, but on Sundays we kneel.
    Cottage cheese every day, we'll be starved out by May.
    Everything that's wrong with every man here is directly
        caused by keeping him near that leaping, screaming, flam-
        ing, raving ass."

Another standby was the *Vance*'s version of the civil rights song "We Shall Overcome." It ended with the words "But we are all afraid."

Electronics Technician Third Class John K. Lundy, who worked for Generous in the combat information center, drew cartoons ridiculing the captain. The caricatures were copied on the Xerox machine in the radio room and circulated among the officers and crew. One cartoon depicted Arnheiter in Indian dress, brandishing a tomahawk and whooping, at a "war council" session. Another had the *Vance* sidling up to a big destroyer, like a small boy with a cap pistol approaching a policeman engaged in a shoot-out with some bank robbers, and pestering her skipper for a gunfire mission. A third showed the captain, in baggy shorts, sunglasses and baseball cap, asking a couple of guerrillas, one of whom was dozing beside a bunker on the beach, "Where can I go to get my boat shot at?"

The underground humor also took the form of Arnheiter stories. Everyone had several. Belmonte's most cherished story concerned the time he was officer of the deck and the captain ordered him to increase speed to 16 knots to generate enough wind over the bow to make the flag on the mast fly in a straight line, as it always does in paintings of ships at sea.

Generous told the tale of the ten bells. He was standing out on a wing of the bridge one morning, maneuvering the *Vance* alongside a junk he intended to board for inspection. The captain was sitting quietly beside Generous on one of his bridge-wing chairs. The ship's bells began ringing the hour of 8 A.M. Generous was intent on not damaging the wooden hull of the junk and paid no attention.

"Officer of the deck," the captain erupted. "That was ten bells."

"All stop!" Generous yelled at the helmsman. "Sir?" he asked Arnheiter in surprise.

"Officer of the deck, I heard ten bells. There should have been eight. I want you to find out who rang those bells. I heard ten bells," the captain repeated.

"Captain, I've got a goddamn junk out here," Generous said.

"Who's the quartermaster of the watch?" Arnheiter asked.

Generous glanced at the junk again and shouted, "All back one third," to the helmsman to avoid ramming it.

"Who's the quartermaster of the watch?" the captain reiterated.

"Right here, Captain," a sailor said.

"Find out who rang those bells," the captain commanded. "I know that was ten bells. I want you to find out who rang those bells." The quartermaster ran below and made a pretense of searching for the culprit. He was never discovered, but Signalman Boson was forever ribbing Generous about the incident. "Mr. Generous," he would say, wrinkling his brow in mimicry of the captain, "who rang ten bells on your watch?"

Somehow the Arnheiter stories always seemed funniest when the participant was someone else. The sight of Smoot coming down from the bridge every morning near tears was comical to the other sailors until the captain pounced on one of them for some fanciful dereliction. And the tribulations of the deck gang amused the snipes in the engine rooms until the water rationing began. The humor yielded only a momentary escape from the captain. "This ship has turned into a concentration camp," Belmonte said to Merkel. "He gets closer and closer all the time. It's like being bombarded. There's always Marcus—Marcus at meals, Marcus on the bridge, Marcus at meetings, Marcus on the loudspeaker, everywhere there's Marcus. You can't get away from him." Simply having to look at the captain, that figure in the billowy, pleated shorts, with the baseball cap on his head, the revolver at his hip, toying with a pipe in his hand, smiling his boyish smile, fresh from a late morning's sleep while they were haggard, became an emotional irritant for the crew.

Of the officers, Mason and Williams were the least affected. Their terms of service on the *Vance* were expiring. They would leave when the ship visited Bangkok on February 20 for a brief five days of shore liberty and rest for the crew. The knowledge that the punishment would end soon made it more bearable for them.

Hardy was in a frightful dilemma. His situation was impossible. He was the classic man in the middle, caught between Arnheiter hammering away from above and the rankling depression of the subordinates below. The traditional role of the executive officer is to administer the ship for the captain and to serve as his lightning rod. He issues the captain's orders in his own name, sees that they are executed and absorbs any resentment that results from the crew. Hardy had been executive officer of the *Vance* for nearly a year before Arnheiter arrived, however. It was obvious to all that the metamorphosis in the life of the ship had not been his doing. He could not sustain the fiction that the orders were originating with him. Yet he could not afford the psychological safety valve of admitting to the subordinate officers and the chief petty officers that the captain's orders violated reason, or were illegal or immoral. He could not join them in their mockery of Arnheiter. His position as executive officer, his power to issue orders and to command compliance would be completely undermined if he put himself on the same level as the other officers by aligning himself with them against the captain. He had briefly experimented with this luxury in early February with Generous, Mason and a couple of the older subordinates whom he thought he could trust, but he had drawn back almost immediately. "I can't have them getting the feeling," he thought, "that they can come to me and appeal and say, 'Come on, XO, this is a lousy, stinking situation and what

are you going to do about it?' because there's nothing I can
do about it."

Ray Sterling Hardy believed in the United States Navy. He
had never been troubled by any doubts about the order of its
universe from the day he had entered the monastery as a
novice midshipman at Annapolis. Its traditions, its codes, its
attitudes were part of his soul. What the Navy wanted and
what the Navy did was good, made sense and was patriotic.
Hardy's self-possessed and forbearing personality, and his talent for things mechanical, his zest for the intricacies of engines, torpedoes and radar sets, were well suited to long sea
voyages. He was a natural naval officer. His fitness reports
from previous superiors were unblemished. Except for the
time he devoted to his wife and four sons, his ambition was
to spend all of his life sailing, and one day commanding, the
ships of the United States Navy. Arnheiter was a denial of all
of Hardy's values, some horrible mistake, a baffling contradiction in a just and rational system. And Hardy could do
nothing to remove the contradiction. He had to serve the
captain. The law, the tradition, the code said so.

Hardy pondered whether he should ask for a transfer and
rejected this alternative as cowardly. He would be shunting
his problem to someone else, who might be less prepared to
cope with it because he would be new to the predicament.
He considered swearing out court-martial charges against
Arnheiter for the false position reports and the other violations of regulations. This was the only officially sanctioned
way for him to proceed against the captain. He would have
to hand the charge sheets to the captain first, however, since
Arnheiter was his immediate superior, and he was certain that
the captain would never permit the papers to leave the ship.
The inevitable confrontation would make matters worse. He
did not ask himself whether the captain was mad. The thought
was always there in the back of his mind, but he suppressed
it. What difference would it make if Arnheiter was psychotic?
The idea was too harrowing to torture himself with. He decided to absorb the stress somehow until his own term of
service on the *Vance* expired the following August. "I'll give

the man what he wants," Hardy said to himself. "I'll do my damnedest to give him what he wants and to keep the ship going at the same time."

Hardy adopted what he mentally labeled his "positive-attitude program." He simply issued an order and insisted that it be carried out. There were very few explanations to give, so he gave none. There was no room for reason and tact any more, so he wielded his authority. Most of the officers appreciated his dilemma and accepted his instructions without much demur. Fuehrer tended to gripe, however, and Generous, who had the mind-set of the intellectual, often wanted to debate the sanity or legality of instructions he knew were originating with the captain. "Talk is fine, Tom," Hardy would say. "But it doesn't mean anything. Just do it!"

Despite Hardy's effort to resign himself to his lot, the anomaly of his position, the sleep deprivation and the compromises with his own integrity put him under an escalating strain. By the end of February he had developed ulcer symptoms—painful bouts of gastritis. Every time the sound-powered phone extension in his compartment would *whup, whup, whup* with that special fast twirl of the crank the captain used, Hardy's stomach would twist up into a knot. "Here we go again," he would say to himself as he rolled off his bunk. "Some sailor has said 'Yes, sir,' instead of 'Aye, aye, sir,' or somebody's hat was dirty, or I'm going to hear more about General MacArthur, and there's a war going on over here and a lot of people are fighting the war and we're shooting at sand dunes and raving about belt buckles . . . Jesus Christ!"

Generous too was in a luckless position, since as operations officer he was the ship's communications link to the outside world. His high-strung personality unraveled rapidly during February and early March. The U.S. coastal surveillance center at the Vietnamese navy station at An Thoi on Phu Quoc Island, which monitored patrol activities in the Gulf of Siam area, unwittingly hastened his decline by relentless nit-picking at the routine reports the *Vance* radioed on the course and speed of ocean-going merchantmen and large cargo junks. Generous suspected that enough rumors of how Captain Arnheiter had operated on the central coast had filtered down the grapevine to An Thoi to make the staff officers there suspicious of anything the *Vance* told them. They incessantly demanded verification of messages and set snares to catch the *Vance* in a lie.

Generous' combat information center would, for example, message An Thoi the identification, position, course and speed of a Liberian merchantman the bridge watch had sighted. A half-hour later An Thoi would ask over the radio, "Do you still have Liberian ship *Whistling Star* in sight?"

"No, we don't," the *Vance* would reply.

"Then find her," An Thoi would direct.

Generous would tell the captain what An Thoi wanted, and the *Vance* would chase the merchantman as fast as her cranky diesels could go. A pursuit of several hours would again bring the Liberian into sight and the CIC would send the merchantman's new position, course and speed to An Thoi.

"According to your original position, course and speed for Liberian ship *Whistling Star,* she can't possibly be where you say she is now. Where is she?" An Thoi would gleefully riposte.

Several things could have happened. Generous' CIC watch could have made a five-degree error in its first computation. By the time three or four hours had passed, this error would mean a significant difference in mileage. Or the merchant captain might simply have changed course and speed. But an exasperating imbroglio would ensue before the matter was arranged to the satisfaction of An Thoi. Messages would shuttle back and forth over the radio, and confusion would be heaped upon puzzlement. As soon as this particular snarl had been undone, An Thoi would be requesting verification of some other message the CIC had sent four hours previously. By then the watch crews would have changed, and because of the commotion, the offgoing watch would not have adequately briefed the oncoming men. The current watch crew would therefore not remember the message, and would have to hunt it out of the message file or wake up the previous watch and ask what it was about.

Meanwhile, since the captain insisted on signing all messages before they were transmitted, Generous would be in Arnheiter's cabin or on the bridge trying to explain what was occurring. With a few details of course and speed, most experienced naval officers can visualize the movement pattern of two or more ships. Arnheiter was an exception. Generous had Lundy draw up and Xerox blank mini-charts that he placed on a clipboard and used to sketch the ship movements for the captain. Even with this aid, Arnheiter's nontechnical mind had difficulty comprehending the situation and his attitude would be antagonistic.

"Well, what does this mean?" he would ask. "Did somebody blow it? Did you have another bust in the operations department?"

When Generous had laid out the fundamentals of one misunderstanding to the captain, he would emerge from the cabin to find a sailor from his CIC crew waiting with a new message from An Thoi. The situation had changed and An Thoi was demanding something else. Back to Arnheiter he would go. On occasion, hardly any sailors would be left on duty in the CIC. They would all be in transit as messengers. "Jesus Christ, I'm going crazy," Generous confessed to Gwynn.

The captain seemed unable to separate personalities from events, and his mind categorized personalities into two groups —those who were for him and those who were against him. Generous was obviously against him. Arnheiter had interpreted as insubordination Generous' balking over the false position reports, his opposition to the shore bombardments and his continued unwillingness to falsify the daily summaries of the number of junks and sampans sighted and boarded for inspection. The captain had never ceased faking these reports to impress Navy headquarters in Saigon with his energy and conscientiousness. The numbers would burgeon each night under his ballpoint pen when Generous brought the correct reports to his cabin. He had suggested without success several times that Generous ought to relieve him of this little task. The

chronic tardiness for rendezvous with oilers and supply ships
was another personal failure by the operations officer. Now
Arnheiter interpreted the difficulties with An Thoi as a plot
by Generous to make him appear incompetent. The captain
complained angrily to Hardy about what a jackass he had for
an operations officer.

Generous worsened his own predicament by collapsing in-
ternally. He ceased caring. "Why try?" he said to himself. "It
doesn't make a goddamn bit of difference." What efficiency
he had preserved dwindled away. The captain gained genuine cause to rail against the sloppiness of the operations department. Generous also abandoned formalities, in which
Arnheiter put great stock. An operations officer schedules
training exercises and other events the ship will perform during the next day and submits a plan to the captain the night
before. Most captains observe the plan, unless there is an
emergency. Arnheiter rarely did, and Generous ceased handing one in. But the captain wanted a plan, even if he forgot
about it the moment he had it.

And Generous was discovered trying to circumvent Arnheiter's rule that he sign all messages before they were transmitted from the *Vance*. Generous resorted to the trick in a
desperate attempt to end the snarls with An Thoi. He sent
a message to the operations officer there:

"If you have some problem about a merchantman or junk,
a routine contact, and you've got a course and position and
speed filed, and you don't think we sent you the right information, send us an ops-to-ops wire note so that I can handle it
and I don't have to bother my commanding officer."

This informal procedure would have been permissible on
most other Market Time patrol ships to save the captain's
time. An "ops-to-ops" wire note does not need the captain's
clearance, because it is addressed to another operations officer,
not to a command. Arnheiter's rule encompassed all messages,
however, and Generous knew that he was scheming to violate it. The operations officer at An Thoi was apparently
suspicious and showed Generous' message to his own commanding officer, a Coast Guard commodore who was in

charge of the surveillance center there. The commodore questioned Arnheiter about it when the captain went into An Thoi one day for a conference. Arnheiter was touchy over his relations with the commodore because the Coast Guard officer, being a full commander, outranked him. The captain usually took pains to please his superiors. He returned to the *Vance* in a fury. "The commodore chewed me out because I've got an insubordinate operations officer," he yelled at Generous. "I ought to keelhaul you!" Hardy sat through another monologue in the captain's cabin in the predawn hours about the disastrous operations officer Arnheiter was saddled with, and then lost his temper with Generous.

"Goddamn it," he said, "shape up or ship out. You're screwing me. Run your own department and stop making work for me or else I'm going to have your ass!"

"I'm sorry, I'm really sorry. I know I've let you down," Generous said. He knew intuitively, as did the other leading subordinates, that Hardy was depending upon them to hold their departments together while he somehow managed the captain. Generous did reform for a few days, until another ruckus with An Thoi took place. Then he relapsed into demoralization. "Screw it," he said to himself. "It's just one big, constant headache. I'm ready to go off the deep end, anyway."

On the afternoon of February 18, the day the ship was to leave for Bangkok and five days of shore leave, the captain took the speedboat into An Thoi for a conference. While he was ashore, yet one more misunderstanding with the operations staff there occurred, and Generous sent a message without the captain's authorization. He was not attempting to trick Arnheiter this time. When Arnheiter returned, Generous pointed out that the captain had not been aboard to sign the message and that an immediate reply was imperative. In the rush he had forgotten to ask Hardy to sign the message in the captain's stead. The explanation was to no avail; Arnheiter accused Generous of again violating his order and tongue-lashed him mercilessly. Generous slept fitfully for about two hours that night. He stood the 12-to-4 A.M. watch on the bridge, waited until Hardy rose at 5:45, and poured out his despair in a long confession in the executive officer's compartment. Before falling onto his own bunk, he sat down and made a tape recording to mail to his wife, Diane. She was six months pregnant with their first child. His voice was barely audible and it broke several times:

"I've been in constant hot water for about ten days . . . just constant, in and out and in and out of hot water. I don't know if I'm equipped to give a fair appraisal of events. I can tell you at least the way it seems to me. It seems to me that because Marcus is such a real ass hole, everybody up and down the coast is after him . . . they do whatever they can to make things a little bit grim for him. Well, I get caught in a bind here, because they're making things tough for us and yet I'm . . . as operations officer . . . I'm the ship's connection with the outside world, communications-wise. So I'm the guy who gets caught in all these flaps."

He recounted his troubles with An Thoi, the debacles over the messages sent without the captain's authorization, and then, as he continued, he began to weep.

"Oh Jesus, it's just sick . . . [He sobbed]. So, I . . . it's more than unhappy, it's a way of life. [His voice broke again] You know . . . you just grit your teeth and say, 'Jesus, you can't let it bother you so much,' but boy, you don't really, Diane. The commanding officer of a ship . . . the relationship of a commanding officer of a ship is much more effective than you have even with your wife. [He stopped to blow his nose] This guy . . . he's not just . . . he's a paranoid. He's too stupid to know what's going on, but he's so paranoid he cares what people think of him, and oh God, what problems that makes for us. Well . . . I'm using this tape because to write these things in a letter would be just too tough. It's so late and I'm so tired . . . Great God, I keep saying to myself, you know, like I haven't written to you in a week . . . and I keep saying to myself, 'The girl's having her baby, you've got to make her feel loved and wanted.' "

He shut off the recorder, left the tape on the machine and slept for five hours. At five-thirty in the afternoon he came back to it.

"I feel better today. I just couldn't continue before. I slept until eleven this morning and got up and had a real enjoyable chat. We're taking four Coast Guard officers to Bangkok with us and we had a good time with them and they were fun to talk to. We were able to laugh about the whole thing, so I do feel better. I'm going to send this along to you today, because I want you to know the kind of tension I'm living with . . . Try to— The thing about this tension that I'm talking about is its . . . its prime cause is insane . . . He's— It's not something I can cope with. I've tried to figure it out and I know all I can do is hang on until he's through berating me and bounce back, but this guy . . . It's a different story and I don't know what the hell the answer is, if there is an answer. Maybe the answer is to dissolve the relationship. I do love you, darling. Please help me live through this. I need your help."

Bangkok was too short a respite to cure the depression sickening Generous and the other men of the *Vance*. The visit began sourly. A Thai harbor pilot lost control while taking the *Vance* up the river. He nearly rammed the ship into some concrete pilings and a Japanese tanker tied up alongside the bank. Generous seized the conn from the pilot and averted a collision with an emergency maneuver. The captain was up on the O-3 deck shooting movies of the golden-roofed Thai temples and having his picture taken again. By this time Merkel had escaped from his personal predicament by persuading an electronics technician who worked in Generous' CIC to become the captain's photographer. The sailor liked the work.

Arnheiter descended to the bridge after the crisis had passed, ignorant of the near-mishap. Generous was backing the ship out into the main channel to resume the journey up the river. He had just instructed the helmsman, "All back one third," when Arnheiter said, "This is the captain. I have the conn. All back two thirds. You're babying those engines again, Mr. Generous."

Some of the crew—Belmonte and a few of the sailors— were not tolerating Arnheiter with Hardy's restraint or sliding into passive despair like Generous. They too believed that the

Navy had deserted them and they foresaw no way out of their prison, no end to their ordeal. They were also despondent. But by late February, when the *Vance* resumed patrol off the Gulf of Siam coast, they had begun to resist the captain.

For Belmonte, resistance was a reflex action. His father had been a soil conservationist for the Department of Agriculture. Belmonte had grown up in small farming and ranching towns in the West. Because he was slight of build, he had been forced into one fistfight after another in school to keep the bigger boys from bullying him. When someone pushed, he pushed back. Arnheiter was pushing. Belmonte followed orders, but his combative nature would not let him do it quietly. He made no secret of what he thought of the captain's antics. If the captain did something that Belmonte considered particularly outrageous, he would feign ignorance of Arnheiter's authorship and noisily ask another officer in the captain's hearing, "Do you know what some ass hole has just done?" Belmonte would describe the incident, embroidering his narration with several more colorful obscenities.

Arnheiter was not fooled. "You know perfectly well I ordered that, Mr. Belmonte," he would say crossly.

Their mutual animosity took on a sharper edge because of a running skirmish between Belmonte's deck apes and Signalman Farnum, the captain's favorite. The deck gang had never forgiven Farnum for turning in three of their comrades for brawling with the enginemen after the sailors' party on Guam. Belmonte sided with his seamen, threatening Farnum and berating him to "leave my men alone." Farnum continued to gall the deck hands with his ostentatious display of naval lore and the other knowledge his reading gave him. They were not about to declare a truce. Farnum confessed his troubles during the hours of conversation he and Arnheiter frequently had in the captain's cabin. Farnum owned a revolver, and like the captain, enjoyed target practice on sharks and sea snakes. Afterward they would clean their pistols together and chat. Arnheiter would try to pump Farnum for tidbits of gossip about the crew. The captain blamed Belmonte for the enmity between Farnum and the deck apes. When someone threw Farnum's jacket into a water bucket that served as a spittoon, Farnum accused one of Belmonte's seamen of the deed—the plowman from South Dakota who had been the one most severely punished at the captain's mast on Guam. The captain told Lieutenant Julian Meisner, who had taken Williams' place as weapons officer and was now Belmonte's immediate superior, that he had a mind to court-martial Belmonte "for gross incompetence."

"Christ, let him do it, let him do it," Belmonte retorted to Meisner. "I'd welcome a court-martial. I want waves. Real bad I want waves. You're not supposed to be controversial in the Navy no matter how bad things get. But this is different. At a court-martial I could tell the rest of the Navy what's happening on this ship. Marcus is an oily, criminal bastard and he's gotten as far as he has because nobody's been willing to stand up to him. If we don't stop him, he'll get to be an admiral with all of this crazy horse-shit."

Meisner persuaded Belmonte not to push the captain to this extremity. Generous argued Belmonte out of typing up and mailing to their squadron commodore random notes about some of the captain's more memorable exploits which Belmonte had been scribbling on the backs of old forms and envelopes. He had even invented a title for his fragmentary scratchings—"The Marcus Madness Log."

Belmonte fell back on guerrilla warfare. He kept up his verbal harassment and pulled other tricks whenever an opportunity presented itself. One tactic he adopted was to slip out of his compartment in the middle of the night to the nearest sound-powered phone station, ring the captain's cabin and wait to hear Arnheiter wake up to a silent receiver. Although the captain had Hardy conduct an investigation, Belmonte was never caught.

Those sailors who had started to resist acted more surreptitiously. The captain forgot pairs of sunglasses on the bridge, just as he absent-mindedly left loaded rifles and Tommy guns there. As soon as an officer had his back turned, a sailor would pitch the sunglasses over the side into the sea.

AFTER A VISIT TO QUI NHON: Lieutenant (j.g.) William "Tom" Generous (*left*) amuses with a song an unidentified American officer who was an adviser to the Vietnamese navy, a Vietnamese officer and Lieutenant (j.g.) Edward "Hoppy" Mason (*far right*), during the ride back to the *Vance* in the motor whaleboat.

VISITING A VILLAGE: Captain Arnheiter poses with two Vietnamese navy officers in a fishing village on an island off the coast of central Viet Nam. The captain is dressed in his tropical working attire.

KIDS AND CANDY: Captain Arnheiter passes out candy to the children of the fishing village. An old Vietnamese woman in a turban (*left*) watches with amusement.

"AYE, AYE, SIR": Lieutenant (j.g.) Thomas Williams (*left*), the weapons officer, in flak jacket, reports to Captain Arnheiter on the bridge during gunnery practice off Viet Nam. Lieutenant Ray Hardy and a Vietnamese liaison officer watch. The captain's .38-caliber revolver has his initials carved on the bone grip.

"ALL HANDS AFT": Lieutenant Ray Hardy at the flag-draped podium on the fantail, leading the second of the "All Hands Aft" Sunday services Captain Arnheiter instituted for the spiritual health of his crew. One sailor with arms folded at the left end of the first row stares off at the sea, while another toward the rear at the right scratches his arm. Signalman Wayne Farnum stands at the right end of the first row.

AWAY THE SCOUT BOAT: The 16-foot speedboat Captain Arnheiter purchased with the crew's recreation money (note shark's teeth painted on the front) cuts through the water off Viet Nam. Gunner's Mate Moses "Tiger" Coleman (*in helmet at rear*) mans the machine gun.

"ONE ROUND, BALL AMMUNITION, LOCK AND LOAD": The Special Fire
Team preparing to shoot at imaginary guerrilla junks in the form of
yellow-painted oil drums while Captain Arnheiter directs the firing
over the loudspeaker from the 0-3 deck above.

BAD BOY: Lieutenant Generous looks out from under the table where he had been ordered by Captain Arnheiter as a joke at one point during the mess night festivities on Guam. Lieutenant Williams smiles at the camera.

ROAST BEEF: Ensign Luis Belmonte plays the imp for the camera at the mess night festivities on Guam.

BANGKOK LIBERTY: Ensign Michael McWhirter, in civilian clothes (*center*), leans on the gangplank rail while waiting to go ashore on the first morning of the five-day visit to Bangkok in February. Behind him Ensign John Hannigan smiles at the camera and Ensign Bernard "Tuck" Black, also in civilian clothes, walks by with a cigarette in his hand.

FAREWELL: Captain Arnheiter *(center, in Bermuda shorts)* saying good-bye to Lieutenants Hoppy Mason and Thomas Williams as they leave the ship at Bangkok in the latter half of February.

COLD BEER: The *Vance*'s motor whaleboat ferries another group of sailors to the picnic in March on an island in the Gulf of Siam, when a seaman got drunk and raved that he would kill Captain Arnheiter and Signalman Wayne Farnum.

A BIT OF SUN AND SAND: (*left to right*) Ensign Bernard "Tuck" Black, Chaplain George Dando and Communications Technician Frank Feeney at the ship's picnic on the island in the Gulf of Siam.

AT SEA: Chief Petty Officer Hector Cornejo squints into the sun during a ceremony on the fantail of the *Vance* off Viet Nam.

The *Vance* under way.

1 After 3-inch Gun Mount
2 Depth Charges
3 Fantail
4 Torpedo Launcher
5 Motor Whaleboat
6 0-1 Deck
7 Captain's Cabin
8 Wardroom
9 Main Deck
10 Forward 3-inch Gun Mount
11 Forecastle
12 Hedgehog Mount
13 Pilot House
14 Bridge
15 0-2 Deck
16 0-3 Deck
17 .50-caliber Machine-gun
   Mount Locations
18 Main Gun Control

One evening the captain forgot a pipe on one of his bridge-wing chairs. It vanished too.

Arnheiter never seemed to attach any meaning to these small disappearances. "Gee whiz," he would say as he searched the bridge for his missing sunglasses, "I'm sure I left them up here." He did become disturbed over one incident, but again he did not sense its significance.

The captain liked to sunbathe in swimming trunks in his hammock on the O-3 deck, above the bridge. A sailor happened to sit in it one afternoon and a suspension rope snapped. An examination showed that the rope had been cut halfway through, weakening it just enough for the weight of a human body to rend the strand entirely. The captain would not have fallen far, only about three feet, but that might have been far enough to injure his spine seriously on the hard deck. The sailor was not hurt. Arnheiter was very angry and sent Hardy off on another fruitless investigation.

Although the incident was small, its ominous overtones were not lost on others in the crew. They wondered when some sailor might decide that he could endure no more and make a serious attempt on the life of Captain Arnheiter.

8

WHAT CHAPLAIN DANDO FOUND

> You shouldn't point a shotgun at
> somebody unless you intend to
> kill them.
>
> —Captain Arnheiter

By March 4, 1966, Lieutenant George W. Dando had been a Presbyterian chaplain in the United States Navy for six months. He was thirty-one years old, a bull of a man, 210 pounds, with a quick mind and a friendly manner. "How many years will I have to serve," he asked himself that morning, "before I see another scene like this?" He was standing on a wing of the bridge of the *Vance* with his host, Captain Arnheiter. The *Vance* had been instructed to rendezvous with a Coast Guard cutter and a Swift boat that were ferrying an American Broadcasting Company television team out from An Thoi. The team was to board the ship to film a program on Operation Market Time. From the higher deck of the DER, they planned to photograph the Swift boats and Coast Guard cutters at work inspecting junks.

As the cutter and the Swift boat hove into view, Captain Arnheiter decided to impress his guests with the fighting power of his ship and perhaps glean some publicity for himself. A few minutes earlier, Belmonte and Smoot had mustered their eight-man deck gang on the main deck and the forecastle to lower the anchor and throw fenders over the side. The captain ran into the pilothouse and grabbed the microphone. "Away the motor whaleboat," he sang out over the loudspeaker.

"Stay here, Smoot, and take care of the anchor," Belmonte said. He took four seamen, left Smoot with the remaining half of the deck force, and rushed up to swing the twenty-six-foot whaleboat out onto its davits and down the side of the ship. He had barely begun when Arnheiter's voice boomed out of the loudspeaker in another command: "Away the scout boat." Belmonte abandoned two seamen to struggle with the whaleboat, a task that normally takes six, and hustled to the speedboat with the other two. Because the speedboat was not on davits and had to be manhandled off its mount on the O-1 deck amidships and lowered into the water with ropes and a torpedo davit, Belmonte needed more men. He ran back down to the forecastle and amidst Smoot's curses seized two of the four deck apes left there. Dando watched Belmonte dragoon into service two mess cooks he bumped into in the scramble along the gangway to the speedboat. By the time they reached the speedboat again, Arnheiter had barked, "Away the Special Fire Team." Two of Belmonte's deck hands who were helping him with the speedboat were members of the thirty-man troop. They dashed off to get their rifles. "Where the fuck are you going?" Belmonte screamed after them.

"We've got to muster," a sailor shouted back over his shoulder.

Dando could see that other sailors in the fire team were bobbing up onto the O-1 deck with their rifles, crashing into Belmonte and his sweating helpers, and shoving sandbags next to the railing where Belmonte and his men were trying to lift out the speedboat and winch it down the side with the torpedo davit. Dando felt as if he were watching a Keystone Cops sequence from a 1920's movie. The pandemonium of an hour had been compressed into a few minutes. Just then Arnheiter brushed past him in a huff. The captain leaned over the railing of the bridge wing and upbraided Belmonte for not having the speedboat in the water yet. "I told you to lower away the scout boat, Mr. Belmonte," he shouted. "You're again not being responsive to my commands."

The speedboat and the motor whaleboat were soon, somehow, in the water. Belmonte and two seamen climbed into the speedboat and another armed crew hurried into the motor whaleboat. The yellow-painted oil drums were flung over the sides. While the sailors in the whaleboat splattered one set of barrels with showers of bullets, Belmonte drove the speedboat back and forth along the other side of the ship and a gunner's mate, an imposing black sailor, stood up in the middle of the bucking runabout and vainly sought to hit a second brace of barrels with bursts from the .30-caliber machine gun mounted on the pole. Next, the captain called off his small-boat flotilla and gave Marcus' Marauders their turn. Dando watched him up on the O-3 deck, marching to and fro with the microphone on the extension cord: "One round, ball ammunition, lock and load." Volley after volley crashed out at the oil drums. The chaplain picked up a pair of binoculars and looked at the Swift boat and the Coast Guard cutter loitering at a distance. He could see the television cameramen sitting on the bows, laughing and pointing at the fray.

At the end of the performance, Belmonte was to be chastised again because the gunner's mate had failed to hit the oil drums. He was summoned to the bridge, where the captain was explaining his tactics to the television team, who had come aboard as soon as the shooting stopped. While he waited to see Arnheiter, one of the cameramen who was standing beside Dando looked at Belmonte with an expression of astonishment on his face and shook his head.

"You don't know the half of it, fella," Belmonte said.

"Marcus is indulging in nautical masturbation again," Generous muttered.

The chaplain noticed that the captain was not unhappy. Arnheiter insisted that the television team interview him on camera, and later wrote to several admirals suggesting that they watch the program when it was screened in the United States.

Dando had boarded the *Vance* four days earlier for a two-week visit. He worked for Commodore Donald F. Milligan, the DER squadron commander at Subic Bay who had operational control over the *Vance* and the other DER's on Operation Market Time. Dando made a regular circuit of chaplain's calls on the DER's off Viet Nam and he would eventually have reached the *Vance* in the course of his rounds. He had come sooner rather than later, because he had encountered Commodore Orlie G. Baird, the commander of the *Vance*'s parent squadron at Pearl Harbor, when Baird was on an inspection trip in the Far East. He had mentioned to Dando that there seemed to be a morale problem on the *Vance*. The Roman Catholic chaplain at Pearl Harbor, Father Osterman, had turned over to Baird the letter from Generous protesting the compulsory Protestant services. There had been similar letters to the Pearl Harbor chaplain from other Roman Catholics on the ship, and Baird had heard through the grapevine that the men were complaining about the captain in letters to their wives. Baird was not alarmed. There was often grousing about a new captain. The crew usually settled down after a while. Baird had written Arnheiter a polite letter in late February that gently cautioned the captain against tampering with religious sentiments. Baird was concerned, though, and he had asked Dando to have a look.

Arnheiter lent Dando a small compartment next to the ship's post office where he could conduct chaplain's counseling. The line formed, and the complaints filled the room. Like most chaplains, Dando was accustomed to bitching. Normally, he was not impressed. For a minister, George Dando was not a particularly fastidious man. His chubby face bespoke a pleasant, intelligent nature. He was what might be called "a regular sort of guy," not above barnyard language and a few drinks ashore. While his Navy service was brief, he had spent three years in the Army as a missile-base security guard in the military police before going to college and the Pittsburgh Theological Seminary. Bored with the duties of a small parish in Iowa, he had volunteered for active duty in the Navy in September 1965. His Army years had taught him that the ritual griping of enlisted men was as much a part of military

life as salutes and bullets. But he had never encountered anything like the volume and nature of the complaints he heard on
the *Vance*. They ranged across the spectrum from the captain's Protestant services and the racket of "Hellcats Reveille,"
"Roast Beef of Olde Englande," and the fire-team practice,
to the phony gunfire missions, the false position reports, the
Boner Box, the purchase of the speedboat with recreation
money, and so on, to Hamaker's abiding dilemma over what
to do about the $11.57 worth of postage stamps Arnheiter
had appropriated at the beginning of the voyage. "Nobody
seems to be happy on this ship," Dando thought.

The captain invited the chaplain to sunbathe with him in
a second hammock slung on the O-3 deck. They had several
discussions. Arnheiter sought to impress upon Dando his concern for the moral and spiritual well-being of his crew. He
was going to delete most of the religious content from his "All
Hands Aft" sessions in deference to Baird's wishes, he said,
although he felt Baird was wrong. The captain was confident
that if the issue ever came to a showdown, the admirals would
support him because chapel was compulsory at Annapolis.
He showed Dando copies of letters he had written while executive officer of the *Ingersoll* to the parents of sailors who were
minors. The letters asked the parents to permit forced church
attendance for their sons. "I have a responsibility to these
fresh-caught lads," Arnheiter told Dando. "I can't leave them
to their own immature desires." The captain said that when
the *Vance* went to Manila at the end of March for two weeks'
repair work, he also intended to stop his sailors from fre-
quenting the prostitutes seamen have flocked to for centuries
in ports around the world. He would have Cornejo give him
the names of all the men who appeared at the dispensary
with venereal disease, he said. Then he would send letters to
their wives, or to their parents if they were unmarried, warning that their husbands and sons would be court-martialed if
they returned to the prostitutes and caught venereal disease
again.

Dando walked down to the dispensary afterward and asked
Cornejo what he thought of the captain's plan to reform the

sexual morals of the sailors. "That's a great way to get your-self shot," Cornejo said. To contract venereal disease is not a court-martial offense in the Navy.

Besides the reception for the television team, the chaplain had other occasions on which to observe Arnheiter's person-ality. One day he accompanied the captain on a visit to one of the sparsely inhabited Vietnamese islands in the Gulf of Siam. The captain gave a Vietnamese fisherman who lived on the island some vitamin pills and antidysentery medicine as a gesture of good will. The fisherman responded by offering Arnheiter some coconut wine. Arnheiter had the *Vance*'s li-aison officer, who was acting as an interpreter, excuse him. He could not drink the wine because he was having stomach trouble, he said. Dando could not recall Arnheiter mention-ing any stomach ailment that morning. "But my chief of pro-tocol," the captain said with a wave of his hand toward Dando, "will have some." The chaplain drank the wine.

The next day Arnheiter stopped Dando in a passageway and asked solicitously, "Are you all right, Chaplain?"

"Sure, I'm fine," Dando replied, puzzled.

"I was worried about that wine yesterday," the captain said. "I've heard that stuff gives you dysentery."

Dando was amazed at the state of rancor into which Arn-heiter had driven his crew. Nine days after Dando came aboard, the captain staged a swimming and beer party for the sailors on an island. The farm boy from South Dakota who had been humiliated at the public captain's mast on Guam became senselessly drunk and raved that he was going to kill Arnheiter and Farnum. The seaman had learned that Arnheiter had written a letter to his parents informing them that their son was an apprentice criminal who could be sal-vaged only by the spiritual guidance of forced church attend-ance. Presumably the sailor was already receiving such guidance at the captain's "All Hands Aft" meetings. Dando watched the seaman roll around on the beach in his swimming trunks, plastering sand into his wet face and hair, screaming that he would even the score with the captain.

"I'm going to kill that son of a bitch. I'll kill him. I swear I'll kill him," the deck hand ranted.

Belmonte's inner tension was leading him into squabbles with the other officers. Two days earlier the captain had axed Belmonte. Because of the war between Farnum and the deck apes, Arnheiter had formally relieved Belmonte of all of his duties—as first lieutenant of the deck gang, as the ship's legal officer, and as Catholic lay leader. Belmonte had been assigned to the engine rooms as an assistant to Fuehrer, who had been promoted to engineering officer since Mason's departure, to handle the paper work for a new computerized preventive-maintenance system the Navy was organizing.

Now Belmonte and Meisner got into a vehement confrontation over what to do about the drunken seaman. Meisner wanted to send the sailor back to the ship. Belmonte wanted to leave the youth on the island until he sobered up a bit so that Arnheiter, who had returned to the *Vance,* would not overhear what the sailor was saying in his delirium. Meisner finally gave Belmonte a direct order to have the seaman put into the whaleboat and carried aboard. When Belmonte refused, Meisner began berating him in front of several sailors. The shame enraged Belmonte. He thrust his face into Meisner's.

"Listen, you son of a bitch," he said in a voice of quiet menace, "if you ever talk to me like that in public again I'll kick the dogshit out of you."

Meisner was considerably taller and heftier than Belmonte and probably would have bested him in a fight. Dando intervened and negotiated a compromise. He persuaded Meisner to leave the sailor on the island for another hour or two. Then Dando slung the youth over his shoulder and hauled him into the whaleboat and back to his bunk on the *Vance.* He spoke to the deck hand the next morning, after the sailor had slept off the drunk, and concluded that he would not carry out his threat, for the present at least.

One afternoon Dando had an opportunity to approach Lieutenant Generous and several of the other officers in the wardroom. "If you guys really feel the way you say you do, then you've got to stiffen your backbone and do something official about it," he said. "If you sign a false report, you're as guilty as he is. You've got to say, 'Captain, what you're doing is wrong. I'm reporting it, and here are the court-martial charges.' Then you've got to go on up through channels with him and fight it out." There was no reaction from the officers. Even Belmonte was momentarily in the doldrums because Meisner had talked him out of seeking a court-martial. He too said nothing. Dando looked at the sullen faces and thought: "These people have withdrawn psychologically to the point where they're dangerous."

The chaplain decided that he had to force the captain to understand what he had done to the emotional stability of his crew and to persuade Arnheiter to change his ways. A couple of nights before his departure he knocked on the captain's door and said he would like to discuss crew morale.

"Certainly, Chaplain, have a seat," Arnheiter said with a wave toward the bunk across from his swivel chair. He offered Dando one of the wardroom's panetelas. Dando declined.

"What about the morale?" the captain asked.

"I hate to tell you this, Captain," Dando said. "The morale on your ship is extremely poor."

"Why?" Arnheiter asked in surprise.

"Well, Captain, I believe that much of the low morale can be attributed to your personality," Dando replied. These were virtually the last words the chaplain said for the next four hours.

In the course of the fervid declamation that followed, Arnheiter conceded that he might have taken a few actions, such as his spit-and-polish program, that had temporarily dampened morale, but on the whole the crew was happy and morale was improving all the time. He summoned the chief petty officers to his cabin one by one.

"How's the morale of the crew?" the captain asked them in turn. Each chief glanced at the chaplain, and back at Arnheiter, and each said, "Morale's fine, Captain."

"You see," Arnheiter said triumphantly when the parade had concluded. "I told you morale was excellent."

Dando knew the chiefs were lying. Privately they had given him a different story. He also realized now that they had long ago learned a lesson about the captain that he was now being taught. "Nobody is going to tell him anything," Dando thought.

"Well, Captain, I've given you my opinion and I want you to know that I just don't agree with you," he said.

On the way to his bunk, Dando stopped in the wardroom and found Hardy there working on some papers. "Oh my God," he said, and described the sensation of being cornered in the captain's cabin while Arnheiter's nasal voice harangued on and on, rising and falling in cadence.

"I know the story. I've been there once or twice," Hardy said. By this time Hardy's incipient ulcer had made him a regular patient at Cornejo's dispensary. He was taking belladonna and Amphojel every day to fight off the bouts of acute gastritis. Cornejo had also put the senior boatswain's mate, Smoot, on tranquilizers for nervous depression. The captain was proving more powerful than the Librium capsules and Smoot's condition was continuing to deteriorate.

On the morning of March 14, Dando transferred to the U.S.S. *Kretchmer,* the next DER he was scheduled to visit on his rounds. "You're young, Chaplain. You'll learn as you go along," Arnheiter assured him as Dando maneuvered his large frame into a boatswain's chair, a portable seat which, mounted on pulleys whose ropes stretch between two vessels, can be used to sling a man from one ship to another.

"Good-bye, Captain," Dando said.

"I won't be much use to you for a week or so," Dando told the skipper of the *Kretchmer* at lunch. "I've got an awfully big problem to think my way through."

Dando knew that he had far more to resolve with himself than the bald decision of whether to tell Commodore Milligan at Subic Bay that morale on the *Vance* was deplorable and then give a few reasons. What he had seen and heard had so shaken him that his conscience would not permit him

to pass off his experience with a perfunctory report. He had
to determine whether he was prepared to risk recommending
that Milligan act drastically against the captain of the *Vance*
to forestall violence. He knew that if he marched that far, he
would have to support his recommendation with specific accusations against Arnheiter and to defend those accusations
under oath if Arnheiter were court-martialed. Suppose Arnheiter won? Dando could be court-martialed for false allegations. This was a perilous course for a young chaplain to
take against the captain of a Navy ship. Dando realized that
he might destroy his own career. He did not want to leave
the Navy. He hesitated.

Dando was afraid that if he vacillated too long, events
might resolve themselves. One of the most disturbing incidents had occurred just a few days before he left the *Vance*.
The captain, ironically, had almost provoked his own assassination because of his conviction that others loved praise as
much as he did.

Arnheiter had a habit of driving the ship at night into the
long nylon nets the Vietnamese fishermen strung out in the
shallow waters along the southern coast and then cutting up
the nets in the screws when he backed the *Vance* away. One
night he managed to wrap a net all the way around the ship.
The fishermen would scream and curse from their junks, because the nets were their means of livelihood and their most
valuable possession besides their boats. The captain paid no
attention to them.

Late one afternoon, as the *Vance* was hurrying at 16 knots,
tardy as usual, toward a rendezvous with an oiler, a vibration
suddenly developed in the shaft from the port engines to the
screws. Arnheiter sought Hardy, very upset. An admitted ig-
noramus in mechanical matters, the captain was afraid that
he might have warped the shaft or loosened a screw, possibly
during one of his shallow-water incursions. Hardy and Fuehrer investigated and assured Arnheiter that the trouble was
likely to be just some fishnetting caught at the end of the shaft.
The netting, Hardy explained, was probably causing the vibration in the shaft. Arnheiter would not believe the fault

could be that simple. Fuehrer knew that Boiler Tender Richard MacSaveny, who was one of his senior enginemen, had scuba gear aboard. He asked MacSaveny if he would dive down and see what was wrong.

"Okay," MacSaveny said, "I'll do it as a favor to you, not for that guy." MacSaveny, slim, with crew-cut brown hair, had grown up in the old fishing towns of eastern Long Island. His parents were divorced when he was a child. Shuttling between them was an unhappy existence, and he had fled to the sea in his boyhood, working after school and during the summers as a crewman on fishing boats and trawlers. He dropped out of high school as soon as he could, at sixteen, and joined the Navy at the minimum age of seventeen and a half. MacSaveny was a natural mechanic. He had spent days down in the bilges cleaning out the silt and muck the captain had forced into the evaporators by his shallow-water incursions. Like the other enginemen, MacSaveny loved his diesels and boilers and loathed the way the captain abused them.

The ship was stopped and MacSaveny climbed down the side. Arnheiter was worried about sharks and posted a rifleman to protect him. The sharks did not concern MacSaveny. He had learned in years of scuba diving that if there was no blood in the water and if you did not thrash about or flash a shiny object at them, sharks were unlikely to attack. He found a piece of fishnetting about a foot by two feet in size caught on the end of the shaft and cut it loose. MacSaveny was hoisted back aboard and the engines were restarted. The vibration had disappeared.

Arnheiter was so relieved that he insisted upon publicly presenting MacSaveny with a letter of commendation. MacSaveny told Hardy that he did not deserve any praise and did not want a letter of commendation, particularly a public one.

"I did it as a personal favor to the engineer," MacSaveny said. "I don't want anything for it. If he musters the crew back there on the fantail and gives me some letter of commendation, I'll be the laughingstock of this ship."

Hardy argued with Arnheiter, but the captain was adamant. "We have to set an example by rewarding audacious-ness, Ray. MacSaveny is an audacious young seaman."

The crew was assembled on the fantail in dress whites before the captain's flag-draped lectern and microphone. Mac-Saveny stood at attention in solitary anguish in front of the ranks. Arnheiter held up the letter and read to the assembly in a parade-ground voice of MacSaveny's "outstanding ex-ample of courage, initiative and dedication to duty . . .

"You, without self-consideration, volunteered to dive be-neath the ship's hull . . . in water known to be infested with sharks and poisonous sea snakes. Undaunted by these known facts and warnings from the engineering officer, you pro-ceeded as directed. Once in the water you conducted yourself in a manner that is a credit to you, your ship and the Navy. On several occasions you dived beneath the hull to inspect the areas in question. Upon finding the cause to be fishnets entwined in the port screw and shaft, you made one final dive and removed the obstruction. You did this even while a leop-ard shark and moray eel slithered into view in your vicinity."

The sailors standing behind MacSaveny were smiling broadly. Although MacSaveny could not see their faces, he could hear some of them snickering. MacSaveny had watched one shark swim drowsily by at a good distance. A couple of poisonous sea snakes had approached uncomfortably close, but he had easily avoided them by ducking behind the sonar dome under the hull. There had not been a glimmer of a moray eel.

"The courage and dedication you exhibited is exemplary of the American Navy fighting man," Arnheiter concluded. "Again, you are commended for your actions and your coura-geous performance of duty, above and beyond the normal expected of you."

"Ridiculous," "stupid," and every other adjective of shame MacSaveny could think of, ran through his mind. He wanted to dive back into the sea. Later that day one of the sailors coined a nickname for MacSaveny—"Thunderball," after the James Bond movie of underwater espionage in the West In-dies. The nickname stuck, and every time MacSaveny saw another sailor in a passageway he would be greeted with "Hey there, Thunderball." MacSaveny was troubled with a private problem as well. He had been married for a year and a half, and his wife was pregnant with their first child. He was upset at being away from her at this time. The combination of his personal concern and the ribbing he was being subjected to overwhelmed him. Within a few days MacSaveny was so nervous and depressed that Cornejo put him on a daily dosage of tranquilizers. The Librium helped, but the razzing from the other sailors chafed deeper than the drug could reach. MacSaveny's shame and anger crystallized into a ferocious hatred of the captain.

At dusk one day about two weeks after his ordeal on the fantail, MacSaveny was lying on his bunk in the first class petty officers' berthing space, tense and jittery. The effects of the last Librium pill were wearing off and it was not yet time for another. The loudspeaker sounded: "Away the boarding party." MacSaveny was a member of one of the boarding sections. His task was to stand on the O-1 deck of the *Vance* with a 12-gauge sawed-off shotgun. From there he could look down on the junk pulled alongside. If the Vietnamese crew turned out by chance to be hostile, MacSaveny could sweep them off their deck with a hail of buckshot, lead pellets about the size of a .30-caliber bullet that spew out of a shotgun like grapeshot from a cannon.

MacSaveny slid from his bunk in that peculiar state of mind the profoundly depressed enter, where perception is fragmentary and spasmodic. He drew a shotgun from the small-arms locker and climbed to the O-1 deck. He could see through the dim light that the men on the junk were having difficulty working their wooden craft next to the *Vance* because of the swells. He was dizzy and slightly nauseated. He weaved a bit with the roll of the ship. Just then he heard the captain's voice yelling, yelling. Arnheiter was standing next to the railing about twenty feet away, screaming at the Vietnamese on the junk to move alongside faster. Almost instinctively, MacSaveny decided to kill the captain. It was time to silence that voice. He pumped a shell into the chamber with a snap of his arm, swerved and aimed the shotgun at Arn-heiter's head. "For thirteen cents, for the price of a shotgun shell, I can end everybody's problems," he said to himself as he looked down the barrel at that familiar head topped with the khaki baseball cap. He could feel the pressure of his index finger on the trigger when he thought of what his act would cost himself and his wife and the baby-to-come. The captain would be dead, but he would go to jail and they would suffer. "It's just not worth it," he muttered.

Arnheiter stopped yelling and turned away from the rail-ing. He saw the shotgun leveled at his face. MacSaveny had been pointing it for about five seconds now. The captain ap-parently thought that MacSaveny was toying with the shot-gun to pass the time and did not sense any danger. "You shouldn't point a shotgun at somebody unless you intend to kill them," Arnheiter said in a tone of mild admonition.

The captain's remark struck MacSaveny as grotesquely comic. Every family on rural Long Island had owned a shot-gun to hunt rabbits and birds. In his boyhood, his father and his uncles had tacked the lesson into his mind: "Never point a gun at anything unless you mean to kill it." He lowered the weapon, turned his head away and laughed hysterically.

MacSaveny put the shotgun back into the arms locker and walked down to the dispensary. He had to talk to someone, and Cornejo was the only man he trusted. Leaning against the bulkhead next to the autoclave that Cornejo used to steri-lize instruments, he began describing how narrowly he had come to assassinating the captain. When he spoke, his body started to tremble convulsively. He slid down the bulkhead, shaking and weeping like a child. "Go ahead, talk, talk, it's good for you," Cornejo said. As soon as MacSaveny had calmed down somewhat, Cornejo gave him a double dose of Librium and sent him to his bunk.

"Jesus," Cornejo said to himself after MacSaveny had left, "it's like walking on eggshells around here. You're just waiting for something to happen."

The next morning Cornejo told Dando about the incident. The chaplain questioned MacSaveny and then instructed Cornejo to keep MacSaveny on tranquilizers until Cornejo could get him to a doctor. Dando decided that with his immediate crisis past, MacSaveny would, like the deck hand who had raved drunkenly on the beach, not harm Arnheiter for the present. But the chaplain was worried that there might be other MacSavenys who had not gone to Cornejo.

9

A SUBMARINE AND A SILVER STAR

It isn't true and I won't be a party
to this.

—Lieutenant Hardy to Captain Arnheiter

While Dando searched his conscience and MacSaveny took more tranquilizers, Luis Belmonte was praying that an American Air Force plane would not strafe him to death. The captain had left him and two sailors in the speedboat in the Gulf of Siam on a Saturday night, at least twenty miles from the nearest shore, to wait for a Chinese submarine.

The genesis of Belmonte's plight had occurred the day before, Friday, March 18, when the captain was summoned to An Thoi for a special, secret briefing. Navy headquarters in Saigon had received an intelligence report that a small Chinese submarine was going to steal out of the port of Sihanoukville, in neighboring Cambodia, and meet several guerrilla junks off the southern coast of Viet Nam to transfer arms and ammunition. The *Vance* and a task force of three Coast Guard cutters and three Swift patrol craft had been ordered into a secret five-day search operation to detect the submarine.

Arnheiter had mustered his entire crew, and the men from the cutters and the Swift boats, on the fantail of the *Vance* Friday afternoon. He read the hush-hush intelligence report from Saigon to the assembly and then launched into one of his most fiery eve-of-battle orations.

"I call upon each and every one of you for a supreme effort," he said. "The men on the beach are depending upon us to discover that submarine before she can deliver her deadly cargo of weapons. The lives of our infantrymen are at stake. We must not fail them.

"You sonarmen," he said to the sonar technicians, whose most interesting work recently had been listening to his twenty-minute showers, "must hone your ears to detect the slightest underwater sound.

"And you gunner's mates," he continued, "must be prepared to go into action in a split second. The depth charges and the hedgehogs will be armed. When we find that submarine, and we're going to find her, we're going to kill her. Our depth charges and our hedgehogs will crush her hull like an egg. If she surfaces, we'll fight her there too. We'll ram her if we have to," he vowed.

The search order said to detect and report the presence of the Chinese submarine. It said nothing about destroying her. A lieutenant commanding one of the Swift boats was not accustomed, as were the *Vance*'s officers, to Captain Arnheiter's imaginative interpretation of orders.

"Captain, you can't go around sinking other people's submarines in international waters. That's piracy," he protested. The *Vance*'s position in the search screen would be about twenty miles to sea, well beyond South Viet Nam's territorial waters.

"I'm the captain of this ship and I know what I'm doing," Arnheiter retorted.

"Jesus Christ, he really means it," Radarman Sides said to Cheadle, his fellow radar technician in the combat information center. "He wants to sink that submarine. It's either them or us."

The search operation had commenced on Saturday morning. That night the captain came upon a large fishing junk at anchor beside its nets. For some reason he decided that the junk looked suspicious and that the submarine might surface near it to transfer weapons. Belmonte was roused from his bunk and told to man the speedboat. He impressed the gunner's mate who had vainly tried to sink the oil drums for the television cameramen, and a seaman, one of his former deck hands, as a crew. The captain walked back to the fantail while they were climbing down the ladder into the speedboat, still half asleep, and outlined his plan. He would tow the speedboat toward the junk until Belmonte could see it and then cut the runabout loose. Belmonte was to creep near, hopefully unseen by the fishermen because of the speedboat's low profile, then shut off his engine and anchor where he could observe. Arnheiter did not say what to do if the submarine appeared. Belmonte assumed that the *Vance* would remain within radio range so that he could call for help if the Chinese submariners did surface with their cargo of munitions.

The experience of being towed behind the *Vance* at 15 knots jarred Belmonte and the two sailors into complete wakefulness. The captain turned the ship sharply a couple of times, and the sixteen-foot runabout skipped up one side of the *Vance*'s wake and down the other like a loose water ski.

"That crazy fucker's going to drown us," the gunner's mate said.

"This is getting a little hairy back here. We're shipping a lot of water and my bow is hard down. I request the ship reduce speed," Belmonte said to the captain over the radio.

"Don't worry about it, Mr. Belmonte," Arnheiter replied.

A few minutes later Belmonte reported that he could see the junk. The captain let them go. They edged the speedboat fairly close to the junk and threw out a sea anchor. The *Vance* disappeared into the darkness. Within ten minutes Belmonte could no longer raise the captain on the radio.

The sound of aircraft engines intruded on the humid stillness of the tropic night. A plane angled down, made a run over the speedboat and swung around for another pass, this time at about two hundred feet, illuminating the runabout in its landing lights. Belmonte recognized its silhouette; it was the type of plane known as "Puff the Magic Dragon," the name given to the World War II twin-engine Dakotas the Air Force had resurrected from an airplane graveyard and armed with extremely rapid-fire machine guns called miniguns, for strafing. There were rumors that the Air Force had been shooting up Vietnamese fishing boats without warning in so-called prohibited zones along the coast. Belmonte was afraid the pilots might mistake the speedboat, with its machine gun mounted in the middle, for some kind of smuggler, or just start shooting anyway. He grabbed the three-by-five-foot American flag the speedboat carried to entice the Viet Cong, stood up and waved it wildly as the plane turned for another low pass with its landing lights on.

"Please God, please don't let them open up with those miniguns," he prayed aloud. "They'll grease us right out of the water with six thousand rounds a minute or whatever they shoot."

The plane shut off its lights and flew away.

A half-hour later they had calmed down enough for one man to stand watch while the other two slept. Shortly before dawn the seaman asked, "What the hell are we doing here, Mr. Belmonte?"

"You know," Belmonte said, shaking his head to come awake, "that's a terribly germane question, because what the hell *are* we doing here? We've got no visual or radio contact with the ship. That plane lit us up so the junk must have seen us. If the goddamn sub does come up, what are we going to do? Storm it with a .30-caliber machine gun, a Tommy gun and an M-1 rifle? They'll blow us to shit." Belmonte and the two sailors had a couple of sandwiches, but no water, no charts, no compass, and they were twenty or thirty miles off a hostile coast. There were only a few places on it to land, because the VC owned the rest. Belmonte didn't even know if they had enough gas to get back to the beach, VC-owned or not.

"Jesus, God above, what the hell is going to happen to us?" Belmonte thought to himself. "That damn fool Marcus was on the bridge and he can't navigate his way around his own cabin. Unless the XO was up there or they had a good watch, they'll never know where to find us." Belmonte spent the rest of the night studying the stars and trying to keep fixed in his mind which direction to head for the coast.

The fishing junk weighed anchor at dawn. An hour of sun made the sailors thirsty. Belmonte was considering the possibility of finding another junk to board for water when the seaman spied a Coast Guard cutter in the distance. "Let's go over there and eat breakfast," he suggested.

They started the outboard engine and crossed over to the cutter. "Can we have some bacon and eggs?" Belmonte asked a Coast Guard ensign as they tied up alongside. The officer looked at him in consternation. Three sailors in a sixteen-foot speedboat do not come hippity-hopping across the waves twenty miles out to sea every morning and ask for breakfast.

They were still eating when another ensign, who commanded the cutter, came below and said, "Your ship's calling."

Belmonte walked up to the cutter's bridge and saw the *Vance* emerging on the horizon. He could hear Hardy's voice over the radio asking the cutter, "Have you seen my scout boat?" He felt a surge of temptation to tell the Coast Guard ensign, "Say you haven't seen us so that you can take us into An Thoi and we can get away from that madhouse."

"Jesus," Belmonte thought, "wouldn't that really shake old Marcus up? Here he's been pulling all these stunts and getting away with them and what would happen, by God, if he had to report that three men and a speedboat were missing? How would he get around that one?"

Perhaps because Hardy, and not the captain, was calling, Belmonte said nothing. They returned to the ship.

They discovered the *Vance* suspended into a state of extraordinary, if relative, silence. Not even the prospect of a Chinese submarine could persuade the captain to stop "Hellcats Reveille" or "Roast Beef of Olde Englande," but paint chipping, the slamming of hatches, and other loud noises had been prohibited in order to help the sonarmen listen for the submarine's propellers. The plan of the day warned: "In other words, *BE QUIET, BE CAREFUL AND THINK BEFORE*

YOU ACT. 'Will I make unnecessary noise?' *DON'T.*" Arn-heiter encouraged the officers and sailors to wear sneakers and rubber-soled boating shoes so that they could tread si-lently about the decks. They were also forbidden to smoke abovedecks at night on the chance that the submarine might see the *Vance* before it was detected. "Darken ship routine must be rigidly followed. A lighted cigarette can be seen for two miles at night through binoculars and the flame of a match or lighter for five miles," the plan of the day warned. The water was so shallow that the captain had the depth charges and hedgehog explosives set to detonate at a mere fifty feet below the surface. Arnheiter wanted to be certain of his quarry. He paced the bridge with anticipation and frequently darted into the sonar compartment at the back of the pilot-house to encourage the technicians listening there.

"It's like a John Wayne movie," Generous said to Fuehrer. John Wayne might have preferred another ending.

On the third night of the alert, the captain's mind appar-ently strayed to his last conversation with Chaplain Dando. He approached a sailor who was leaning up against the rail-ing on the O-1 deck a few feet away from where the speedboat was mounted.

"How's your morale, sailor?" Arnheiter asked.

"Pretty shitty, Captain," the sailor said.

"Oh yes?" the captain asked suspiciously. "Why?"

The seaman pointed to the speedboat. "Well, there's nine hundred and fifty bucks of my recreation dough sittin' over there and it ain't doin' me a fuckin' bit of good."

At lunch the next day the captain asked Fuehrer and Merkel, "How would you like to take some of the crew riding in the scout boat?"

The submarine alert was still in force and Fuehrer as-sumed the captain was joking. "No, I wouldn't care for that. That wouldn't be much fun," he said. "But I'd like to go water-skiing." Merkel agreed.

"Would you go skiing in these waters with those poisonous sea snakes and the sharks around?" the captain asked.

"Hell, there aren't that many of them," Fuehrer said.

"Then take the scout boat and go ahead and water-ski," Arnheiter said.

"You don't mean it, Captain, do you?" Merkel asked, suddenly apprehensive.

"Certainly I mean it. Go ahead. Go water-skiing," the captain said. They tried to draw back. It was too late. Arnheiter grew insistent. Fuehrer and Merkel went to their compartments to change into swimming trunks.

The captain declared a general holiday for the crew. He had Ensign McWhirter, who now ran the deck gang, launch the motor whaleboat as well and load it with cases of beer. The sailors took turns drinking beer in the whaleboat and learning to water-ski with the speedboat. From one of his open-air chairs on a wing of the bridge, the captain provided a running narration of events over the loudspeaker—sportscaster fashion—for three hours, until his voice finally gave out. "There goes Currier, Electrician's Mate First. He's struggling, he's struggling. He's up! He's on the skis and doing beautifully. Oops! Currier's in the air. He's down in a hard fall." Belmonte retreated to the junior officers' compartment at the stern to escape into his statistics for the computerized preventive-maintenance program. He ripped the compartment's loudspeaker extension out of the bulkhead.

Hardy watched the spectacle in disbelief. He doubted that any Chinese submarine would risk smuggling arms to the guerrillas in waters as shallow as those in the Gulf of Siam. The submarine would probably have had to make a surface approach, not a very feasible undertaking. But Admiral Ward in Saigon obviously thought there might be an attempt. The orders were clear. And neither An Thoi nor Navy headquarters had any idea that Captain Arnheiter had become bored with submarines and had put the crew of the *Vance* to water-skiing and swilling beer in a whaleboat.

"You know," Generous said to Hardy, "if there is a Chinese submarine around here and those Chinamen see this whacky shit they'll turn tail and run for Shanghai as fast as their diesels can carry them. They'd never believe the United States Navy had a nut in command of one of its ships. They'd think this was some kind of devilish occidental ambush we'd set up for them." Hardy shuffled off to his compartment and threw himself on his bunk, exhausted.

The sonarmen quit listening for the submarine and lined up for a place in the whaleboat. The odds of distinguishing the noise of a submarine's propellers over the racket of a speedboat's outboard engine weren't worth the effort. Besides, the sailors didn't give a damn at this point. The captain was like the Greek gods to them. If the gods were laughing today and handing out iced cans of beer, who was foolish enough to refuse the largesse? By nightfall, when the water-skiing ended, half the crew was tipsy.

Early the next morning, the fifth and last day of the alert, the *Vance* was relieved on station by another DER, the U.S.S. *Brister,* and set sail for Manila for two weeks' maintenance work on her equipment by the technicians of a repair ship moored there. While the beer-drinking and water-skiing gala had been in progress, the *Vance*'s teletype tapped out a message from Rear Admiral Donald G. Irvine, the commander of the Seventh Fleet's flotilla of cruisers and destroyers. The message was addressed to the *Vance* and to all the other destroyer-type ships off Viet Nam. It noted that the Navy had awarded the smallest number of medals for the Viet Nam war of any of the three major services. The admiral urged his ship captains to recommend any deserving officers and seamen for awards. On March 23, as the *Vance* headed toward Manila, Hardy was summoned to the captain's cabin. Arnheiter gave him a list of twenty medals and awards he intended to propose: a Silver Star for gallantry, four Bronze Stars for valor, five Navy Commendation Medals, and a number of letters of commendation. Hardy was flabbergasted. His own name headed the list for the Silver Star.

"Captain, I don't see that we've done anything to receive any medals for," he said. "We haven't encountered any hostile fire to justify these recommendations."

"We sent in hostile-fire reports, didn't we?" the captain replied, cocking his head to one side.

Hardy remembered the press releases. "That's true," he had to agree. "We did send them."

"Well, there it is," Arnheiter said.

"But why are you proposing me for a Silver Star?" Hardy asked. "I don't deserve any medal like that." The Silver Star is the Navy's third-highest combat award.

The captain explained that Hardy had exposed himself to enemy bullets one day by climbing the mast as a lookout while the *Vance* chased ten sampans filled with Vietnamese who refused to stop for inspection. Despite the fact that Arnheiter had his crew open fire on the sampans with rifles and the .50-caliber machine guns, the Vietnamese had escaped unscathed into an enclosed lagoon. They had not shot back. Hardy suspected that they had refused to stop because of the captain's reputation among the fishermen for abuse.

"I don't merit a medal for that, Captain. That was just something to do. I didn't want to send someone else up the mast, so I went myself."

"That's for me to judge, Ray," Arnheiter said.

Belmonte, as the captain had promised him when he had volunteered to man the speedboat for the forays close to shore, was being recommended for a Bronze Star. Mason was also to receive one, for the venture ashore to foil the supposed submarine landing; Generous, McWhirter and Gwynn were being proposed for Navy Commendation Medals for expeditions in the whaleboat. The other awards were to go to enlisted men.

"Now you've got to listen to me, Captain," Hardy said. "I don't rate the Silver Star and I don't want it."

"I told you, Ray," Arnheiter said firmly, "that's for me to decide and I've decided." The captain's remark ended the conversation and loosed a thunderstorm of paper work.

Arnheiter composed the basis citations for each incident. Hardy gathered from the officers and sailors two sworn eye-witness statements to accompany each citation. Using the captain's press releases as a guide, Hardy outlined to each witness what he was to include in his affidavit. He was surprised at how adroitly the men faked their accounts, although the captain improved on each before a final version was typed and signed. The crew had learned what Captain Arnheiter wanted.

Right after dinner on March 24, the captain called Hardy and Generous to his cabin. They sat on the bunk opposite his swivel chair.

"Well, we've got everybody taken care of here, haven't we?" he asked. They said nothing, and he looked intently from one face to the other.

"We've got everybody taken care of now, haven't we?" he asked again, slowly and deliberately this time. Hardy took the cue.

"No, we don't, Captain. You're not taken care of," he said.

"Well, now," Arnheiter replied, permitting himself a grin. "That is kind of a problem, isn't it?" He asked Hardy and Generous if they recalled one of the rare movies he had allowed the wardroom to see the previous week. It was called *To Hell and Back,* and was the story of how Audie Murphy had become the most-decorated American soldier in World War II. Did they remember, the captain continued, that Murphy had received his first medals when he was a sergeant because the other men in his infantry squad were always recommending him to the platoon leader, a lieutenant, for awards? Yes, they said, they remembered that.

"Right, now does this suggest anything to you?" the captain prodded.

"Are you implying that you want us to recommend you for a medal, Captain?" Hardy asked.

"Well, now, I'm not saying that, but now that you mention it, that has interesting possibilities. Let me think about it," the captain replied, indulging in another boyish smile. He reached over to the wardroom cigar box on his desk, selected a panetela and lit it with satisfaction. Hardy and Generous left.

"By God, he really handled that one, didn't he?" Hardy said as they walked down the ladder to the main deck. "We suggested to him that we recommend him for a medal, and now he's going to think about it and let us know. Jesus, I don't know whether to go and hit my head against a bulkhead because it'll feel so good when I stop, or what." Hardy returned to the wardroom to work on the flurry of citations already in the paper mill. Generous, speechless, retired to his bunk.

Three hours later the captain summoned Hardy back to his cabin. He had the executive officer sit down on the bunk and gave him a pad of lined yellow foolscap and a pencil. "Now, don't interrupt, just write what I'm going to dictate to you," Arnheiter said. Reading from a sheaf of papers in his hand, he began dictating a letter to the *Vance*'s operational squadron commander at Subic Bay.

"Dear Commodore Milligan,

"I know this is not the generally approved method for recommendations for awards to be submitted. However, neither you nor an immediate superior to Commanding Officer, *Vance,* is on board to evaluate meritorious action in combat of this officer.

"On the other hand, I and certain other men attached to this ship, being in a position to observe the Commanding Officer during combat action, believe it would not be in the best interests of the naval service to not submit the accounts of some of his actions in combat to date, which we have observed and which have served to inspire others on board to perform their duties with more audacity, aggressiveness, and verve, to the end that we do all we can as vigorously as we can, to make felt our imprint in this war.

"This letter to you is my idea, and I myself penned it after consultation with other men whose signatures follow and who also desire to attest to the citation, if that's what you want to call it, which is herewith appended."

Hardy's indignation forced him to interrupt. "Captain, I'm not writing something like this. I can't write a letter like this."

"Now, just be quiet and keep writing," the captain said. He resumed dictating.

"Recommendation is very respectfully made that award of the Silver Star medal be made to Lieutenant Commander Marcus A. Arnheiter, 5544819/1100, U.S. Navy, Commanding Officer, U.S.S. *Vance;* otherwise, the Legion of Merit. A special note should be made of the fact that aggressiveness, imagination, and fearlessness in all operations is the routine character reflection of Lieutenant

Commander Arnheiter. Short of sinking an enemy submarine, which the whole crew knows he wants very much to do, there is not much that any other destroyer-type commanding officer could do—if he really worked at it—that ours has not already done. There is no doubt that the presentation of a decoration in this case would be most decidedly approved by all observers on board *Vance*. Not to recognize his gallantry in action would be a disservice to the Navy as well as to him."

Hardy stood up, his bland features distorted with rage. He thrust the pad of yellow foolscap at Arnheiter. "I'm not going to send any letter like this to Commodore Milligan, Captain. It isn't true and I won't be a party to this."

"Ray, what did I tell you about MacArthur and how he won his Silver Stars?" Arnheiter asked calmly.

"So what? What does that have to do with us?"

"I don't see that what he did is one bit more than what we've done out here," the captain replied in a cold voice. "This is working out fine. You sit down and keep writing." There was threat in his tone now. Hardy sat down. Arnheiter dictated the citation that was to accompany the letter:

"The President of the United States takes great pleasure in presenting the Silver Star medal to Lieutenant Commander Marcus Aurelius Arnheiter . . . for constancy in forging the highest combat *esprit de corps,* by himself setting a resolute example of gallantry and intrepidity in action through persistent displays of boldness, audaciousness and courage in the leadership of officers and men . . ."

The citation forged on, a notable improvement in extravagance over the earlier press releases. The dune in the sand-crab bombardment of January, which had acquired machine-gun bunkers and entrenchments in the press release, now bristled with "a company of Viet Cong hard-core soldiery." Again, near the destroyer *Bache* on January 30, when "enemy soldiery hiding in a jungled area close by opened fire on the ship," the officers and seamen had been inspired by the sight of the captain, "stationed in an exposed manner atop the pilothouse . . . acting in his customary pattern of inherent disregard of personal safety when vigorously leading the crew in combat action. With complete personal control over the situation, he coolly directed a prompt and intensive return fire which succeeded in quelling all enemy action." There was no mention of Arnheiter's uncaptainly dive behind the gun-control shielding after he mistook the ricochets of the *Vance's* armor-piercing .50-caliber machine-gun bullets for the muzzle flashes of guerrilla automatic weapons.

Arnheiter took more than an hour to dictate the citation, eight typewritten pages long. At the end the captain explained to Hardy that he had dictated the letter and the citation so that the ship's senior yeoman, who would type the final copies, would see the drafts in the executive officer's handwriting. "That way he'll think you thought of this and believe it's sincere and genuine," the captain said. Hardy nodded dumbly. After the citation and the covering letter were typed, the captain instructed, Hardy was to return them to him for proofreading. Hardy would then sign the letter and find another officer and an enlisted man as co-signers.

Hardy attempted a last protest before leaving. "How can I get people to sign something like this, Captain?" he asked.

"Now, don't tell me you can't get people to sign anything you want them to sign. You're the executive officer, aren't you?" Arnheiter snapped.

Since the captain had brought Generous into the first act of the charade, Hardy thought he should co-sign the letter. On the way to Generous' compartment, he ran over in his mind once more the possibility of swearing out court-martial charges against Arnheiter, and rejected this alternative for the same reasons he had earlier. The captain would never permit the charge sheet to leave the ship and the act would provoke the confrontation Hardy had sought to avoid all along. He reiterated to himself that he could endure until his scheduled transfer in August. In the meantime he would obey the captain and hold the ship together. He convinced himself that the captain's Silver Star scheme was so patently spurious that Commodore Milligan would see through the fraud and toss the letter and the citation into his wastebasket, or at least send for Hardy and question him about them. Hardy could then, with a clear conscience, tell the commodore the truth. He knocked on Generous' door, and when the operations officer opened it, Hardy silently handed him the pages of foolscap covered with his handwriting. Generous read them. Hardy explained how he had played secretary in the captain's cabin. He asked Generous to co-sign the letter.

"I won't do it, XO," Generous said. "It's a farce."

"I'm not debating whether it's a joke or a farce or whatever it is and I'm sure it won't go through, Tom, but that letter has got to be signed to keep things going."

"What do you mean, 'keep things going'? What the hell is so great about the way things are going?" Generous asked.

"Things have got to keep going even if they aren't so hot, or the top will blow off, and I say the top is not going to blow off," Hardy replied.

Generous agreed to sign if Hardy would also co-sign an affidavit telling the truth. "We'll seal the affidavit in an envelope and type on the outside that it is to be opened only with our permission," Generous said. "The sealed envelope will go in with Marcus' phony letter and his citation. If it looks like he's going to get the medal, then we'll ask the commodore to open the sealed envelope and let him read the affidavit. If the commodore's got sense enough to realize that the citation couldn't possibly be true and throws it away, the envelope will stay sealed. I'm sure he wouldn't open it without our permission."

"All right, I'll do it," Hardy said.

Generous sat down at his typewriter and composed the affidavit:

The idea for this award was generated by Lieutenant Commander Arnheiter himself, despite what the letter says. The words of the letter were dictated to Lieutenant Hardy by Mr. Arnheiter. The letter is anything but a spontaneous attempt to cover a deserving officer in glory. It represents, rather, a shameful farce and a degrading of all those brave men who have earned the award.

We further state that we, as the most senior officers under the command, signed the letter in order to preserve peace in the ship; and we did so in the belief that some action would take place to prevent the actual bestowing of the award.

They signed the affidavit and Generous sealed it in an envelope. He asked a petty officer who worked for him to sign the captain's Silver Star letter as the enlisted crew member. The man did so without a question.

Lieutenant (j.g.) Uldis Kordons, a laconic, self-possessed Princeton graduate of twenty-four who was the communications officer on Commodore Milligan's staff, was making a circuit of the DER's off Viet Nam and had joined the *Vance* after Dando's departure. Kordons had been aboard for the past few days, trying to resolve some recurrent problems in communications. He rode the *Vance* into Manila Bay on March 26 and was given the packet containing all of the citations, including the captain's, to deliver to the commodore at Subic Bay. Just before he went ashore, Hardy handed him the sealed envelope and asked him to carry it to Milligan in confidence. The executive officer offered no explanation of its contents, and Kordons did not ask for one. He simply slid the envelope into the packet with the citations.

If Captain Arnheiter had any doubts about his game, he did not make them known. He seemed quite sure of himself.

10

THE RECKONING

He that walketh uprightly walketh surely: but
he that perverteth his ways shall be known.

—Proverbs 10:9

(Quotation selected by Captain Arnheiter
to head the *Vance*'s plan of the day for
March 31, 1966)

All of the ships in Manila Bay knew the U.S.S. *Vance* had
arrived. Belmonte was up early the first morning in port. The
Vance was tied up next to the repair ship U.S.S. *Markab*,
in what is called a "nest" of ships. The vessels were anchored
side by side, with connecting gangways so that the *Markab*'s
repair crews could walk back and forth from one ship to another. Three destroyers and a couple of sister DER's of the
Vance were also undergoing repairs by the *Markab*'s technicians. A number of sailors on the other ships had risen
before reveille and were sleepily swabbing decks and polishing
brass fittings. At 6:30 precisely, they froze at the cacophony
of "Hellcats Reveille" bursting from the *Vance* at the peak decibels that could be heard a mile away at sea. It did not occur
to the captain, now that he was in port, to wake his crew
and his neighbors more gently to the day. The sailors on the
neighboring ships whirled and stared in amazement at the
Vance. A few dropped the mops they had been wielding.

Other seamen came running up onto the decks to see what the alarm was all about. One sailor from a destroyer had been halfway across the *Vance*'s deck on his way to the *Markab* when the captain's musical eye-opener sounded. The seaman apparently thought he had intruded upon some important ceremony. He halted, braced to attention and saluted the air.

"What the hell is going on over there?" the sailors from the other ships shouted toward the *Vance* as soon as silence returned four minutes and ten seconds later. Belmonte hid behind a vent on the quarter-deck. Several *Vance* seamen who were on deck ducked into compartments and passageways.

At lunch and dinner, "Roast Beef of Olde Englande" started the digestive juices flowing throughout the nest.

Johnnie Lee Smoot's nerves snapped on the second morning in port. Another tongue-lashing from the captain, for a tarnished belt buckle, rent the frayed strands. Trembling and forcing back the tears, he went to see Hardy and told the executive officer that he was going to jump ship. Hardy instructed Cornejo to take Smoot over to the doctor on the *Markab* and see if he could be sent ashore for psychiatric treatment. The *Markab*'s doctor talked to Smoot for an hour that afternoon. He sent for Cornejo and said that he would arrange for Smoot to enter the psychiatric ward at the Clark Air Force Base Hospital, near Manila. The doctor said that he could not believe the stories Smoot had recounted about Captain Arnheiter.

"What kind of stories did he tell you?" Cornejo asked.

The doctor mentioned the towing of the motor whaleboat at 12 knots in choppy seas with a crew aboard, and the captain's tornado-like commands to simultaneously drop anchor, launch the speedboat, lower away the whaleboat and muster the Special Fire Team.

"Oh, those are all true," Cornejo said, "and there are a lot more." He treated the doctor to a few Arnheiter anecdotes. "In fact, I'd like to have you come over and take a look at our captain," he added.

The doctor quickly declined. "I'm not a psychiatrist. I'm

just an M.D., and that's a very touchy thing to do." He pointed out that if Arnheiter did submit to a psychiatric examination and was proven sane, he and Cornejo could find themselves in serious trouble.

"Why don't you just come over for dinner some evening and watch him during the meal?" Cornejo persisted.

"No thanks," the doctor said.

"What the hell am I going to do?" Cornejo said. "You're at least a doctor. I'm just a corpsman."

"That's your problem," the doctor said.

Cornejo returned to his problem, Captain Arnheiter, convinced now that only an explosion from within the ship would solve it. He took MacSaveny to the doctor on the *Markab* as well. The doctor decided that MacSaveny's most severe depression had passed and that he was no longer dangerous. Still, like Chaplain Dando, Cornejo feared that there might be other MacSavenys who would not hesitate. His intuition told him that some kind of upheaval was approaching.

Hardy had become so haggard and nervous from lack of sleep and the emotional strain that Generous and Meisner were taking turns keeping an eye on him, for fear that he might do something rash. Generous was afraid Hardy might eventually harm himself. "He's getting so heavy with the troubles of everybody else, he's like St. Christopher in the middle of the river," Generous said to Meisner.

Belmonte was drinking himself sodden every night that he could escape from the ship on shore liberty. He wandered from bar to bar in Manila in an alcoholic fog, vowing he would send a telegram to Commodore Milligan appealing for help. "Please God, somebody come and rescue us," he muttered to himself. At the end of one evening Merkel and Gwynn found him slumped unconscious across a table in the Ugly American Bar and carried him back to the ship.

In their darkening mood of isolation and imprisonment, some of the officers began to plot puerile acts of defiance against the captain. While none of these childish plots bore fruit, they were the beginnings of that desperate state of mind and emotion that ultimately contrives a serious conspiracy.

Except for Hardy, and for Belmonte, who was usually too drunk, the officers took to meeting at the American Embassy Bar near the pier around midnight for a few more drinks before the shore-liberty launch made its final trip to the *Vance* at 1 A.M. They would anesthetize their senses with the last glasses of a hasty bender and commiserate with one another. One night someone suggested that they should all jump ship together when it came time to sail back to Viet Nam. Mass desertion by the ship's officers certainly ought to create enough consternation at squadron and flotilla headquarters to force the captain's removal, they reasoned.

"We've been deserted by the whole goddamn Navy," Generous said. "They're blind to the problem. Marcus has been spending the last three months trying to attract attention to himself, and if they haven't gotten the message by now about what a kook they have running this ship, they're never going to get it." The disenchantment of the next morning's hangover made them think the scheme was not so wise after all. The captain would be removed, but they might go to jail.

A plot hatched amidst the alcoholic reveries of another evening came closer to fulfillment. Merkel owned a bawdy record from his college-fraternity days entitled "Hot Nuts." They would filch the tape the captain used to play "Hellcats Reveille" over the loudspeaker system and splice in the most ribald lyrics of "Hot Nuts" after the first thirty seconds of Arnheiter's bugle mishmash. After Generous did the splicing with his tape recorder, they would slip the doctored tape back onto the little recorder the captain had hooked up to the central loudspeaker control on the bridge. They laughed themselves giddy at the imagined reactions of the sailors and officers on the other ships in the nest when "Hellcats" ceased after thirty seconds, and three minutes and forty seconds of "Hot Nuts" resounded over the harbor at full volume. "Jesus, that'll drive Marcus right over the side," Merkel said. "He'll have five cat fits at once."

Back on the ship, one of the officers quickly snitched the tape. Then they lost their nerve. They found the captain writing letters in the wardroom. They were afraid that in some unpredictable sortie up to the bridge, he might catch them fitting the doctored tape onto the recorder. They hastily returned the tape to the bridge untouched.

Some sailor was bolder. The tape disappeared, apparently tossed into Manila Bay. The theft was discovered in the late afternoon as the captain was returning from one of his daily excursions in the speedboat. He cried out for Hardy. "Someone on this ship is trying to defy me," he said. "I won't stand for it." The sting of suspected opposition propelled him into an inquisition that lasted most of the night.

The captain transformed the wardroom into an interrogation chamber, with Hardy sitting beside him at the table, mutely nodding assent each time Arnheiter reiterated the urgent necessity to apprehend and punish the culprit. One by one, every sailor the captain could imagine as a possible suspect was brought in for questioning by the chief master-at-arms, the senior petty officer responsible for discipline. The petty officer of the bridge watch finally said he had seen a young fireman walk through a passageway earlier that day with a wad of recording tape in his hand.

"Arrest that man and bring him to me immediately," Arnheiter ordered Chief John Wesley Blake, the master-at-arms. Chief Blake learned that the sailor was in Manila on liberty.

Not to be denied, the captain ordered Chief Blake to round up a shipfitter and have him cut open the sailor's locker with an acetylene torch. The master-at-arms objected that this was against regulations in the man's absence, unless the captain was willing to write out an order stating that the locker was believed to contain narcotics or other contraband.

"Cut it open!" Arnheiter hollered.

Inside, the captain found a tangled ball of recording tape. "That's it," he yelled gleefully, holding it up for Hardy to see. "I've got him. I've got him."

"That tape looks a lot longer than the one we used to record those bugle calls, Captain," Hardy demurred.

"Well, we can play it and find out," Arnheiter said. They untangled the tape and set it on a recorder. Both sides were filled with rock and roll and country-and-western music.

Hardy later established that the engine gang had a communal tape recorder. The machine had gone haywire that morning and snarled a tape. The sailor had put the tape into his locker with the intention of untangling it. Despite the absence of bugle calls, the captain was convinced that the tape was proof of the fireman's guilt.

"He left this here to throw us off the scent. He flung the real tape over the side," Arnheiter said.

"I don't think so, Captain," Hardy said. "That doesn't make sense. The petty officer of the watch said he saw the kid with a wad of tape in his hand. We found the tape and it isn't the bridge tape. The bridge tape was short. This one is long."

"That's the trick, Ray," the captain said, wrinkling his brow and wagging a stiff forefinger at the executive officer. "That's how he thought he'd cover his tracks."

The sailor, a beanpole of a youth with a bad case of acne, returned from liberty a bit tipsy shortly before midnight. He was seized on the quarter-deck and hustled to Arnheiter champing in the wardroom.

The fireman stood as near to attention as his fear and trembling would permit while the captain paced back and forth during the interrogation. "Admit it, admit it, admit it!" he commanded in a harsh, penetrating voice. "Confess! You stole that tape. I know you did it. You're a sneak thief. Here's the proof," he said, brandishing the tape he had found in the fireman's locker. "You stand convicted."

The sailor stammered, apparently seeking to explain the origin of the tape.

The captain cut him off. He poked his face into the youth's, his round eyes dilating with anger. "I know all of you snipes secretly hate that reveille. You stole that tape and maliciously threw it over the side!"

The sailor stammered once more and again he was cut off. Arnheiter raved on, roiling himself into a fury. He began to threaten the sailor with dire punishment if he did not acknowledge his guilt. "I'll court-martial you. I'll court-martial you and have you drummed out of the Navy."

Hardy could see the sailor's hands and knees shaking uncontrollably. He was afraid that the fireman might faint. "Good God," Hardy muttered to himself, "even if he did toss that tape into the bay you couldn't do that to him."

After the better part of an hour the captain seemed to exhaust himself. The sailor mumbled a denial, and Arnheiter ordered a petty officer into the wardroom to take the youth under guard to his bunk. He noticed that the sailor had a few smudges on his white uniform from the dirt of Manila.

"Look at yourself, you're filthy," he said, pointing at the smudges with disgust. "You're restricted to the ship for the duration. And don't think I'm finished with you," he warned. "I know you did it. I'll make you admit your guilt before I'm through."

"Do you think I ought to confess?" the fireman whispered to the petty officer outside the wardroom door.

"Did you steal the tape?"

"No, but maybe he'd go easier on me if I said I did," the sailor answered. The petty officer advised him to remain silent and to take his chances. The captain had not resealed the sailor's locker after having it cut open. Some other sailor had rifled it in the meantime and stolen an $80 ring. The captain set Generous to work in the predawn hours transcribing another tape of "Hellcats" from the record Arnheiter kept in his cabin.

The next morning Cornejo spotted Hardy in the wardroom slumped in a chair, his arms hanging limp over the sides. The executive officer's eyes were opaque with fatigue and stress. "Christ, you look like some boxer's taken you out and punched you around real good," Cornejo said.

"I don't think I've slept in a week," Hardy whispered.

Perhaps frightened by the fireman's ordeal, several sailors decided the law was a lesser risk than Captain Arnheiter. They did not return from shore liberty that day and went AWOL in the slums of Manila.

On the morning of March 29, Smoot left for the psychiatric ward at the Clark Air Force Base Hospital. He might have stayed on board ship if he had known that the god who had goaded him to the edge of madness was himself being judged by higher, more majestic deities that morning and would be found flawed. Time and tolerance had expired for Captain Arnheiter. He would not become a certified hero with a Silver Star. Nor would he end as a martyred captain, assassinated by some deranged sailor or overthrown in a mutiny by his officers. His would be the worst of endings for a naval officer—dishonor. He would be expelled from his ship in disgrace.

After a week of examining his conscience on the *Kretchmer,* Chaplain Dando had braved the risk that reason and intellect demanded. He had returned to the squadron headquarters at Subic Bay a few days before the *Vance* docked in Manila on March 26, described his experience to Milligan and urged the commodore to act swiftly to forestall rebellion. If the ship was allowed to resume Viet Nam patrol with the forces now boiling within it, the closed cauldron of emotions would blow apart, Dando warned. He did not specifically recommend Arnheiter's removal, but his implication was obvious. While by far the gravest, Dando's was not the first worrisome report on Arnheiter that Milligan had received. During visits to Subic Bay, several of the destroyer captains had complained about being harassed by Arnheiter for "an urgent naval gunfire mission." They had mentioned that the *Vance*'s captain seemed to behave in a queer fashion. Ironically, a confidential, "for officers' eyes only" report from the skipper of the *Mason* on Arnheiter's antics was pigeonholed in the files of the Navy bureaucracy and had never reached Milligan. But another destroyer officer had been very blunt. "You've got a nut running around out there," he said. Every few days for the past month the phone from Pearl Harbor had also rung with news from Commodore Baird, the commander of the *Vance*'s home squadron, that another batch of seething letters had reached the wives. One distraught sailor's wife had called Hardy's wife, Mary, and announced that she was going to telephone the Pentagon "and tell somebody there that my husband's ship is being run by a lunatic." Mary Hardy had persuaded the woman not to make the call.

Donald F. Milligan was not a man to act precipitately. Forty-one years old, with light, thinning hair, a round, cautious face, and a short, compact build, Milligan had enlisted in the Navy as a sailor during World War II. He acquired a regular commission through a wartime officer-training course and college ROTC and rose by building a reputation for competence and discretion. His instincts led him to doubt that the situation was anywhere near as grave as Dando had described it. He was afraid that the chaplain's meager six months of Navy experience had left him gullible enough to believe exaggerated tales about the captain from the junior officers and sailors.

"Are you sure you know what you're talking about, George?" he asked.

"I'm absolutely certain," Dando replied. "I'm sure that if there's an investigation, the officers and seamen on that ship will testify freely against Arnheiter."

Then Lieutenant Kordons, who had been entrusted with the sealed envelope from Hardy, reached Subic Bay. He confirmed Dando's account and filled it out with more revelations. He too advised the commodore to act urgently. He told Milligan that in early February, shortly before the Vietnamese navy commander for the central coastal region refused to imperil any more liaison officers on the *Vance*, Admiral Ward had dispatched a staff officer from Saigon to admonish Arnheiter against further shore-bombardment exploits or beach landings. The staff officer informed Arnheiter that he was not to interpret literally the admiral's polite "well done" for the foray against the suspected submarine smuggling point. Privately, the admiral frowned on such expeditions ashore as dangerous and foolhardy, the staff officer said.

Besides conveying the information that Saigon had been upset about Arnheiter, Kordons corroborated Dando's report that Arnheiter had apparently sailed into a prohibited area to bombard the coast and had sent false position reports to conceal these violations of orders and of the rules of engagement. A careful young man, Kordons had read the *Vance*'s CIC log and noted the discrepancy between the positions transmitted and the ship's true locations at the time.

Milligan had looked at the letter and the eight-page citation recommending Arnheiter for the Silver Star. He had received several letters from Arnheiter in the past and was well acquainted with the captain's distinctive style. He knew immediately that Arnheiter had written both. A glance at the sealed envelope with the words, "To be opened only by the direction of Lieutenant R. S. Hardy, USN, or Lieutenant W. T. Generous, USN," typed on the outside, was all he needed to guess that Arnheiter had coerced Hardy and Generous into recommending him for the medal. Even for a man of Milligan's circumspect temperament, the bits and pieces began to fit together into a harrowing tale. He was particularly disturbed by the report that MacSaveny had almost murdered the captain. He ordered Dando and Kordons to write out and sign statements listing their own observations and the accusations they had heard against Arnheiter.

Milligan had determined to give the captain a tongue-lashing and to spend a few days aboard the *Vance* after she returned to Viet Nam patrol to make certain that Arnheiter reformed. He had rejected any thought of asking for Arnheiter's removal from command. The commodore believed in giving any man a second chance, and he did not know anyone who had suffered the disgrace of being relieved. Because command of a warship is so sacrosanct within the Navy, reliefs are rare. When they do occur, they are almost always controversial. Milligan's mental radar guided him away from controversy.

For two days, however, the commodore was prevented from flying down to Manila by the folderol of exchanging one flotilla commander for another. Rear Admiral Thomas S. King, Jr., was replacing Rear Admiral Irvine as the commander of the Seventh Fleet's cruiser-destroyer flotilla. When a flotilla commander moves, his staff often moves with him, and the shuffle is complicated by paperwork and ceremony. On the night of March 28, Milligan, without specifying the ship or the skipper, described his worry to an old friend who had just arrived with the new flotilla staff. "Arnheiter's got the *Vance,*" the friend said immediately. "Are you talking about Arnheiter?" Milligan, who had spent much of his career in communications, learned to his surprise that Marcus Aurelius Arnheiter was quite a legend among professional destroyer men. "I wouldn't sit on that if I were you," the friend advised. "I'd go to the boss with it right away." Early the next morning, March 29, Milligan went to see Admiral Irvine.

The captain's scheme to award himself the Silver Star now helped to seal his undoing. Donald Irvine was a submariner by trade. He had never heard of Marcus Aurelius Arnheiter until Milligan appeared in his flag quarters on the cruiser U.S.S. *Topeka* that morning. But unlike the prudent Milligan, Irvine was an independent spirit. Decisions, once considered, were not difficult for him to make. Slim, with wavy gray hair, prematurely aged at fifty-five years from an incipient case of emphysema, Irvine had grown up in small towns in Iowa where his father was a Presbyterian preacher. His father had resigned from a fraternal lodge in one community in which they lived to protest local anti-Catholic and anti-Jewish prejudice, and Irvine was harassed by his schoolmates for his father's nonconformity.

He had read the accusations against Arnheiter with wonder. In Irvine's thirty-one years of service, he had never seen anyone dare to put into writing allegations like these against the captain of a ship. The written statements from Dando and Kordons, and the variety of verbal reports that Milligan had given him, suggested that the charges might well be true. Irvine was struck by how bizarre many of the incidents were. The name "Queeg" had flitted into his thoughts as he read and Milligan talked. The question of whether Arnheiter was abusing his crew quickly became a secondary consideration for Irvine, however. He had encountered abusive captains before and had reined them in sharply with a few harsh words. What mattered to Irvine was that Arnheiter was apparently disobeying orders, shooting up places where he wasn't supposed to be, and lying about it all with false position reports and phony press releases. Milligan had shown him Arnheiter's Silver Star recommendation and explained his

reasons for believing that the captain had written the letter
and citation and forced Hardy and Generous to sign.

For Irvine the fraud was "the straw that shows which way
a big wind is blowing." Arnheiter seemed to be a man of such
overweening ambition that he had lost sight of why he was
commanding the *Vance* and what duties the United States
Navy expected him to perform. The accusations appeared
to be genuine. In any case, until their truth or falsity had
been determined by an investigation, it was too dangerous to
leave Arnheiter in command of a warship off Viet Nam. He
had done nothing serious yet, but what if he decided to blast
hell out of some friendly village on the pretext that the place
was full of Viet Cong? Irvine had been emphasizing over
and over again in newsletters to his ship captains that Viet
Nam was not "a hell-bent-for-leather fight" like World War
II. The rules of engagement that told them how and when
they were to open fire meant exactly what they said. The
rules were to be obeyed literally. So there would have to be an
investigation, Irvine decided. This meant that he would have
to either relieve Arnheiter or keep the *Vance* tied up at Subic
Bay for weeks while the testimony was reviewed and a decision made. Pacific Fleet headquarters in Hawaii demanded
that Irvine keep every designated position in Operation Market Time filled by a ship. This had proven very difficult with
twenty-year-old DER's that were always breaking down because of their age and the shortage of spare parts. If the
Vance were off the line, another ship would have to replace
her. Irvine did not have another ship. Arnheiter would have
to be relieved; someone else would have to take the *Vance*
back on patrol as soon as the officers and sailors had finished
testifying. Besides, Irvine reasoned, if Arnheiter was the glib
and cunning man he appeared to be, he might destroy evidence and coerce his crew into silence if he was left in command while the investigation was in progress. The men would
only testify freely when they did not fear the captain. If the
review of the testimony showed that Arnheiter was not
guilty, he could then be given another ship somewhere else.

On the morning of March 29, as Smoot left the *Vance* for the psychiatric ward, Irvine discussed the problem with Admiral King, and King agreed. Since Irvine would be relinquishing command of the flotilla the next day, King would have to convene the investigation and review the findings. The chiefs of staff to the two admirals also argued out the pros and cons with each other and reached a similar conclusion.

Navy regulations state that before action like dismissal is taken against an officer, every effort should first be made to correct whatever incompetence or misbehavior is involved. Obviously no such effort was going to be made in Arnheiter's case. Irvine had a senior Navy lawyer brought in who searched the regulations and found an exception, under which the Bureau of Naval Personnel could be asked to dismiss a ship captain summarily if wartime operations necessitated doing so. Irvine asked himself if he should confront Arnheiter with the accusations and give the captain a chance to answer before removing him. A man had a right to be told of allegations against him and to defend himself. But in this case, Irvine decided, Arnheiter's right had to bow to circumstances. He would have to be relieved. To confront him with the accusations, to let him make a short response and then to dismiss him would be an empty legal formality. Arnheiter's right to a fair hearing would have to be protected during the subsequent investigation and formal review of its findings.

By now the weighing of Captain Arnheiter's fate had lasted into the early evening. Irvine summoned Milligan back to his flag quarters. "You're going to be relieving Arnheiter until we can find another skipper for the *Vance*," he said. Milligan was taken aback. He thought that he would be instructed to fly to Manila, give Arnheiter a verbal keelhauling for the admiral, and then ride the *Vance* for a week or so off Viet Nam to make certain that Arnheiter mended his ways. Instead, Irvine instructed Milligan to sit down with his flag secretary and draft the relief message. The admiral quickly signed it and the message went to the cruiser's radio room for transmittal to Washington. The officers and men of the

Vance would have thought the message hilariously banal in the light of what they had endured for the past three months:

It has come to my attention that the commanding officer U.S.S. *Vance* (DER-387) has engaged in certain irregular practices and established some policies which are definitely seriously detrimental to the morale and combat efficiency of his command. Accordingly, I consider it mandatory that he be relieved immediately . . . pending investigation of the allegations made to date.

The Bureau of Naval Personnel took another day to digest this information and issue the relief order.

Around 10 A.M. on March 31, 1966, a teletype machine in the radio room of the *Markab* tapped out four coded lines addressed to the captain of the *Vance*. The *Markab* was receiving the *Vance*'s message traffic while the ship's teletypes were being repaired. One of the repair ship's radiomen brought the message to Chief Grissom, the *Vance*'s senior radioman, and he carried it directly to the captain's cabin. Arnheiter was there in his short-sleeved shirt and pleated Bermudas, ready to don his baseball cap and set off for another day's speedboating around Manila Bay. An hour later the captain sent for Hardy. "Look at this," he said, thrusting the slip of yellow teletype paper at the executive officer. "What do you make of it?"

As Hardy read the message, he mentally translated the Navy abbreviations into common English: "Lieutenant Commander Marcus A. Arnheiter . . . hereby detached as Commanding Officer U.S.S. *Vance*. Proceed immediately and report to U.S.S. *Dixie* (Destroyer Tender-14) for temporary duty and for further assignment by Chief of Naval Personnel . . ." The *Dixie* was moored at Subic Bay.

In his physical and emotional exhaustion, it did not occur to Hardy that the cumulative effect of the captain's actions had finally worked his downfall. "Maybe they've got some secret, hush-hush assignment for him," Hardy thought, "and this is the way they're sending him. Or maybe he's going over to Subic Bay for a five-day briefing and he'll come back after that."

"Well, Captain, it says you will detach immediately and report to the *Dixie* for temporary duty," he answered Arnheiter inanely.

"Yes," the captain said impatiently, "but what does it mean?"

"I don't know," Hardy mumbled.

"I'm going to find out. Have them lower the scout boat right away." Arnheiter snatched up his baseball cap and headed for the fantail, bellowing for Belmonte to ferry him to the naval air station at Sangley Point across the harbor, where he could make long-distance telephone calls on the main trunk lines. The captain disappeared into an office building there. After a couple of hours Belmonte ventured inside to ask Arnheiter if he could radio for another officer to ride over in the motor whaleboat and relieve him, since he had to stand quarter-deck watch. As Belmonte rounded one of the long rows of file cabinets in the building, he spied the captain sitting at a desk with a telephone receiver to his ear, obviously listening to someone on the other end. Arnheiter's boyish features had a desperate cast Belmonte had never seen before. "Are you sure this is final, Commodore?" the captain asked in a pleading voice. "Are you sure this is final, Commodore?" he repeated a moment later. Belmonte instinctively guessed what had happened.

"You've bought it, you bastard," he said to himself with a surge of joy. "You've had the cotton. They finally caught up with you."

He backed away so that the captain would not notice him, and returned in another ten minutes. Arnheiter was off the phone now, and Belmonte asked if he could radio for a relief. The captain consented. "But before you go, Luis," he said in a friendly tone, "I'd like to take advantage of the fact that we're alone to talk to you for a few minutes."

He beckoned Belmonte to a battered Naugahyde sofa near the desk. The captain sat beside him and put his arm on the back of the sofa behind Belmonte's shoulder. "You know, Luis, you've got a great deal of talent and potential. You're an audacious, imaginative officer, and you have a fine career

ahead of you," he said amiably. "I'm doing everything I can
to help your career along. I want you to know that the reason
I relieved you as first lieutenant and sent you to the engineering department was to broaden your experience. A professional naval officer must be well acquainted with engineering
problems. That's an absolute requirement, you know. This
summer, I'm going to broaden your experience some more
and make you assistant navigator. That's a splendid position.
You'll benefit enormously."

"Yes, Captain, thanks a lot. I'd really appreciate that,"
Belmonte said sarcastically. He thought: "Now I know for
sure you've gotten the ax. You've got that big, bullshit, public
relations smile of yours on and you're oiling me up for the
inquiry you know they're going to hold to find out about all
the crazy stunts you've been pulling on that ship."

Just then Hardy appeared. He told Belmonte he could
go back to the ship.

Hardy's arrival had been precipitated by an event that
occurred shortly after Belmonte had taken the captain to
Sangley Point. The skipper of the U.S.S. *Koiner,* another DER
in Manila for repairs, had boarded the *Vance* and offered to
lend Hardy and Generous one of Commodore Milligan's
squadron pennants if they did not have one.

"Why?" they asked.

"Because the commodore's coming aboard," the captain
of the *Koiner* said. "Didn't you know that? He's on a plane
to Sangley Point right now. You'll have to fly his pennant."

"Square away the ship, Tom," Hardy commanded. "I'll
go over to Sangley Point and take the captain to the airfield
to meet the commodore." Hardy scrambled into a set of
dress whites and disappeared over the side into the whaleboat with the skipper of the *Koiner.* Generous was baffled.
Hardy had not told him or the other officers about the fateful
four-line message that morning.

As soon as Hardy sent Belmonte back to the *Vance,* the
captain put an emergency long-distance call through Navy
circuits to his wife in San Diego. He instructed her not to sell
their house there and move to Hawaii with their five children,

as she was about to do. Although he could not tell her why he was changing their plans, she was not to worry.

"Here, Ray," he said, handing Hardy the receiver, "you tell Janice there's nothing to worry about, that you're here and everything's going to be all right."

"Mrs. Arnheiter, I'm here and everything's going to be okay, so don't worry," Hardy said mechanically.

"I don't know what it is, but you take care of him," Janice Arnheiter replied.

Standing beside the airstrip waiting for the commodore, Arnheiter told Hardy that he had been unable to reach Milligan on the phone at Subic Bay. Commodore Baird at Pearl Harbor had said, however, that he was being relieved for an investigation.

"Why? Why are they relieving me and investigating me, Ray? I can't figure it out," Arnheiter said despairingly.

"I guess it would have to be some big thing that happened, and I don't know of any big thing, Captain," Hardy said. Hardy's brain was so boggled from coping with one and two and three and four crises a day for the last ninety-nine days that he could not yet comprehend the significance of what was occurring. He searched his mind numbly for the single aberration that might have provoked the captain's summary relief and could not find it.

"Could it have been that time Admiral Ward had to send his operations officer out from Saigon to see you, Captain?" he asked.

"No, it couldn't be that," Arnheiter replied.

"Well, maybe it was because of those church services, Captain. You got a letter from Commodore Baird about those."

"No, it wasn't that either," Arnheiter said.

"I don't know, Captain." Hardy gave up. "I'm puzzled."

Milligan's plane was hours late. As they continued their conversation in a desultory manner for the rest of the afternoon and into the early evening, the realization that Captain Arnheiter was to leave the *Vance* and that he was to leave it for good, that he would never be back, filtered into Hardy's consciousness. "There's going to be a change," he said to himself with a tuckered-out sense of relief. "There's going to be a change and any change will be for the better."

The moment he reached the ship, Belmonte told Generous what he had overheard of the captain's telephone conversation. "Marcus has had it!" Belmonte whooped. Generous had noticed a curious exhilaration among the sailors while they were sprucing up the ship for the commodore. He had asked one seaman what they were all so happy about and the man replied craftily, "That guy got a special message this morning." Generous suppressed the suspicion that the United States Navy might at last have learned what Captain Arnheiter was doing on the *Vance*. "Don't believe it," he had said to himself. "It's April Fool's Eve and somebody's just playing the big-stinker rat and tantalizing us."

At Belmonte's news, Generous ran to the radio room. "I want you to level with me," he said to the radioman on duty there to handle the traffic brought over from the *Markab*. "Did we get some kind of unusual message for the captain today?"

"Yes, we did, Mr. Generous," the radioman said, "but Chief Grissom told us not to talk to anybody about it."

"Liberation! Liberation!" Generous yelled. He bounded to the bridge and grabbed the captain's microphone. "This used to be the number-one DER in the Navy. Let's show the commodore she can still be, despite all suspicions to the contrary. Make her sparkle!" he called out to the crew over the loudspeaker. The sailors needed no encouragement. Although the captain had sworn Grissom to secrecy, the word had leaked out. The news had spread quickly through most of the crew. The cleanup was probably the fastest in the history of the *Vance*.

Milligan was hardly polite to Arnheiter at the airstrip. He refused to ride out to the *Vance* in the captain's scout boat, and insisted on using the *Markab*'s launch. During the trip to the ship the commodore snubbed the captain and made small talk with Hardy and the skipper of the *Koiner* about the difficulty of obtaining spare parts for the antiquated DER's.

The boatswain's whistle piped Milligan aboard shortly after 8 P.M. Belmonte looked at the commodore's face with anticipation and noted that Milligan seemed grim and determined. The commodore deposited his bag in the wardroom and turned to the captain, saying, "Mr. Arnheiter, I want to see you in your cabin."

A few minutes later, Milligan sent for Hardy. "Have the quartermaster log that at 2015 this evening I relieved Lieutenant Commander Arnheiter and have assumed command of the U.S.S. *Vance*," he said, handing Hardy a copy of his orders to this effect from the Bureau of Naval Personnel.

Generous, who was the duty officer for the evening, claimed the honor of entering the event in the log. Belmonte, Gwynn, Fuehrer, McWhirter, and the other officers crowded around to read over his shoulder.

"How long was he captain?" someone asked. They added up the days since Arnheiter had taken command on December 22, 1965, at Pearl Harbor.

"I guess we'll all have to write books and call them *Ninety-nine Days and a Wakeup*," Belmonte said.

They all felt a strange emotional letdown. The ordeal had ended. Somehow, they had survived.

The captain packed his belongings the next morning in a defiant mood. He showed Hardy a copy of his novel, *Shadow of Peril*, and recounted how he had ghostwritten the book as part of a Pentagon intrigue to divert budget funds from aviation into antisubmarine weaponry. "I've been in fights before, Ray, and I've always won them by making sure everything was wired in advance. I'll win this one too. You watch," he said.

He asked the commodore for permission to make a farewell address to the crew. Milligan reluctantly consented. The officers and seamen were mustered on the fantail one last time. The captain was dressed in a khaki uniform this morning instead of his Sunday-best whites.

After breakfast, he began, one of their petty officers had approached him and said he was the best skipper the petty officer had ever sailed under. He reminded the crew that he had nominated twenty of their number for bravery in action under his leadership and promised to see that the Navy presented the awards. (All were subsequently invalidated.) "Under my command the Communist enemy felt the presence of the U.S.S. *Vance* along the Viet Nam coast. We engaged the enemy and we destroyed him. All of you were part of that great adventure."

A destroyer berthed next to the *Vance* was scheduled to put to sea that morning. The destroyer could not maneuver out of the nest of ships until the *Vance* got out of her way, and the *Vance* could not move until Captain Arnheiter finished speaking. As usual, the captain had more words than there was time. His valedictory passed the half-hour mark and the skipper of the destroyer became extremely restless.

"What the hell's going on back there?" the destroyer captain shouted at one of his ensigns who was standing on the stern with a large group of the destroyer's sailors, fascinated by the spectacle on the fantail of the *Vance*.

"You wouldn't believe me if I told you," the ensign yelled back.

"Christ, why doesn't he just leave," Cornejo said to a petty officer beside him. "It's so embarrassing."

Milligan was also embarrassed. The commodore tugged at Arnheiter's sleeve. The captain's time was up. "You've said your piece. Let's get moving," Milligan said.

"You will never forget me," the captain called out in a ringing farewell to the crew. "For I took you into harm's way. I led you where the shells were falling."

Hardy escorted the captain to the quarter-deck. Halfway down the ladder to the bobbing whaleboat, Arnheiter lost some of his confidence. He stopped and looked up anxiously at Hardy, who was leaning over the rail.

"You'll back me up in this, won't you, Ray?" he asked. "You'll make the commodore understand, won't you? If you see me through on this thing I'll make sure you're taken care of."

"Sure, Captain, sure. As much as I can," Hardy said.

EPILOGUE

These people really think we
shanghaied that guy off the
ship.

—Boiler Tender MacSaveny

At lunch in the wardroom the day after the captain's relief,
someone remarked, "Boys, this is going to be the end of it."

"Like hell," Generous rejoined. "There'll be lots more before
this thing is over. Marcus won't give up that easily." Generous would learn to his own chagrin that he had a talent
for prophecy.

For March 31, 1966, the day of the captain's disgrace,
was in one sense the beginning of the Arnheiter Affair. Over
the months and years to follow, the captain would demonstrate once again that if you make a hoax look and sound
plausible enough, a lot of people will believe you. You must
know how to play upon fears and prejudices, to exploit
motives and limitations. Arnheiter was adept at this. The
captain took naturally to fraud because his mind had difficulty distinguishing reality from delusion and right from
wrong. The deliberate lie blurred into the unconscious fantasy. The events, the chain of cause and effect that he cut
from the cloth of his imagination, became very real to him.

His narrative acquired an inner logic that was convincing unless you looked at it through the memories of other, rational men who had been there too. Most of those who accepted the captain's version of events, particularly those who publicized it, never took the precaution of seeking out other participants. They believed what the captain told them.

During the six-and-a-half-day inquiry at Subic Bay, which resulted in forty allegations against him, the captain evaded what he could not deny and blamed on someone else what he could not evade. There certainly had been a Viet Cong machine-gun bunker on the sand dune near the *Mason*. Before he ordered the *Vance* to open fire at the mountainside near the *Bache* he definitely had heard the crack of enemy bullets overhead. Hardy and Merkel were to blame for any exaggeration in the press releases; they had written them, not he. If the sailors were unhappy about the speedboat purchase, that was Hardy's fault; he should have convinced the seamen of how wisely the captain had spent their recreation money. The candelabras were stolen by his ensigns as a drunken prank against his wishes. He had not had himself recommended for the Silver Star. He had never transmitted false position reports; they were "localized general area" reports, and so on. He was an innocent man, being scurvily maligned.

The hearing was what the Navy's Manual of the Judge Advocate General defines as "an informal investigation." While the testimony was tape-recorded and sworn, the judge, jury and board of inquiry consisted of one officer—a destroyer-squadron commodore, Captain Ward W. Witter, a graying professional of forty-nine, forbearing and sophisticated in the ways of ships and sailors after three wars and twenty-five years of service. As the defendant, Arnheiter was assisted by a Navy lawyer. He and his attorney had the right to cross-examine all witnesses. The captain's cross-examinations often degenerated into indignant tirades at the accusations of his subordinates or bulldog rushes calculated to intimidate them into conceding they were at fault and not he. The psychic reflexes of his mind quickly invented the hoax which he was to elaborate thereafter: his downfall was the work of a conspiracy, a clandestine mutiny. He badgered away at Hardy about Generous' failings as an operations officer and then closed for the *coup de grâce:* "Anyway, what I'm trying to get at here is: why didn't I have Mr. Generous' loyalty? Why wasn't he doing a job? Why were you continuing to protect him? *At what time did you enter into conspiracy with him?"*

"I beg your pardon, sir—" Hardy tried to interrupt.

The captain thrust ahead, not seeming to need an answer. "At any time, to not bring me all the facts. And you were protecting him, not bringing his actions to my notice. And other things were going on like this. This is a conspiracy of people designed to thwart someone, namely the commanding officer, from knowing all the facts . . . to prevent him from doing his job the way he must do it. In order to do my job, or for any commanding officer to, he must know the facts. The exec has got to tell the captain all the facts. Then, the man can make a decision. Without the facts, the man can't do anything. And I was relying on you as any commanding officer would rely on his exec. This is what I'm saying."

"Yes, sir," Hardy said meekly.

Commodore Witter broke in. "Do you feel that you and the operations officer had anything that could conceivably be described as a conspiracy of any kind?" he asked Hardy.

"No, sir, with the exception of the letter, the sealed letter [the affidavit] that I talked about. And I consider that to be my conscience wrapped up."

In his zeal to discredit his subordinates and their accusations the captain betrayed himself. After Arnheiter had harried Hardy for half an hour over the candelabra episode, Witter asked, "Mr. Hardy, is what I have just heard here in the last half-hour typical of the way Commander Arnheiter approached many of his problems in running the ship?"

"Yes, Commodore," Hardy said.

Witter concluded that when the captain could not conveniently delude himself, he lied. The result, in either case, was a man who became a menace to himself and others when armed with authority. He recommended that Marcus Aurelius Arnheiter never again be given command of United States naval officers or seamen, "either ashore or afloat." He attached a verbatim transcript of the testimony as evidence of the emotional havoc the captain had wrought among his crew. If sustained by Vice Admiral Benedict J. Semmes, Jr., the Chief of Naval Personnel in Washington, after reviews by lesser admirals at various echelons of the hierarchy, the judgment meant that the young midshipman who had dreamed of emulating Nelson would stain his fingertips with carbon paper in the oblivion of some clerkdom until the Navy could retire him.

Captain Arnheiter, like another of his heroes, John Paul Jones, had not yet begun to fight. Over the months to come, he composed a sea scandal entitled "The Vance Mutiny." An overpopulation of cockroaches at Pearl Harbor inspired the tale of a filthy tramp, her guns rusting and her equipment in disarray, "a ship of McHale's Navy" where slovenly officers "watched wardroom movies every afternoon" and the crew ran wild, "squads of goons" terrorizing the other sailors with their fists. Lieutenant Generous, the Phi Beta Kappa and military-honors graduate of Brown, became an antiwar intellectual with the criminal genius of Professor Moriarty . . . "a Berkeley campus type of Vietnik/beatnik." He had other unseemingly attributes—"a psycho case . . . an atheist . . . a coward." Hardy was "a weakling" who had been the pawn of Generous in the conspiracy. Belmonte was "a beatnik . . . unshaven . . . reckless." The other officers were "a bunch of dissident malcontents." Captain Arnheiter, "a hard-driving, hard-charging skipper," reformed the ragtime *Vance* into "a man-of-war . . . a fighting ship . . . a live wire in the Viet Nam war." To frustrate this patriotic endeavor and to recapture the life of ease he and the other officers had known before, Generous conceived and led a masterful conspiracy "to stab the captain in the back." With letters to the Roman Catholic chaplain at Pearl Harbor and to others yet unknown, and with whisperings in the ear of another "do-gooder" preacher named Dando, Generous instigated a campaign of "false and clandestine complaints" which he knew would eventually reach Arnheiter's superiors. Commodore Milligan and Admirals Irvine and King then panicked and summarily relieved an innocent man, in violation of Navy regulations. They realized their mistake but decided to mask it with a rigged inquiry. Commodore Witter was "prejudiced," and the accusations of the officers and sailors who testified against Arnheiter were all "malicious lies." Generous' letter to the Pearl Harbor chaplain, which Generous had submitted to Witter because it indicated how the captain had violated his constitutional rights, was "documentary evidence" of collusion between him and Hardy and of "mutiny via the mails." The captain minted a new verb to describe his unjust demise. He had been "Vanced."

On temporary assignment in San Diego until his fate could be determined, Arnheiter unfurled the first version of this conspiracy tale in tens of thousands of words; the completed work constituted a two-inch-thick "letter of rebuttal" to the Subic Bay testimony and Commodore Witter's findings. As he was entitled to do under the regulations, he wrote the volume on three and a half months of Navy time, with the assistance of Navy stenographers and a senior Navy lawyer. To prove the conspiracy, the captain attached a file of "documents" to the letter. There were affidavits from Arnheiter's personal photographer and nine other enlisted men on the ship, three or four of whom genuinely liked the captain. A few of the compliments were backhanded, but the statements in general said that Arnheiter had been a splendid skipper.

The documentation appeared plausible until it was examined closely. One sailor, an obliging man who finished his tour of sea duty and was reassigned to the United States shortly after Arnheiter's dismissal, readily admitted to me that the affidavit he had signed was not true. Arnheiter wrote it, he said, and he surrendered his signature to stop the captain from pestering him. "The guy was driving me nuts, man. I wanted to get him off my back." I remembered Arnheiter telling me at his home in San Rafael how persistence paid off.

Another affidavit ostensibly demonstrated that Hardy and

Belmonte lied when they testified that the captain had instructed them to steal the candelabras from the Guam officers' club. Signed by two waiters at the club, the affidavit
stated that the *Vance*'s ensigns had indeed filched the candelabras in a drunken prank and that the captain disapproved of
their act, the same story Arnheiter had told at Subic Bay. A
friend of Arnheiter's who obtained the signatures on the
affidavit for him told me that the captain had written this
one too. The Guamanian waiters, who do not read English
well, had hardly glanced at the document before signing it,
Arnheiter's friend said. I read the affidavit again and realized that I should instantly have suspected it was spurious.
What English Guamanian waiters do speak does not include
phrases like "rollicking good spirits," an authentic Arnheiter-
ism.

As evidence that his shore-bombardment exploits were
not faked, as his subordinates had claimed, the captain attached copies of the same affidavits concocted to win him the
Silver Star in March. Arnheiter found a Chicago psychologist who had served with him on the *Ingersoll* as medical
officer to provide a "psychological analysis" of the mutiny.
Hardy's "weak personality" had been unable to contend
with the rebellious conduct of Generous and had made him
"easily succumb to the pressures and mount the bandwagon
of the side which appeared headed incontestably for victory,"
the psychologist explained.

When his enthusiasm is aroused, Arnheiter is a man of
lavish energy. Writing this voluminous opus on the "mutiny"
comprised only half of his work in San Diego. The other half
consisted of marshaling a band of influential supporters who
would see that his version of events prevailed. His seventy-
one-year-old friend and mentor, Vice Admiral Settle, for
one, needed no encouragement or convincing. He welcomed
the contest and let Arnheiter use his name to rally other retired and active-duty admirals. The captain tailored his fable
to the ingrained political bias of these men, most of whom
held pronounced right-wing opinions. Later he would exploit the anti-military bias of the liberal. He would become

the little man victimized by that sinister row of gold-braided hats that rules the Navy.

Now he was as traditional as a barnacle. At stake in his case, he wrote to one senior admiral on active duty, was not only his career, but the question of whether a dangerous precedent could be tolerated, a precedent which acknowledged that a commanding officer was no longer supreme on his ship, but was henceforth to be a mere puppet to the will of the majority of the crew. He raised the specter of a rash of mutinies spreading through the Navy if he was not vindicated. To the subalterns of the fleet the Light had been lit and the Way had been paved, he wrote in another letter. Worse, his overthrow by dissident, irresponsible, none-war-motivated junior officers was of a piece with hippie beards, LSD, student riots and those other defilements of life in America as it used to be portrayed on the cover of the *Saturday Evening Post*. The plot that had worked his downfall, he intoned, was an example of a new kind of mutiny designed for the modern Navy, the product of an anarchistic mind which, encouraged by the fight for civil rights, had toppled university chancellors, as at Berkeley, and had gone on to engineer the demise of the commanding officer of the *Vance*.

Soon the captain had a band of devoted partisans, led by Admiral Settle, who busied themselves writing endorsements to attach to the captain's "letter of rebuttal" and sending personal letters off to the active-duty admirals in the chain of command who would review the Subic Bay inquiry and Commodore Witter's verdict. The letters, of course, urged these admirals to clear Arnheiter of any wrongdoing and to give him another ship to command. With these retirees lending the prestige of their names to his cause, Arnheiter's case became a matter of principle within the Navy.

The first important success was with Rear Admiral Baumberger, to whose staff in San Diego Arnheiter had been attached after the investigation at Subic Bay. Admiral Baumberger, as Commander, Cruiser-Destroyer Force Pacific, was to review the verbatim transcript of the testimony and the findings.

The admiral had sensed Arnheiter's hyperenthusiasms for glory when the captain was attached to Baumberger's staff for several weeks prior to flying out to Pearl Harbor to take command of the *Vance*. Worried about how Arnheiter might behave as a ship's captain, he had invited him to lunch just before the captain's departure for Pearl Harbor and advised him to temper his enthusiasm with discretion. Until the captain's abrupt dismissal, however, nothing occurred to justify Baumberger's concern. His knowledge of the *Vance*'s doings was all obtained from Arnheiter's keen letters and from the captain's press releases about his ardent and apparently successful prosecution of the war. Those who know Admiral Baumberger describe him as an eminently fair-minded man. He was too astute to credit the mutiny tale, but his conscience troubled him over the way the regulations had been skirted in Arnheiter's relief. And there was the suspicion that even if his subordinates had not conspired against Arnheiter, the captain's removal might somehow have been improperly related to surreptitious complaints to Dando and others. Furthermore, the Arnheiter that Admiral Baumberger now talked to in San Diego was a different man from the tyrant of the hearing room who had so repelled Commodore Witter. Baumberger did not discern *that* Arnheiter in the typewritten transcript of the testimony he read in an air-conditioned office in San Diego 7,500 miles from Subic Bay. The Arnheiter that Baumberger listened to was an obviously overwrought officer in mid-career. His judgment might be somewhat immature, and he had clearly made mistakes and alienated his crew. Yet he seemed resourceful and talented, and he was arguing passionately and persuasively for help to salvage his professional life. After several long private talks with Arnheiter, the admiral persuaded himself that he had convinced the captain of his errors and that Arnheiter had learned from his unfortunate experience.

Baumberger dismissed all except six of the forty allegations against the captain that Witter had summarized in his verdict, and mitigated half of these. Arnheiter's lawyer would therefore claim afterward that the admiral had dismissed all but three of the charges against the captain. Baumberger recommended that Admiral Semmes, the Chief of Naval Personnel, give Arnheiter command of another destroyer escort, in a conventional squadron "to provide an opportunity for reassessment of his abilities" under the supervision of a squadron commodore.

Baumberger subsequently realized his mistake. Enlightened by prolonged contact with the captain, he disavowed Arnheiter a few months later with a bad fitness report and an attached letter confessing naïveté in his original evaluation. It was too late. Forevermore, Baumberger's recommendation was held aloft by the captain and his supporters as proof that Arnheiter should be exonerated and restored to command.

With Baumberger in hand, the captain and his partisans began to activate the circuits that Arnheiter had so adroitly wired, as he had promised Hardy he would on that last morning on the *Vance,* to jog Admiral Semmes in the right direction. His decision would be the one that counted. To this end, Arnheiter's supporters turned on the Congress. They mailed off to various congressmen and senators letters to which were attached lists of loaded questions for the Navy to answer. To make certain the legislators would see the scandalous proportions of the injustice done Arnheiter, the words "The *VANCE MUTINY"* were typed at the top left-hand corner of many of the letters. Admiral Semmes and his staff were shortly answering inquiries about Arnheiter's case from the late Representative Lucius Mendel Rivers of South Carolina, the chairman of the House Armed Services Committee; the late Senator Richard B. Russell of Georgia, the chairman of the Senate Armed Services Committee; Senators Margaret Chase Smith of Maine, Edward M. Kennedy of Massachusetts, the late Robert F. Kennedy and Jacob K. Javits of New York, Jack R. Miller of Iowa, Charles H. Percy of Illinois, and Clifford P. Case of New Jersey; and Representative Bob Wilson of California, a member of the House Armed Services Committee whom Arnheiter had approached directly because his district included San Diego.

The captain filed formal court-martial charges of "mutiny and conspiracy to commit mutiny" against Hardy and Generous. He withdrew them at Baumberger's incensed demand. The captain then filed the accusations a second time after the admiral in charge of the entire Pacific Fleet, who ranked, for purposes of judicial review, between Baumberger and Semmes, overruled Baumberger's recommendation that Arnheiter be given another ship, and sustained Witter's verdict that the Navy should never again risk officers and men under Arnheiter's command, on land or sea. The court-martial charges were dismissed, but the captain left hanging the threat that he would raise an outcry in the press and demand "a full-scale court of inquiry and/or general court-martial" to uncover "the full extent of subversion aboard U.S.S. *Vance*" if Semmes did not follow Baumberger's lead and clear him. The Navy did not have to endure the shame of unfavorable publicity: Arnheiter suggested a genteel compromise. "I shall consider my honor in essence to have been upheld if I am shortly returned to command of a destroyer-type ship," he wrote in an official letter.

Arnheiter occasionally accompanied this cattle-prod technique with a lump of sugar. The captain wrote a private appeal to Admiral Semmes. He reminded Semmes, a destroyer man like himself, that the admiral had once complimented Arnheiter on his magazine articles exposing the weaknesses in the Navy's antisubmarine defenses, a circumstance that appears to rule out the possibility that Arnheiter's role in this Pentagon intrigue as a junior staff officer influenced Semmes against him. Commodore Witter, the captain blithely continued in his letter, had informed him after the hearing that Witter had seen no culpability in anything Arnheiter had done as commanding officer of the *Vance*. What had really happened, Arnheiter explained, was that he had taken the ball and had run like hell, apparently where some dissident characters didn't think he should have gone. He had taken his ship where the guerrillas were most likely to be found and he had prosecuted the war with the utmost vigor. He was writing Semmes informally and in this personal manner because the admiral had once asked him to keep in touch and because he trusted Semmes' wisdom and sense of fair play. As in his letters to other admirals, he was,

"Very respectfully yours,
"Marc Arnheiter"

An obstinate man himself when his suspicions are aroused, Semmes was not disarmed by the letter, nor was he intimidated by the captain's threat to take his case to the press. And his wisdom and sense of fair play told him that something was very amiss with Captain Arnheiter.

In early February 1967, nearly a year after Arnheiter had been ejected from the *Vance,* Semmes confirmed the captain's disgrace. He upheld Witter's verdict by approving orders that would transfer Arnheiter later that month from San Diego to a tombstone post as communications planning officer on the staff of the Commander, Western Sea Frontier, at Treasure Island, San Francisco. The Western Sea Frontier is that undisturbed portion of the Pacific which extends halfway to Hawaii and down to the South Pole. The closest thing to a naval action there is handling a complaint about a Japanese trawler poking into an American fishing ground.

Semmes had made up his mind, but to try to mollify Settle and the other retired admirals whom Arnheiter had rallied to his standard, Semmes invited Arnheiter's elderly mentor to read the transcript of the testimony at Subic Bay. "Look at that mess, Admiral," he said when Settle had finished. "How can I give that man another ship and put young men under his authority?"

"Well, don't put him in the Pacific Fleet. Transfer him to the Atlantic and give him a ship there," Settle replied.

"Thank you very much. I appreciate your advice, Admiral," Semmes said.

Arnheiter flew to Washington at the beginning of March to plead his case to Semmes in person. Their confrontations in Semmes' office reinforced the admiral's judgment that appointing Arnheiter the captain of the *Vance* had been an appalling mistake.

"We have quite carefully preserved the power of a captain to discipline his crew, because his responsibility is so absolute," Semmes said when I talked to him in the summer of 1968. "If anything goes wrong, it's his fault. You can't order young men involuntarily into a situation like that unless you have absolute confidence in that skipper. I had to ask myself, 'Would I want my son to be a member of his crew?' I couldn't say yes, and that's why I couldn't put him on another ship."

Any other dishonored naval officer might have struck his colors at that blow. Captain Arnheiter hoisted his in the press.

His former skipper on the *Coolbaugh* had told me with amusement that Arnheiter, as a junior lieutenant and the destroyer's public information officer, had achieved considerable success with the local newspapers in Florida and Alabama by writing imaginative press releases that the papers would print without much question. With this lesson in mind, the captain exploited a weakness of the country's press that government propagandists and public relations men discovered long ago—most journalists work on short deadlines. If you keep them busy until they have to write something, they may write what you want. Those long hours of reading to me from the *Congressional Record*, the hundreds of pages of spurious documents, the constant veering of the interviews back to his narrative of the mutiny, and the frequent invitations to dinner were not unintentional as far as Arnheiter was concerned.

A couple of weeks after Semmes personally sentenced him to limbo, Arnheiter managed an introduction, through a family friend, to the Middletown *Times-Herald*, an upstate New York newspaper in the Ottaway chain with a daily circulation of about 40,000, the largest in its area. The first of a series of sympathetic articles appeared on March 20, 1967.

A young naval officer, fighting to regain his lost command, has raised an issue which strikes at the very heart of the war effort in Viet Nam: Can a competent commander be cashiered for prosecuting the war too hard?

Lt. Cmdr. Marcus A. Arnheiter says he was.

By the time that Cmdr. Arnheiter learned that he had been secretly smeared by a group of disgruntled junior officers, he had already lost his command and a chance for promotion.

The Navy's abrupt dismissal of Commander Arnheiter and its indifference to his pleas for a full-scale court of inquiry to clear his name also casts grave doubt on the integrity of the Navy. What kind of a system would permit a career officer—with a record good enough to have earned him a ship to command in the first place—to be relieved of it three months later without so much as a warning that charges had been filed against him, an opportunity to confront his accusers, or the chance to obtain adequate legal defense to counter the charges?

The captain thoughtfully came up with a picture of himself, taken with Navy-bought film, dispensing the candy to the refugee children in the junk. The myth was in print, and the captain kept it there.

The San Francisco *Chronicle* was next. By mid-April, Arnheiter had this newspaper publishing articles about a malicious "58-page Captain's madness log" that Belmonte had compiled because Arnheiter sought to curb "a gang of goons who were beating up fellow seamen." Then there was Generous, "who had a mental problem." The captain went to work on other papers, and soon his fraudulent account was appearing in newspapers elsewhere around the country.

The Middletown *Times-Herald* secured Arnheiter his greatest public relations boon by interesting the late Congressman Joseph Y. Resnick in the captain's cause. The *Times-Herald* was the biggest newspaper in Resnick's district and he paid attention to it. A self-made man, a millionaire inventor, Resnick was an ambivalent Democrat who represented an essentially Republican and conservative district. Arnheiter's case seemed a worthy cause to him. Later, the affair would provide an opportunity for Resnick to wedge his own way into the news columns in preparation for the Democratic senatorial primary fight in the spring of 1968. Arnheiter would appeal to the upstate conservative vote as a champion of law and order, and the civil-rights and anti-brass-hat angles

of the captain's case would go over well with the downstate
Jewish liberals. A gross injustice had been done a decent
man, and Joe Resnick would take on the entire naval es-
tablishment to set things right. One of his campaign adver-
tisements in *The New York Times* read: "Washington is full
of lobbies for the rich, for big corporations, for special interests. But who's lobbying for the people? . . . Joe Resnick
is a fighter for the people." While the Navy fended off the
other congressmen and senators whom Arnheiter and his
friends had approached, it had no success with Resnick.
The captain had a congressional champion.

That April of 1967, Resnick's administrative assistant
passed Arnheiter's conspiracy fable to Jack Anderson, the
associate columnist of the late Drew Pearson. In the first of
several nationally syndicated columns which Anderson and
Pearson were to publish in Arnheiter's behalf over the next
year or so, Anderson had the junior officers of the *Vance*
enjoying "a leisurely life . . . they went joy riding and water-
skiing in an outboard motor they had acquired ashore." In
another column, Drew Pearson suggested that the Navy was
persecuting Arnheiter because he was a Jew. The Navy's
handling of the case, Pearson wrote, "has overtones of anti-
Semitism." Arnheiter hastened to send Anderson a letter
thanking him and Pearson for their kind intentions, but informing the columnist that his ancestors had all been solidly
Protestant gentiles, Lutherans in Germany and Episcopalians
in the United States.

No one bothered to talk to Hardy, or Generous, or Belmonte before publishing articles accusing them of mutiny, a
serious crime in any man's navy. The San Francisco *Chronicle* did not ask Generous about his "mental problem" or request a look at Belmonte's "58-page Captain's madness log."
Jack Anderson did not even interview Arnheiter. "Drew and
I were always for the little guy," he said when I asked him
why he had printed the story so quickly.

James Jackson Kilpatrick, the right-wing columnist, compared Arnheiter to Dreyfus. He too dispensed with talking
to the captain, let alone the radical young slobs in rumpled

and ketchup-stained shirts whom he described as having engineered their skipper's downfall. Kilpatrick said he drew his
information from Arnheiter's letter of rebuttal and other
documents supplied by a sympathetic lawyer.

With each retelling, of course, the account of the mutiny
acquired more detail and less truth. At Resnick's public
hearing for Arnheiter in May 1968, on Capitol Hill, Rear
Admiral Daniel V. Gallery, a nemesis of Nazi submariners in
World War II who had turned to writing novels and magazine articles since his retirement, said that he had learned all
he knew about the case from the newspapers. Thus informed,
the admiral had written a philippic for the Chicago papers
the previous December on the "disgracefully ragtime, sloppy
and inefficient ship" Arnheiter had inherited, manned by
junior officers "who should have been wearing beards and
picketing the White House. One of them was a psycho case.
One is now a member of the LSD hippie colony on Haight
Street."

I and the other reporters who covered the Resnick hearing
that May of 1968 were equally guilty of perpetuating the
fraud. None of us thought to telephone any of the men who
had sailed under Arnheiter. We were all too preoccupied with
getting into print Arnheiter's charges that Admiral Semmes
was a liar and that his former subordinates were mutineers.
Since the Navy had nothing to say, we settled for silence from
the other side. I too, without a qualm, wrote stories citing
Generous as "the alleged ringleader of the conspiracy . . ."
The "alleged" did not make Generous' guilt any less real to
the readers. By this time the captain had also found Seaman
Cicerich to lend plausibility to his claim that brutality and
anarchy had ruled the *Vance* prior to his arrival and had
burst forth again as soon as he was ousted. On investigation,
Cicerich appeared to be one of those unfortunate (there is
one in most infantry companies on land and on most ships at
sea) who annoy their fellow sufferers for any number of reasons and become whipping boys to slake the misery of their
forced companions.

In front of the television cameras, Resnick interspersed

protests against the outrageous injustice the admirals had wreaked upon the captain with parallels between the *Vance*'s junior officers and the radical student rioters at Columbia University that spring. He ended the hearing by demanding the resignation of the Secretary of the Navy, Paul R. Ignatius. On the strength of the publicity, Resnick persuaded eighty-five other congressmen to sign a petition calling upon the Navy "to give Arnheiter his day in court" by convening a court of inquiry. What Resnick did not tell his colleagues, possibly because he did not know, was that the captain and his partisans had no intention of settling for an ordinary court of inquiry of active-duty officers who might, perchance, find against Arnheiter. They had a special court in mind. Settle had described it in a letter to the captain. Once the Navy had been shamed into ordering a court convened, they would insist that it be composed of retired admirals temporarily recalled to active duty for that purpose. The president would be a retired flag officer residing on the West Coast, another of Arnheiter's partisans. Settle hinted that he would not be averse to membership. The court would lack for nothing but suspense.

Despite his concern for law and order and justice for the ordinary man, Joe Resnick proved more persuasive with his fellow congressmen than with the voters. He finished third in the New York State senatorial primary in June, and a year and three months later died in his sleep in a Las Vegas hotel while on vacation there.

Captain Richard G. Alexander's support of Arnheiter undoubtedly raised the gullibility quotient of all but that relatively small group of officers within the Navy who knew the true circumstances of Arnheiter's dismissal. Marcus Aurelius Arnheiter might sound a bit strange. Richard Alexander did not. He had been awarded the captaincy of the U.S.S. *New Jersey*, the world's only operational battleship. He had been marked for membership in that college of beribboned cardinals which is at the apex of the Navy, perhaps even as a future Vice Chief or Chief of Naval Operations. When he had declared war with the twenty-seven-page denunciation of Arnheiter's dismissal which he delivered to Secretary Ignatius in November 1967, the conclusion of the public, journalists and many naval officers had been that if a man like Alexander was willing to risk professional suicide to vindicate Arnheiter, the Navy must have erred dreadfully. It was Alexander who had furnished the title for Kilpatrick's full-length chronicle of Arnheiter's unjust demise, "He Might Have Been Another Halsey," in the *National Review,* two months before the Resnick hearing. "Arnheiter has the spark of naval genius. God knows the Navy has need of such men," he had told Kilpatrick.

Exactly why Alexander had held Arnheiter's hand aloft was a question that mystified me in the light of what I had discovered. Eight months before his polemic to Secretary Ignatius, Alexander had cast Arnheiter adrift with a "Dear Marc" letter urging the captain to forget the Navy and "prepare for a new career."

"Your assignment to command was, quite frankly, a calculated risk," he had written Arnheiter. "I was happy to support you. After the *Vance* incident, I must ask myself, what sort of risk would reassignment to command entail? Could I support the risk now? I could not."

Eight months later, Alexander, in effect, vehemently advocated taking just such a risk in his plea to Secretary Ignatius. While seeking the reasons for Alexander's about-face, I found myself dealing with another essential and unanswered question. Why had Arnheiter been made captain of the *Vance* in the first place? Command at sea is the goal of every Navy line officer, a goal only a minority achieve. There were approximately 3,500 lieutenant commanders in the United States Navy in 1965. Arnheiter's bizarre record would not appear to have justified his elevation into the seventeen percent for whom ship commands were available. Before an officer is given command of a ship, his record is scrutinized by a command clearance board, a committee of five or six seniors, precisely in order to weed out the Arnheiters.

I gradually worked my way to Captain H. Lynn Matthews, Jr., forty-two, an unassuming but articulate officer who was at the Bureau of Naval Personnel in 1965 as lieutenant commander detailer, the officer who supervises the assignment of all lieutenant commanders in the service, a kind of personnel manager for this grade of officer. At this time Alexander was the Bureau's destroyer detailer, the man who assigns officers to destroyer-type ships once they have been cleared for command.

According to Matthews, Alexander had maneuvered Arnheiter onto the *Vance* by short-circuiting the Bureau's protective machinery.

Alexander, Matthews said, had first prodded him into placing Arnheiter's name before the command clearance board. Unlike Alexander and Arnheiter, who were both destroyer sailors, Matthews was a submariner. He said he had never heard of Arnheiter until Alexander proposed him for a command. He was therefore able to judge the captain solely on the basis of his fitness reports and the other records in his file. He told Alexander that Arnheiter was obviously unfit. Alexander pestered him and then "accused me of setting myself up as a 'judge and jury' as to who should get command," Matthews said. "He implied that other people, higher than either of us, felt Arnheiter should be given a command."

"Who were they?" I asked.

"I don't want to name them. They were admirals outside of the Bureau of Naval Personnel," Matthews said.

After reading the record of the officer who has been nominated for command, each member of the clearance board writes his opinion on what is called a "boarding sheet." Matthews said he had been a member of the board because of his position as lieutenant commander detailer. He remembered writing on the boarding sheet that he was submitting Arnheiter's request "against my better judgment." He recalled noting that the captain's fitness reports showed that Arnheiter had exhibited "screwball tendencies from time to time throughout his career. What is important to remember is that heretofore he has operated under wraps and he has had a commanding officer looking over his shoulder. I shudder to think of what could happen if this officer were suddenly turned loose in command."

Alexander, Matthews said, had countered with a three-page argument that Arnheiter should be awarded a command. Alexander contended that Arnheiter was being punished because he was unorthodox and refused to conform to the round Navy mold. Matthews remembered Alexander obliquely comparing Arnheiter's career to that of Vice Admiral Hyman G. Rickover, the father of the nuclear submarine. Alexander had not suggested that Arnheiter was a Jew and a victim of anti-Semitism, but he implied that Arnheiter, like Rickover, had provoked the animosity of superiors from time to time by being more intelligent, imaginative and enterprising than they were.

According to Matthews, the command clearance board had consisted of himself, Alexander and three other officers. He said that two of the others voted with him against Arnheiter. Alexander had now stood alone, one against three, and the dispute went for resolution to the fifth member, a senior captain who headed the board. In the Navy's not-so-democratic system, the opinion of the head of the board outweighed all the rest. This officer had listened to the loggerhead views of Alexander and Matthews and then worked out what Matthews thought was a fine technicality that saved everybody's face. He approved Arnheiter for a command only in an "emergency," where no other qualified officer was available. "This was a neat solution," Matthews said. "I was the lieutenant commander detailer and it would be up to me to determine when a personnel emergency existed. Alexander might have won the battle, but I could preclude him from winning the war. I was going to make damn sure Arnheiter didn't fill any emergency."

Two months after this "neat solution," Matthews said, in September 1965, Alexander suddenly told him that Admiral Semmes had decided to give Arnheiter a ship. Arnheiter had written directly to Semmes that August requesting a command, and Alexander displayed to Matthews the file copy of the admiral's reply.

Dear Arnheiter:

I am informed . . . that the board has reached a decision in your favor, albeit with some reservations, but nevertheless with the hope that your evident virtues as a destroyer officer can be put to good use . . . you are being ordered to command U.S.S. *Vance* in the next few months . . . Please accept my congratulations and best wishes for a successful tour of duty.

Sincerely,

B. J. Semmes, Jr.

"Arnheiter is going to get his command," Matthews recalled Alexander remarking with satisfaction.

"I figured somebody had just overruled me," Matthews said. "So I said to myself I had fought the good fight and lost, and I wrote the orders assigning Arnheiter to the *Vance*." Matthews said he assumed that the letter was, in effect, an order from the admiral to assign Arnheiter to the *Vance*.

A year later, Alexander and Matthews were still working in the Bureau. They had changed jobs. Alexander was now chief of planning in the plans and programs division, and Matthews, as administrative assistant to Admiral Semmes, was reviewing the testimony of the Subic Bay hearing. His premonition that Arnheiter might run amok in the giddiness of a ship captain's power had proven all too accurate. In retrospect, he could not conceive why the Bureau's screening process had not somehow caught Arnheiter. He searched the records in an attempt to reconstruct what had happened. "I found the file copy of that letter from Admiral Semmes," he said. The notations on the file copy showed that Alexander had actually written the letter for the admiral's signature, a normal staff practice. But the initials of the senior member of the command clearance board and those of other officers on the board, who had known of the emergency-only restriction, were missing from the chain-of-command ladder on the side of the file copy, Matthews said. There were just two sets of initials on the ladder—those of Alexander and another captain, who had been Semmes' administrative assistant in September 1965. "Somehow the letter had gotten around

everybody and up to the front office. I was able to piece together that Captain Alexander had done this pretty much on
his own. He had presented the admiral with what appeared to
be a finished piece of paper for his signature," Matthews said.

As I flew up to Boston in the summer of 1968 to interview
Alexander at his place of exile as assistant chief of staff for
operations of the Boston Naval District, I ran Matthews' story
through my mind again and again. It had amazed me, for
one professional naval officer does not, to a journalist, lightly
accuse another officer of this kind of behavior.

Alexander told me that he first met Arnheiter in 1959,
when they were in the same destroyer squadron at Newport,
Rhode Island. Alexander was a lieutenant commander and
captain of a destroyer escort, and Arnheiter a lieutenant and
the operations officer of the destroyer *Abbot*. "He was quite a
standout compared to the other junior officers in the squadron," Alexander said. "He produced some very fine staff work
for ASW [antisubmarine warfare] exercises we were engaged
in and his briefings were excellent. It was very unusual to
hear a young officer this articulate. He was a good writer and
he seemed to have a keen interest in our profession." Then
and later their relationship, while amiable, remained the professional one of two men who admired each other's work.
Alexander gave the captain some editorial advice and perhaps a few ideas for Arnheiter's magazine articles in 1961
and 1962 on the deficiencies in the Navy's submarine defenses. The articles had pleased Alexander. "Many men think
of some need, but very few will go to the trouble of champion-
ing it," he said. Alexander and another officer had written
a somewhat similar article in 1958 for the journal of the
United States Naval Institute. It was personally vetoed for
publication by Admiral Arleigh Burke, then Chief of Naval
Operations, at the insistence of the aviators. He and Arnheiter lost contact for the next several years, Alexander said,
until he became the Bureau's destroyer detailer in 1964 and
Arnheiter was made executive officer of the *Ingersoll*. They
met and talked again while Alexander was touring naval

bases on the West Coast to try to persuade talented young officers to stay in the destroyer force.

Arnheiter requested a ship of his own in late 1964 and again in 1965. Alexander's version of what happened next collided head-on with the account Matthews had given. Arnheiter's name came before the command clearance board in the normal manner, Alexander said, like that of any potentially qualified officer, because Arnheiter's record merited consideration, not because of his, Alexander's, intervention. The extraordinarily fine fitness reports Arnheiter had received from the *Ingersoll*'s captain, and the enthusiastic endorsement of the admiral in command of the flotilla, convinced Alexander that he should urge approval. He said he interpreted these endorsements as evidence that Arnheiter had matured to the responsibilities of a ship's captain. "He added up to a very able and in some ways brilliant officer who showed that the more authority and responsibility you gave him, the better he would perform," Alexander said. The roller-coaster pattern of Arnheiter's career had been a mark in his favor, as far as Alexander was concerned. "There must be some people in the Navy who are willing to operate at the full limits of their authority to offset the majority who operate at the bare minimum," he said. "If you operate at the limits, you are occasionally going to cross the boundaries or at least brush them. Arnheiter is the man who's not satisfied with the acceptable and wants to excel. His kind may make the Navy turbulent, but they keep the organization alive."

There was a restlessness about Alexander as we talked. The July day was unusually hot and humid. With the petty penny-pinching that is typical of great institutions in small matters, the Navy had not installed air conditioning in many of its offices in northern New England, on the grounds that the summers there were bearable without it. The air hardly moved in Alexander's office on the ninth floor of the Boston Naval District headquarters. He swung his long, lean frame out of the chair behind his desk from time to time and strode over to the window to look down at the tall cargo cranes and the masts of the ships in the harbor, their gray paint dull even in the brilliant sun. I began to sense that this man was far more complicated than the calm, aristocratic-looking officer he had appeared to be at the Resnick hearing. Alexander's aloof, ascetic exterior, the controlled tone of his voice, belied a spirit of passion and instinct.

The majority of the board had voted in favor of Arnheiter, he continued. "Two officers, including myself, were for him, and two other officers said, 'Wait until he becomes a full commander.'" The fifth and senior member of the board then heard both sides "and he voted to give Arnheiter a command." None of the board members objected that Arnheiter was too unstable for the psychological burden of a captain, Alexander said. "They were against giving him a command as a lieutenant commander because they felt others were better qualified." Contrary to Matthews' assertion, Alexander said, Matthews had not been a member of the board. Matthews objected to Arnheiter ex officio, as the lieutenant commander detailer. Matthews' objection was limited, however, to an uncomplimentary comparison of Arnheiter's record with those of other lieutenant commanders who had never aroused a superior's ire. "I had a feeling that Matty had unfavorable opinions about anybody who did things with a flair," Alexander said. Matthews had never raised any questions that Alexander could recall about Arnheiter's mental equilibrium.

"That's the true and complete story of how Arnheiter got on the *Vance*. And contrary to all lying insinuations of someone in Washington, there was absolutely no restriction on his command clearance as being for emergencies only. Absolutely none at all," Alexander said.

Somebody certainly seemed to be deceiving, I thought on the plane back to Washington. Alexander had hardly agreed with Matthews about any essential point. I telephoned every other participant I could reach and rummaged through their recollections to compare the two stories. Although none would confirm Matthews' accusation of trickery, there were great gaps in Alexander's account.

The senior member of the board and the two other officers involved all contradicted Alexander on one fundamental point. They said that Matthews had definitely been on the board. Two of the officers also distinctly remembered objecting that Arnheiter should not be given a captain's power because he was psychologically dangerous. Their opposition was not based solely on a comparison of Arnheiter's record with those of other lieutenant commanders. The first time Alexander proposed Arnheiter to them, one officer recalled, "we just laughed him out of the room." The majority of the board therefore voted against Arnheiter, and Alexander was his sole advocate, they said. A fourth officer whom Alexander had named as a member of the board told me he had not sat on the particular board that considered Arnheiter.

The memory of the senior member of the board, now retired, was vague on most aspects of the episode. He had been on the verge of hospitalization for cancer in the summer of 1965. He recalled something about an emergency, but could not recollect whether it concerned an unforeseen need to replace Ross Wright as captain of the *Vance* or a restriction on Arnheiter's command clearance.

The other two officers remembered precisely that Arnheiter's clearance had been restricted to an emergency only.

The officers at the Bureau of Naval Personnel swore that the record of the command board proceedings, which is secret, documented the emergency-only limitation. I looked at the file copy of the letter from Semmes to Arnheiter, the artifice Matthews had accused Alexander of contriving to trick him and Semmes and circumvent the Bureau's check-and-balance system. The letter had been drafted by Alexander, and all initials, except for his own and those of Semmes' administrative assistant in 1965, were missing from the chain-of-command ladder off to the side.

I telephoned Admiral Semmes, then commanding the Second Fleet in the Atlantic, at the naval base at Norfolk, Virginia. Had he known Arnheiter's clearance was restricted to emergencies only when he signed the letter? I asked.

"No, I didn't," he said. "I really thought it was a due-course nomination."

Would he have signed the letter if he had known about the restriction?

"I would have asked some questions first," he said. "The front office is inclined to take the views of the man on the spot unless they know otherwise."

I telephoned Alexander and confronted him with what I had found. I related Matthews' accusation of chicanery and the testimony of the other witnesses.

"That is absolutely wrong," Alexander said. "What I gave you was a true version of events. I did draft an answer to a letter. We did not write that letter until the board action was complete. There were two for and two against, and [the senior member of the board] broke the tie. He said to put Arnheiter on the *Vance*. He knew Marc and he thought that his tour on the *Ingersoll* had matured him and he would do well. There was absolutely nothing about any kind of emergency. I'm adamant about that." He also could not remember any emergency arising because of a sudden need to find a successor for Ross Wright.

What about the missing initials on the file copy of the letter? I asked.

"I can't explain that," he said. "This is an aspect of the case that has not been brought up to me before. I can't deny that on the file copy those initials are not there, but I deny trying to go around anyone. This is a very disturbing implication, and I think it's greatly unfair and not at all true. Whether Semmes signed that letter I don't recall. I'm certain that whatever happened there, I was acting in very good faith."

Was Alexander telling the truth? I asked myself. Or had he misled Semmes and tricked Matthews with the letter? Or had he somehow convinced the head of the command board that an emergency existed over finding a successor for Wright and persuaded the senior member to order Arnheiter to the *Vance?* Matthews had told me that earlier in the summer of 1965, he had prepared orders assigning another officer to the *Vance* to succeed Wright, and Alexander had induced him to send the man to a different ship. Or did Alexander simply have a poor memory? Despite the basic contradictions between Alexander's story and the testimony of the other witnesses, the principal evidence of trickery Matthews had mentioned—the file copy of the letter—was still circumstantial. Several officers pointed out to me that the omission of the initials from the chain-of-command ladder did not signify anything underhanded in itself. In hurried cases, or where there is a verbal agreement, letters like this would sometimes not be carefully routed through the entire chain of command.

I very briefly summarized the conflicting accounts of Alexander and Matthews in the article on the Arnheiter Affair I wrote for *The New York Times* Sunday magazine of August 11, 1968, and then resumed the search for an answer to these questions. Alexander had reacted angrily to the publication of Matthews' allegation. Since the appearance of the magazine article, he said, he had obtained new information that cast doubt on Matthews' statement that the letter drafted for Semmes had been used to put Arnheiter on the *Vance*. Alexander now claimed that the letter had never been sent.

The other participants, including Admiral Semmes and another captain who was his administrative assistant in the summer of 1965, again contradicted Alexander, however. They remembered that the letter had been sent. An officer who was Alexander's assistant in 1965 partially supported Alexander's claim. He doubted the letter had been mailed. But his testimony was inconclusive and his information had been obtained from Alexander.

In the meantime I was able to ascertain independently that the secret record of the command board proceedings did state that Arnheiter's clearance was solely "for emergency contingencies." Alexander was obviously wrong about that.

I abandoned the search. There seemed no way to resolve the question of whether Alexander was right, or Matthews was right, or both men had fallible memories. Even if Semmes had not sent a reply to Arnheiter's letter, Alexander could still have hoodwinked Matthews with the file copy. Yet there remained the equally puzzling question of why an officer

as eminent as Alexander had chosen to snuff out his professional life for a man as flawed as Arnheiter.

During the original interview in Boston, Alexander had
quickly explained why he had disavowed Arnheiter with his
"Dear Marc" letter of March 1967. "It was a pusillanimous
step," he said. Prior to Semmes' condemnation of Arnheiter
that February, Alexander had been quietly working within the
Bureau to try to convince the admiral to reject Commodore
Witter's verdict and to restore Arnheiter to command. Arnheiter and Settle had mentioned Alexander to several congressmen and senators as a senior captain who supported
them. Semmes began to view as disloyalty the opposition of
one of his leading staff officers to his own views. "My friends
warned me that the case was too dangerous and would ruin
my career," Alexander said. "I was in trouble up to my neck
and it was going to get worse if I kept going. There were some
leads, but not enough to overturn the allegations against Arnheiter. I decided I would either step out or take the other side
and then I took the other side. I guess I rationalized it as the
best way to get out of hot water."

Had the temptation of commanding the only battleship in
operation, the *New Jersey,* been too much for him? I asked.
No, he replied, he had not heard that he would be given the
New Jersey until several months later. His motivation had
been a general wish to retain the favor of those in power.

"Let's say," he remarked with an ironic smile, "that I joined
the firm."

Then why had he resigned from the firm eight months
afterward with his polemic to Secretary Ignatius?

In March 1967 his suspicion that Arnheiter had been victimized by a cleverly staged mutiny "was a feeling in my
bones," Alexander said. It was not a conviction. During the
summer and early fall, however, Arnheiter had gathered
"new evidence that tipped the scales for me." Alexander had
concluded that there had indeed been a conspiracy on the
Vance.

"What was the new evidence?" I asked.

He mentioned additional affidavits from Farnum and other

sailors accusing Hardy, Generous, Belmonte and company of disloyalty. He did not have the statements with him in Boston, but mailed copies to me later. By now I was a practiced textual critic of the Arnheiter affidavit. These were more of the captain's contrivances.

The documents that had convinced him beyond a doubt that Arnheiter's disgrace had been engineered by a campaign of slander, Alexander said, were a spoof familygram and a bogus plan of the day. Arnheiter had received copies of these lampoons anonymously through the mail over a year after he had been relieved. They were the most plausible evidence he was to present of a conspiracy because he had obviously not manufactured them. A familygram is a circular newsletter some captains periodically write to the wives and parents of their crew members. Among other barbs, the parodied familygram poked fun at the captain's noble ancestor, Baron Louis von Arnheiter, of whom he had boasted in the press release on his first shore-bombardment exploit. The spoof had Arnheiter announcing that Baron Louis "married my grandmother, who was Baroness Bungus von Buttbrusher and I have their marriage license to prove it." The bogus plan of the day was filled with like mockery. Arnheiter had told me during the interviews at his home in California that Generous had composed both parodies and had cunningly mailed copies to the families of the entire crew to make him appear an idiot. They were dated March 13 and March 15, 1966, two weeks before his dismissal. According to Arnheiter, a typewriter expert had compared the spoofs with Generous' letter to the Pearl Harbor chaplain and had determined that all three documents were probably typed on the same machine.

"Those were evidence of a willful and malicious effort to subvert the commanding officer by holding him up to ridicule in front of an unknown number of dependents," Alexander said.

Like the rest of Arnheiter's partisans, Alexander had never talked to any of the officers who had served under the captain. Because I wanted to learn what *he* believed to be the truth, I did not tell him that Generous had apparently not written either lampoon, that they had been composed after the captain's dismissal, and that none had been mailed to any of the families, as far as I could determine.

Julian Meisner had admitted to me that he was the author of both spoofs in a moment of rejoicing at the captain's demise. He recalled typing them on a portable machine he did not purchase until April 6, 1966, six days after Arnheiter had left the *Vance*. As evidence he produced the purchase slip for the typewriter, and a familygram and a plan of the day which he said were the originals. They were worded the same as the two Arnheiter had given me, but were typed on a different machine and dated April 15, 1966. Generous explained that he had copied Meisner's originals on his own typewriter as souvenirs and had backdated his copies a month, to March 13 and 15, for a touch of realism. The Xeroxes someone anonymously mailed to Arnheiter a year later had been made from the copies Generous had typed.

One of the events described in both the bogus familygram and the plan of the day, the water-skiing and beer-drinking festivities in the midst of the hunt for the Chinese submarine, did not occur until March 22. The captain would have been the last to notice this discrepancy with the March 13 and 15 dates, and the last to point it out to his friends if he had. Meisner, Generous and the other officers said the lampoons had been passed around only on the ship and had not been mailed to any of the families. I asked a number of wives if they had received copies and was told they had not.

"Are you certain those parodies were written while Arnheiter was still captain of the *Vance?*" I asked Alexander.

"Yes, I am. I'm sure of it," he answered.

He was equally certain, he said, that Generous was a psychotic. His reasons puzzled me, because he cited Generous' medical record as evidence. I had also seen Generous' medical record and it was evidence to the contrary.

During my interview with Arnheiter in California he told me that Generous had been incarcerated in a mental ward in a naval hospital for over a month in 1964 after "he beat up a woman so badly, she had to be hospitalized for five weeks."

On the *Vance*, Arnheiter said, Generous had manifested "a psychotic urge to undermine all established authority." Alexander had made a similar accusation against Generous in his statement to Secretary Ignatius, contending that the operations officer had been hospitalized for thirty-five days for a mental disorder.

I had confronted Generous with these accusations. He told me that he had gone to the psychiatric section of the naval hospital at Camp Pendleton, Calif., in August 1964 to seek help for what he considered an emotional breakdown. A psychiatrist there had reassigned him to the hospital for a little over a month from his job as gunnery officer on a destroyer at Long Beach so that he could undergo a battery of psychiatric tests and weekly analytical sessions with the psychiatrist. Except for the first few days of processing, Generous lived at the hospital like an outpatient, coming and going as he pleased. After a little more than a month, he had been sent back to duty and transferred to the *Vance* at Pearl Harbor. The woman Arnheiter claimed Generous had beaten up was a young lady he was dating at the time. Generous said he had broken open the door to her apartment when they quarreled in the midst of his emotional trouble. She had been standing behind the door and had got a black eye, he said, but had gone to work with a shiner that day. The incident, however, had convinced Generous that he should turn himself in to the hospital.

I had asked to see his medical record and Generous let me read it. The record corroborated his story. The psychiatrist's report said Generous was suffering from a temporary emotional disorder, that he did not have a psychiatric problem, and that he was sane and rational. The psychiatrist attributed Generous' emotional problem to the scars left by a difficult childhood and to the inner turmoil of a prior, abortive romance. "During a month of psychiatric hospitalization, the patient was observed, interviewed and tested," the psychiatrist wrote. "His behavior in the hospital was quite satisfactory, and he at no time revealed any significant emotional illness. . . . The patient continues to be quite eager to return to duty, and his motivation for the naval profession is excellent. He appears to have gained some genuine insight and control regarding the emotional problems of his personal life, and he is felt to be fully fit to return to full duty and handle the responsibilities of a naval officer."

Ross Wright said that he had known about the incident but that during the nearly fourteen months Generous worked for him aboard the *Vance* prior to Arnheiter's arrival, Generous had shown no signs of mental instability, had matured and had performed exceptionally well. I had questioned Generous' shipmates about his actions during their ninety-nine days under Arnheiter, and they had seen no indication of psychotic behavior. Arnheiter, it turned out, had first learned about Generous' hospitalization while Arnheiter was assigned to Admiral Baumberger's staff at San Diego after his dismissal from the *Vance*. Generous had mentioned his emotional breakdown two years earlier in a letter of resignation from the Navy. The letter had passed through Baumberger's headquarters on its way up through channels and Arnheiter had read it.

Generous and the young lady whose door he had broken down were married in October 1964, two months after she received her black eye. They had a two-year-old daughter when I met them in 1968.

Now I asked Alexander why he was certain that Generous was a psychotic. He had seen Generous' medical record, he said, and had also asked a senior Navy psychiatrist whom he knew to read it. The psychiatrist had told him that Generous was a "dangerous" person. Alexander's voice had the calmness of a man who has drawn a conclusion from unimpeachable evidence.

I asked four officers who had known Alexander and worked with him over the years to explain why he had sacrificed himself for Arnheiter. They found his actions as difficult to comprehend as I had.

Some thought he had been deluded by his own crusading instincts. One officer noted that throughout his unusually fine career as a staff officer and destroyer commander, Alexander had always been outspoken on issues where others had preferred the safety of silence, and he had almost invariably been proven correct. "You are dealing with an individual who has been wrong very few times in his life and he's not going to let go of this dying cat yet. He's still backing up his original decision to put Arnheiter on that ship," this acquaintance said.

"There is a quixotic side to Dick," another officer said. "He's a very serious man, and sometimes when Dick forms an opinion it becomes a matter of principle that others accept that opinion. You could discuss something with Dick to a certain point and then it became a hard issue."

Farnum, who had since sickened of the captain and come to regret much that he had done at Arnheiter's beckoning, thought Alexander had been gulled by Arnheiter's spurious evidence of a conspiracy. "He was tricked by a lot of phony documents that were all stacked. I know, because I was a cog in the Arnheiter propaganda machine and I helped stack some of them. I was also naïve. I was led like a sheep," he said.

Alexander may have been the biggest victim of the many who were taken in by Arnheiter's mutiny tale. Or he may have tried some manipulating himself. Or he may have been that peculiar kind of military officer, and there are some, whose professional death wish sooner or later finds a cup of hemlock. In the end, however, Richard Alexander remains an enigma, an elegant sphinx.

Admirals Irvine and King inadvertently gave Arnheiter the opportunity to play the role of a wronged man by running him off the *Vance* before he had been confronted with the accusations against him. Under the circumstances, the act would have constituted a mere legal formality. But this procedure is central to the American concept of justice. In handing to the captain the appearance of an injustice, they provided him with the means to cast doubt on the fairness of Witter's investigation, to convince others, like Admiral Baumberger, that he had been treated shabbily, and to lend credence to his fable of a conspiracy.

A more serious tactical error the naval hierarchy now regrets was the failure to court-martial Arnheiter immediately for the false position reports and other offenses the testimony at Subic Bay disclosed. At the time, the admirals felt that disgrace and the destruction of his career were sufficient punishment for a Naval Academy graduate and regular officer of the line. Later, however, when the captain and his partisans began demanding a court of inquiry or a general court-martial (never saying, of course, that they would settle solely for one rigged in advance in their favor), the Navy could not sink Arnheiter with his own mine by convening an objective court. To order a court of inquiry might be to concede the possibility that his accusations of mutiny, unjust dismissal and an official conspiracy to conceal both were true. Also, to court-martial the captain might appear to be vengeance, not justice. The Navy had to fall back on the lame defense that the one-man investigation at Subic Bay had established Arnheiter's aberrations, that the findings had been carefully reviewed, that the case was closed. While the statement was true, it begged the dilemma.

There were other, unstated reasons for the Navy's refusal to convene a court of inquiry or a court-martial. Either would have had to be a public event under the circumstances. The testimony of Hardy, Generous, Belmonte and the other officers and sailors would have exposed the magnitude of the error the Navy had committed in placing 14 young officers and 135 sailors under the command of Marcus Aurelius Arnheiter in a small ship at sea. No organization cares to air its private sins, and the peculiar character of the Navy officer corps makes it more reluctant than most. That fraternity of men who have chosen to spend years in the isolation of the oceans is a brotherhood set apart. The sense of separateness, of loyalty to an uncommon tradition and code, is especially true of the nucleus of officers who enter the brotherhood as impressionable youths on the parade field at Annapolis. From that day forward, they are never permitted to forget that to them will pass the responsibility to safeguard and to command the mightiest fleet in the history of the world. They rarely seek publicity for themselves. They seek it for their institution, to make deadlier its weapons and more majestic its power. In some ways, their attitude is akin to that of the members of an old-fashioned men's club. When a black sheep appears among them, they hesitate to throw him out the door for passers-by to see. Instead, if they can, they quietly cashier him and exile him to the clacking of typewriters in some dreary office in Boston or San Francisco. Courts of inquiry and courts-martial are a last resort. Throughout the building of Arnheiter's conspiracy fraud in the news media, the Navy refused to make public either the transcript of the testimony at Subic Bay or the other distasteful evidence, such as the tapes of Arnheiter's radio transmissions during the shore-bombardment incidents which the captain of the *Mason* had recorded. Details of the captain's sins were leaked to *Time* and to *Newsweek* in an attempt to counterattack, but the records of his gravest offenses were kept locked in the file drawers at the Bureau of Naval Personnel. It was not until Arnheiter had driven the admirals to the wall by calling Semmes a liar at the Resnick hearing that the Navy opened the files and offered to let the world see what Marcus Aurelius Arnheiter had done.

A court-martial would, in fact, have been a grotesque process for meting out retribution to Captain Arnheiter. To punish a man for transgression of the law is to presuppose that he can distinguish right from wrong. In Arnheiter's mind, right and wrong, deception and candor, fact and fantasy, tumbled together like the colors in a kaleidoscope. He stole and deceived knowingly, but with a mad innocence. And he was never conscious of his greatest crime—goading other men to near-madness. He was a figure of fiction, that whimsical tyrant in the captain's cabin who emerges at some point in every navy. No admiral credits his existence, until he appears. Captain Queeg was a character in a novel. Captain Arnheiter was alive and in command of the U.S.S. *Vance*. Once relieved, he had to invent a conspiracy because, psychologically, it was the only way he could explain his disgrace to himself.

Before writing the article for *The Times* Sunday magazine,

I telephoned Arnheiter in California and asked him about the white toilet seat. At first he denied its existence. "That's just another damn lie," he said. "I didn't have any white toilet seat." I related the detailed accounts of Hardy and Gwynn. His answer changed. He said he could not remember the incident. A few days later, a letter arrived. Arnheiter's memory was more fertile now. He explained at great length how he had ordered Hardy and Gwynn to get white toilet seats for all the latrines on the ship, because the regulation black seats were "cruddy" and covered with "hardened fecal matter." Contrary to what he had told me in our telephone conversation, he now seemed to remember that they had acquired white toilet seats for the entire ship. He was not certain, however. His memory was firm only about how unwilling Gwynn had been to take the time on Guam to try and find a number of items the captain had instructed him to purchase, like white mess jackets, candelabras and weather balloons. (I had told Arnheiter that Gwynn and Hardy claimed they had requisitioned the white toilet seat for him at Pearl Harbor, before the ship left for Guam.) The important thing, Arnheiter concluded, was that Hardy's and Gwynn's accounts, wrongly introduced, could raise false questions about why the captain alone had a white toilet seat.

The *Vance* was still on patrol off Viet Nam in 1968. I sent a telegram to her skipper and asked him if there was a white toilet seat in his private bathroom and if it was the only white toilet seat on the ship.

"Affirmative," he telegraphed back, "on board and in use."

In the end, whatever slighting of the regulations in the relief of Arnheiter and the equivocation over why Alexander had been deprived of the *New Jersey,* the Navy accomplished the essential. It rectified its original error of putting Arnheiter on the ship by expelling him from the *Vance* in time to avert a mutiny or his assassination. And it kept him from conniving his way onto another ship. "We were lucky we caught him in ninety-nine days. This thing just shook me to my boots afterward," Admiral Semmes confessed.

That a mutiny did not flare before Arnheiter was legally ejected was probably due to the fact that throughout those ninety-nine days the officers and sailors of the *Vance* never stared at the life-or-death choice of deposing the captain to survive or continuing to submit to his authority with the certainty that they would perish. In such primeval moments, legality becomes a luxury that men can no longer afford. The men of the *Caine* endured Queeg's madness until the ship was about to founder in the typhoon. Then Maryk, the executive officer, had to seize control to preserve the lives of all. The closest parallel on the *Vance* occurred just before the captain's third shore bombardment, on February 1, 1966, when he became so enthralled with the bursting bombs and the flowering napalm inland that he forgot he was driving the ship toward a collision with the Tam Quan Peninsula. Hardy's instinctive shout to the helmsman—"This is the exec. I have the conn"—was a symbolic act of revolt that he was able to dissolve once he had taken command for the few minutes necessary to save the *Vance*. Arnheiter flayed Hardy's nerves, but he never forced him to that climactic decision point Maryk reached after Queeg's cowardice gripped him in hysteria and the mountainous seas reached out to engulf the *Caine*.

I asked Hardy what he would have done if the sonarmen had located the Chinese submarine in international waters in the Gulf of Siam and Arnheiter had ordered the sub destroyed with depth charges and hedgehog explosives. "In the state of mind I was in, I wasn't looking that far ahead," he said. "I guess I must have subconsciously thought he would go to pieces if he found the sub, just as he had that time he saw the flashes of our own shells on the rocks and thought the Viet Cong were really shooting at us. I must have thought he'd fall apart and I'd be able to persuade him to do what I wanted."

"But what if he hadn't gone to pieces? What if you had discovered the sub and he'd commanded the gunner's mates to fire the depth charges? At the least, he'd have committed an act of piracy and multiple murder. At the most, he'd have started another war. What would you have done?"

I had been interviewing Hardy for two days with almost no rest, in the kitchen of the house where he and his family were living at the Key West Naval Base. It was 2 A.M. He was very tired and seemed depressed at having relived those three months and nine days under Arnheiter while we talked. He rubbed his hand over his eyes slowly and looked at the table for a moment. "I don't know what I would have done," he said.

Undoubtedly there are lessons to be drawn from the Arnheiter Affair, however unique a personality Captain Arnheiter may be. The Navy might well consider the possibility of subjecting the behavior of its captains to scrutiny by some independent authority, perhaps through a mechanism similar to that of the Army's Inspector General. The Inspector General system often falls short of the ideal in practice, but a representative of the Inspector General's office does periodically visit every unit of company or similar size in the Army to listen to complaints. The soldier or officer who thinks he is being abused by his superior has an institutionalized channel of appeal the superior cannot deny him. He can see the Inspector General's representative without asking anyone's permission. The sole, officially sanctioned resources, aside from sending letters to chaplains, available to the officers and seamen of the *Vance,* were to write a formal complaint or to swear out court-martial charges against Arnheiter, hand the papers to the captain as their immediate superior, and hope that he would forward the charge sheets to Commodore Milligan. Hardy knew what the result of that step would have been.

The Navy must preserve the authority of its captains to discipline their crews because of the awesome and absolute responsibility a captain has for the safety of the ship and the lives of all aboard her in the solitude and ever-present danger of the sea. Yet the traditional system of appeal through court-martial presupposes that all officers are Victorian gentlemen.

At the end of the 1960's the Navy, like many of the country's institutions, was afflicted with a kind of arteriosclerosis, an insensitivity to the social environment in which it existed. While Arnheiter may have sounded like a Victorian, he did not behave like a gentleman. The officers and sailors of the *Vance* had to pray that their wives, the eyes and ears of other destroyer captains, and the consciences of men like Chaplain Dando, Lieutenant Kordons and the Pearl Harbor chaplain who received Generous' letter, would eventually rescue them.

The nation's newspapers suffer from the same hardening of the arteries. The techniques of the government propagandist and the public relations man, which Arnheiter utilized so cleverly, long ago outraced a tired community of hemmed-in reporters, editors who ask the wrong questions and publishers who are more interested in profits than in the quality and accuracy of the information they print. The time-honored newspaper technique of scribbling a few details in a notebook, hustling them into something readable on a typewriter, casting the words into a column, and then rushing on to another story the next day, was appropriate to police-beat reporting in Chicago in the 1920's. It is an anachronism today. Those of us in the trade know that the consequence of the cycle is the daily publication of falsehood and bias in favor of those who know best how to exploit its weakness. Systematic deception has become a sanctioned practice of government and industry, a reality of modern life that the established newspapers have, for the most part, found convenient to ignore.

The *Vance* no longer guards the Viet Nam coast. In October 1969 she was decommissioned and once more wrapped in mothballs. Age retired her, as well as one of those economy drives that marked the retrenchment of the ill-fated American venture in Viet Nam. She is moored in silence now among her cocooned sisters in a retirement community at the San Francisco Naval Shipyard, resting and waiting for new fears to put old ships to sea again.

The burial place of the captain's aristocratic grandfather, the late Baron Louis von Arnheiter, that early pioneer in manned flight, could not be ascertained. His place of birth was equally elusive. The archives at the Library of Congress, the *Almanach de Gotha,* and various German and Dutch genealogies held no trace of the noble family of von Arnheiter. Histories of man's conquest of the air do not mention a plain Louis Arnheiter, before or after the Wright brothers.

Four years after Arnheiter's abrupt dismissal as captain of the *Vance,* Tom Generous was settling into work on a thesis on the evolution of the Uniform Code of Military Justice, the body of military law, for a doctorate in history at Stanford University, in Palo Alto, California. He was troubled by his own record under Captain Arnheiter.

"I'm not proud of what I did," he said. "I gave up. In a lot of ways I feel I betrayed my own standards. In some things I feel I wasn't prudent enough, and in other things I feel I wasn't courageous enough. There are about eight different sides to my feelings. Maybe I should have just played the game with the guy, done whatever he wanted. He was the captain.

"But that's where the Nuremberg thing comes up, and for the Germans it wasn't as easy as it was for us on the *Vance.* The war-crimes tribunal required the Germans ex post facto to live up to a higher law than their own damn country required of them. In my case, all I was required to do was to live up to Navy regulations, and our operations order, and the Constitution of the United States. It was pretty clear what was right and what was wrong. I didn't have to compare what Arnheiter was telling me to do with any subjective standards of morality and ethics. He was saying, 'Do this,' and the law said, 'That's wrong,' and a commanding officer can't legally make you obey an unlawful order.

"Still, it wasn't a simple situation, because you were constantly torn, sometimes over the most minor things and sometimes over really major things, between obeying him and obeying the law. If you obeyed him you were taking the easy way out, but then you've got to live with your conscience about breaking the law. And if you didn't obey him and you appealed to the law, then you were in a tremendous scuffle, where you were risking your own liberty, your own future life. Supposing I had gone to war with him about those false position reports. Supposing I'd said, 'Captain, these are false reports. It's against the law to make false reports and I'm charging you,' and I pressed court-martial charges. Practically speaking, that's absurd. That makes a nice kind of novel, that kind of stand, but that doesn't happen in the real world.

"On the other hand, you can't just send the phony message and become an accomplice. So what you end up doing is something sneaky, like I did, and that's send the goddamn thing and then make a log entry of the true position. That's Pontius Pilate."

Luis Belmonte grew tired of amassing mortgage payments and few riches renovating Victorian houses in San Francisco. By the fall of 1970, his life was no longer the casual and tousled one it had been when I had first interviewed him two years before. He took a wife in February 1970. Perhaps she helped him to change his life-style. He became the Nevada manager for a large interstate warehouse company and moved to the town of Sparks, near Reno.

"I loved the sea," Belmonte said. "I would have stayed in the Navy if it hadn't been for Marcus. It was too risky after him. Some year when I was up for a promotion one of Arnheiter's buddies might be sitting on my selection board. He'd take one look at my name and say, 'This guy's one of those sons of bitches who did in my friend Marc Arnheiter!' He'd shitcan me and I'd sit at some goddamn desk for the rest of my twenty years."

The captain's vengeance hurt Ray Hardy. Hardy was wedded to the Navy as an Annapolis graduate, and Arnheiter's mutiny tale damaged his career. He was to have received a command of his own, a DER like the *Vance,* in the fall of 1968. The admirals withheld it from him because Arnheiter was still filling news columns then. They were afraid the Navy might appear to be rewarding Hardy for his testimony against the captain at Subic Bay, and they knew Arnheiter would claim just that. Hardy was instead made executive officer of a new guided-missile destroyer, the U.S.S. *Towers.*

He was promised a ship in another eighteen months. But the economy drive that retired the *Vance* affected Ray Hardy too. Nearly two hundred ships were decommissioned, and Hardy was not among the fortunate who got what commands were left. In the fall of 1970, Hardy was languishing in a staff post at Long Beach, California.

Richard Alexander did not rise from "the Elephant's Graveyard" in Boston. He retired on July 1, 1970. The newspapers did not notice his going. At the outset of the Nixon Administration, in February 1969, Alexander's family attorney, an old acquaintance of the new Under Secretary of the Navy, John W. Warner, had inquired about the possibility of resurrecting Alexander's career. He had been told that nothing could be done. The admirals do not forgive those who violate the code. "No one will ever forget what he did," one senior officer said.

I traced Johnnie Lee Smoot, the *Vance*'s leading boatswain's mate, to Oklahoma City. He was a civilian, working as a painter at an aircraft-repair shop there. Smoot had spent a month and a half in the psychiatric wards of military hospitals in the Philippines and Guam after leaving the *Vance* just two days before the man who had driven him ashore was himself ordered over the side. Released from the hospital, he was transferred to a Naval Reserve training destroyer at Long Beach. He had wanted to sail the Navy's ships for another ten years. Instead he retired with the twenty-one years of service he already had, because he was afraid he might encounter another Captain Arnheiter. "I knew I couldn't take a second skipper like him. He'd finish me," Smoot said. The psychiatrists in the Philippines and Guam, like the doctor on the *Markab*, wouldn't believe the stories that Smoot told them about life under Captain Arnheiter. "They said I must have talked that way about all my captains . . . Arnheiter should have been in there instead of me," Smoot said.

In the fall of 1970, Captain Arnheiter was assigned to a hospital, an ordinary one—the surgical ward of the Oak Knoll Naval Hospital at Oakland, California. He was an out-patient, living at home and recovering from severe fractures of the right hip, leg and ankle, and a dislocated shoulder. He had slipped on a rock and fallen twenty feet down a cliff while leading a group of Boy Scouts on a hike in the mountains east of San Francisco in the summer of 1969. His injuries seemed a gratuitous misfortune for a man who had already sustained the greatest misfortune of his life—the loss of a captain's giddy power.

Arnheiter also lost his suit against the Navy in the civil courts for alleged violation of his constitutional right to due process. A Federal District Court judge in San Francisco dismissed the suit and said that the admirals had treated the captain fairly. Arnheiter's removal, he found, had been "in substantial compliance" with Navy regulations. And contrary to what Arnheiter and his partisans had been contending, the judge held that command of a warship, with its inherent power to deal death and to involve the nation in conflict, was not among the "rights" guaranteed by the Constitution. Arnheiter appealed the judgment to the higher Circuit Court of Appeals and lost again. The Circuit Court sustained the District judge.

The captain could take some satisfaction, however, in the wide credence given his story of a mutiny. Once in print, fraud has a way of acquiring the appearance of truth. Much of the Navy, and a wide segment of middle America, were convinced that Captain Arnheiter, a gallant skipper, had been "stabbed in the back" by hippies and student radicals posing as naval officers. Boiler Tender MacSaveny, who almost made the captain's mutiny fable come true prematurely, found this to be the case among his fellow sailors and the officers at the Great Lakes Naval Training Center in Illinois, where he was stationed in 1970. "These people really think we shanghaied that guy off the ship," he said.

Commander Lloyd M. Bucher's pliant surrender of the U.S.S. *Pueblo* to the North Korean navy in January 1968 had been a godsend to Arnheiter. Few regular naval officers condoned Bucher's capitulation, even under the pitiful circumstances in which he found himself. A navy that surrenders its ships without a fight ceases to be a navy. In newspaper interviews, on radio and television programs, Arnheiter probed at this tenderness. Had he been the captain of the *Pueblo,* he would have battled her to a flaming hulk. "If those North Koreans had come after us, I'd have been ready for them. I'd have fought to the last round in my cartridge belt," he would say in a phrase taken from his elderly mentor, Admiral Settle. His readers and listeners had not been there that day near the *Bache* to see him dive behind the gun-control shielding at the flashes of the *Vance*'s .50-caliber bullets on the cliff.

There was a kind of truth to what Captain Arnheiter said. He fought to the end. As soon as he could rise from his hospital bed, he swore out formal court-martial charges against Admiral Semmes—ten counts of fraud, nineteen counts of writing false official statements, six counts of dereliction of duty, five counts of being an accessory to a crime after the fact, three counts of conduct unbecoming an officer and a gentleman, and one count of criminal libel. The charges were dismissed.

The captain retired on February 1, 1971.

APPENDIX A

STATEMENT OF CAPTAIN A. M. HAZEN, USN, COMMANDER FLEET TRAINING GROUP, WESTPAC

To Whom It May Concern:

In response to COMUSMACV 181140Z JAN 1966, CTU 70.8.9's 240158Z JAN 1966 (NGFS Availability) assigned the USS LEONARD F. MASON (DD-852) to the northern II Corps (Operation MASHER) for the period 27 January–1 February 1966. CTU 70.8.9's 291145Z JAN and 031620Z FEB extended MASON in Operation MASHER for the period 2–5 February and 5–10 February, respectively. The undersigned was in command of MASON throughout this period.

On 27 January 1966, the MASON was working with a II Corps airborne spotter off the South Vietnamese Coast in the northern portion of the II Corps Area in the vicinity of Point KIM BONG and Isle Buffle. It is not believed that any NGFS missions were conducted on this date for this writer neither holds records or remembers firing on 27 January. It is remembered, however, that upon departure the air spotter advised MASON to remain in the vicinity for a possible mission on the morning of 28 January. By previous mutual agreement, "vicinity" was defined as within one hour's steaming of the position of the ship upon the spotter's departure. At 0730 on the morning of 28 January, MASON was assigned a fire mission. Due to the unusual nature of this mission, a verbatim record of the Spotter Net (Circuit C-7) was maintained in CIC for historical purposes. Enclosure (1) is a copy of this log. In addition, enclosure (2) is MASON's 280640Z JAN (NGFS in RVN) which indicates the special nature of this mission. Some time prior to 1243, USS VANCE (DER-387) (Silk Point) appeared on the scene. At that time she reported to the spotter that she was "able to assist in a direct fire mission", and approximately one hour later Silk Point was placed on a standby basis. Shortly thereafter in a flashing light message to MASON, VANCE asked for PEPPER report format followed by another flashing light request for spotter frequencies (enclosure (3)). VANCE did not fire in the vicinity of MASON on 28 January and departed the area about sunset. MASON fired missions from 1345 to 1400 by airborne spotter (USS L. F. MASON (DD-852) 280730Z JAN) and from 1928 to 1958 by ground spotter (USS L. F. MASON (DD-852) 281420Z JAN). Spotters reported that friendly troops were under fire during all fire missions on 28 January. Enclosure (4).

On 29 January MASON fired a night "H" and "I" mission from 0043H to 0400H and an indirect fire mission from 1123H to 1335H. MASON's position for this latter mission was approximately 2,000 yards south of Point KIM BONG. Some time prior to 1123H, VANCE appeared in the immediate vicinity and about 1138H sent a flashing light message (enclosure (5)) stating that he was prepared to provide "direct fire in view friendly forces being under hostile fire" and requesting "can you arrange with spotter for suitable target." VANCE remained in close vicinity to MASON during this mission and, though not interfering with the mission, did, on occasion distract this writer's attention from the business at hand in order to check her position and movements.

On the afternoon of 29 January, MASON received a fire mission (enclosure (6)). At this time MASON was again about 2500 yards 150° true from Point KIM BONG, while VANCE was closer in-shore and fouling MASON's range. VANCE was requested to clear the range and by flashing light, at 1505, replied that she would "close the beach to the south . . . to get within direct fire range." (Enclosure (7)). MASON commenced her mission at 1514H and completed at 1715H. At 1537H while about 1200–1500 yards off the beach, VANCE communicated to the airborne spotter that she held "some bunkers and trenches . . . on top of a sand dune" and that "it looked like a good mission . . ." Enclosure (8) is a copy of the log for Circuit C-7 (4268 KCS) maintained by CIC commencing with this transmission. In addition, enclosure (9) is a copy of the log maintained in CIC of 233.8 MCS (circuit designator unknown) covering portions of the same time period that VANCE was conducting a fire mission. In as much as the latter transmissions appeared to be a possible violation of engagement rules, a magnetic tape recording was ordered made and was obtained. It is not known where this tape is now located, possibly it is in USS MASON. VANCE completed her mission at about the same that MASON completed her mission—1715H. MASON commenced another mission at 1836H and completed at 1915H. VANCE departed the area immediately prior to or during this mission. MASON commenced her final mission this date at 2352H and completed at 0400H on 30 January.

On 30 January this writer does not recall observing VANCE in the vicinity of MASON and it is not believed she was present. In view of the interest generated in VANCE's activities the previous two days, it is most likely that her presence would have been noted. On this day, MASON continued to fire missions in support of the 1st Air Cavalry Division. All were fired from a position 2–4 miles from Point KIM BONG, 2–6 thousand yards off shore. The first mission was completed at 0400H. Other missions were fired from 0950H to 1258; from 1510H to 1855H and from 2114H until 0025H on 31 January. Some time during the day, USS VANCE's 290841Z JAN 1966 (enclosure (10)) was brought to my attention. What was described in this message was greatly at variance with what actually took place. Major discrepancies known to be untrue as witnessed by this writer and several others in MASON are:

a. "delivered urgent naval gun fire support"
b. "urgent fire request"
c. "issued by II Corps U.S. Navy Gun Fire Support Team"
d. "responded to the call by proceeding at full speed"
e. "highly accurate"
f. "known Viet Cong machine gun bunkers and entrenchment area"
g. "very first round fired was observed to hit"
h. "upon destruction of target area"

Items a., b., c., and d. are covered factually in the enclosure hereto. Item e. is questionable. In her press release, VANCE reported expending 17 rounds, while on 233.8 MCS she reported to the spotter 8 rounds were expended. This writer observed VANCE's mission closely from about 800–1000 yards from VANCE and from 2000–2500 from the target. The number of rounds fired is not known, however, there were very few observed bursts. The number of misses and not observed rounds were sufficient to arouse comment by other MASON bridge personnel. MASON observers did not consider VANCE's fire to be "highly accurate" and the spotter did not report fire effectiveness. Due to the close range to VANCE's target and the very flat trajectory of the rounds over very flat terrain and the fact that friendly troops were operating 3–5 thousand yards inland from the target, this writer became concerned from a safety-to-friendly troops standpoint. The ground situation to the West of Route 1 was so fluid in the early days of the Operation that even though requested for every mission, MASON received friendly front line positions only in "danger close" situations. VANCE did not request friendly front line information.

During the seven days MASON participated in Operation MASHER, 1739 rounds were fired in 21 missions on 237 targets. These were all fired from a position within 1–5 miles of VANCE's target. VANCE's target and immediate area were very carefully and continuously observed throughout this entire period. At no time was any person or activity observed in this vicinity even though the situation ashore covered the entire BON SON plain, into the hills and further west in to the AN LAO valley. At no time was there any friendly or hostile action in or near the VANCE target area. At no time was MASON given that target though available continuously and with heavier fire power. In her target description to the spotter, VANCE used the "suspected" rather than "known." With regard to item g., the very first round was observed not to hit. Item h.—other than some dislocation of sand on the dune, no discernible damage was done to the target.

On 31 January MASON continued fire support missions, completing one at 0025H and conducting others from 0054H to 0348H and from 0548H to 0705H. It is believed no further missions were conducted this date for this writer neither recalls nor has records of any. In like manner, it is not believed the VANCE was on the scene this day. As best recalled, it was either on this day or on 2 February that 1st Air Cavalry Division air and ground spotters, CO's of Huey batteries and LTCOL AMOS, ground artillery commander, came aboard MASON for situation briefings and support coordination matters. As a result of these meetings, MASON had a much clearer picture of the general situation ashore and her support role. In like manner these units became aware of MASON's fire support capabilities and limitations.

Some time in the forenoon of 1 February 1966, USS VANCE again appeared in the vicinity of MASON off Point KIM BONG and at 1145H advised the spotter that she was available for an urgent mission on a target provided by her. The CIC logs of both circuit C-7 and the spotting frequency (233.8 MCS) are attached as enclosures (11) and (12). A magnetic tape was recorded of the transmissions on 233.8, however, its location is not now known. It is possibly still in MASON. At 1202H VANCE sent a flashing light message thanking MASON for courtesies (enclosure (13)). VANCE completed her mission and at 1415H MASON commenced a mission and completed at 1550H. USS ORLECK (DD-886) was in the vicinity during this period and was firing concurrent missions with MASON. MASON's targets were in the vicinity of HUNG LONG village 4500 yards NNW of KIM BONG point. (Sheet 17, 472-31 Combat Chart HOA NHON (BON SON)). The spotter desired MASON to remain south of the Point with ORLECK north. From this position it would be very difficult to hit the target. In maneuvering to get the best possible gun range and GTL, MASON advised VANCE of the situation and requested that she stand clear. VANCE remained in close proximity to MASON and her movements were a source of concern and distraction during the early minutes of the mission. At 1453H VANCE advised MASON via flashing light that she would station astern of MASON and did so for a short time. At 1504H VANCE advised MASON that she would move ahead of MASON to change her GTL. Enclosure (14) contains these two messages. MASON advised VANCE not to cross MASON's GTL. VANCE then proceeded to cross MASON's gun target line. Though MASON was not firing at this time due to the spotter working with ORLECK, it was a momentary lull in a continuing mission, and MASON expected to resume fire at any minute. MASON could not resume fire due to VANCE's position on the GTL and fouling the range. At this time this writer ordered VANCE to clear the area immediately. VANCE withdrew to a position 2–3 thousand yards south of MASON. MASON's mission was completed at 1550H. It is believed that VANCE remained in the area a short while attempting to get another mission, but departed when the spotter returned to base. MASON fired another mission from 2008H to 2020H. MASON continued to provide support in Operation MASHER in four missions on 2 February, three missions on 3 February and one mission 4 February. At this time the major effort had moved so far inland into the hills to the west and into the AN LAO valley that targets were beyond effective 5″/38 gun range. CTU 70.8.9's 042215Z FEB provided that USS

BARRY (5"/54 guns) relieve MASON. On the morning of 5 February, the relief was effected and MASON moved north to the CAP SAHOI area to provide support in Operation DOUBLE EAGLE. VANCE was not again in the vicinity of MASON after her departure on 1 February.

Some time subsequent to 1 February, VANCE's 011300Z JAN [should be FEB], enclosure (15), was brought to my attention. Again, this message bore no relation to events as they actually occurred. The major distortions are:

a. "hot Viet Cong target"
b. "machine gun on KIM BONG peninsula"
c. "urgent direct fire mission at the request of . . ."
d. "stitched the beaches"
e. "hits were observed on the fortified emplacement"
f. "target was finished"

VANCE's target was a small stone or masonry structure on the southern slope of KIM BONG point. In the five previous days of close, direct and continuous observation, MASON did not detect any persons or activity within 1500 yards of the target. It was not a "hot" target and it was not a "machine gun." Item c. is covered in enclosures. Item d.—during seven days off the beach at BON SON, MASON observed no action in the beach area other than VANCE's direct fire mission. Troops, helos and aircraft did not stitch the beaches. Although the structure was severely damaged, the spotter actually reported that he was finished for the day and going home, not that the target was finished.

After receipt of VANCE's 011300Z FEB and a review of VANCE's activities the previous few days, this writer considered that he had witnessed events of such significance that collectively they required an official report. I prepared a Confidential-For Officers' Eyes Only message which was typed by Lieutenant Ronald L. SEGERBLOM, USN, Operations Officer. The message was assigned a date/time group and logged out. When next in company with ORLECK, believed to be 3, 4, or 5 February, this writer hand delivered the message, along with much of the material contained herein, to Captain Edward H. HEUER, Commanding Officer, USS ORLECK and CTU 70.8.9. A copy of this message was not retained by me, however, it is believed a copy is in MASON files. The VANCE situation was discussed briefly with Captain HEUER and at that time this writer considered that since the matter had been officially reported, no further action was necessary and none was taken.

Since two years have elapsed since occurrence of the incidents cited, the above statement is as factual as recollection and records will serve. To the best of my knowledge, it is complete and nothing within recollection has been intentionally omitted. Enclosure (16) is an overlay indicating times, targets and positions described herein and in the previous enclosures. Other U.S. Navy officers who were present and witnessed all or portions of the incidents described herein are:

LCDR Stanley L. HAVENS, USN, Executive Officer, USS MASON (DD-852)

LT RONALD L. SEGERBLOM, USN, Operations Officer and GQ OOD

Mr. George WOLFE (then LTJG), Weapons Officer

[signed]

A. M. HAZEN
Captain, U.S. Navy
COMFLETRAGRU WESTPAC

APPENDIX B

26 MAR 1966

From: Chaplain G. W. DANDO, LT. USNR

To: Commander Escort Squadron SEVEN

Subj: USS VANCE: morale situation

1. As squadron Chaplain COMCORTRON SEVEN I also give the use of my services to ships of COMCORTRON FIVE. In the course of carrying out my duties I did during the month of October visit the USS VANCE where it was in Homeport, Pearl Harbor. I found the situation on board the VANCE to be normal and morale to be average. My contacts with the VANCE were limited and my impression of the ship was that she was a good ship.
2. On 28 February 1966, I went on board the USS VANCE in the Market Time area to ride her and give her the coverage of a Chaplain. While on board the VANCE I found that the morale was the lowest of any ship I had ever ridden. The problem seemed to center on the new Commanding Officer who had reported on board since I had last seen the VANCE.
3. The following complaints were received by me from the officers and men. I have listed what I did if anything about the complaint to verify it and my own impressions related to the complaint.

    a. That the CO leaves the bridge when he has the Conn. This I was told by several officers and I saw it happen myself. I asked officers to verify this and could not find one officer that would deny the fact. I was told that on one occasion the CO had the Conn and was found asleep in his stateroom by the OOD who then assumed the Conn.

    b. That the CO causes danger to the ship when he has the Conn. I was told that the CO had to be relieved of the

Conn by the XO when the ship was about to run aground. The CO was looking through binoculars from the 03 level at a battle going on the beach and was unaware of the movement of the ship. He gave an order to bring the ship closer to the shore without being aware of what was ahead of the ship. The XO in taking the Conn brought the ship back around. Several officers witnessed this and told me that only the quick action by the XO saved the ship from being run aground in a known hostile area.

c. That men were denied their rights under UCMJ at Captain's Mast. One man who talked with me and said that he was not even told of his offense until he was brought to Mast, was not told of his rights or given the aid of the legal officer. I talked with the Legal Officer and division officers and they told me that they were not even aware that the man was coming to Mast.

d. Takes ship into area where he is told not to go. I was told that the CO would order the ship into areas where he had been told not to go and to cover for being there order that false position reports be sent to higher command. I questioned officers again about this and as before I could not find one officer who would deny that the CO had done this. I was also told that a record of this was made in the CIC watch log.

e. The CO endangers the life of his men by using them and ship's recreation boat as bait. The speed boat is used to try and draw fire from the shore by sending it in close to the shore. During the time I was on board I read the Coast Guard WPB operating with the VANCE. On one evening the CO placed the XO and an enlisted man on board the WPB with the VANCE's speed boat to go in close to the shore and to then patrol in the area so close that the PCF's and WPB's could not go. We were told that the purpose was to draw fire to allow the VANCE to have reason to fire on the Beach.

f. Fired on Shore without cause. I was told that the CO had fired on beach with small arms fire and when tracers were deflected off the rocks claimed the ship was being fired upon. This was common knowledge of both officers and men and when asked no one said that they saw any fire from the shore. The CO ordered that the VANCE take the beach under fire because he determined that they had been fired upon.

g. CO uses OpTar money for personal film. I was told

by XO that CO had ordered $300.00 worth of film for his camera. The Photos he had taken were placed in Kodak mailers and sent for processing with the return address being that of his wife. Other officers said they had seen this. I could find no officer who would deny this.

h. Creates a general problem in area where he is serving. While riding WPB's and PCF's I was asked about CO of the VANCE and if he was as bad as they say. I was told that the officer in charge of these small craft had been warned about the CO VANCE before they came out to patrol with him. When other ships are in the area conducting Naval Gunfire Support CO of the VANCE bugs them to give him something to shoot at. Message traffic shown me by the Operations Officer reflected this. Also had to be told by CO of one ship to get out of the way as he had a job to do.

i. Ordering the submitting of false reports. While on board I was approached by the postal officer who had a problem he wanted to discuss with me. The CO had taken stamps from the post office to mail what he considered official mail. The postal officer submitted his monthly statement showing the post office short the funds. The CO would not accept the report and told the Postal Officer to submit a new report showing that the books balanced. The Postal Officer did not feel that he could do this and came to me for help. My advice to him was not to sign any false report. The problem had not been solved when I left the ship.

j. Manipulation of Mess fund and general handling of mess. I received numerous complaints about the way the CO ran the mess as Mess President. This included the fact that he would not buy into the mess until he had brought the value of a mess share down from $30 to $2. Had held a required Mess Night that cost each man $14 but would only pay $2 as his share. Changed menus so as to restrict the diet of the officers to the point of having cheese sandwiches three and four days in a row. The use of brandy and cherry heering on several different occasions even when I was on board under the name of "Honey" or "Guava Juice."

k. Makes comments about former CO. This has a very poor effect on the wardroom as the officers generally liked the former CO and felt he was a good officer. These comments are generally childish and seemed to be aimed at making himself look good by tearing down the former CO.

l. CO does not know the ship as he should. The Engineering Officer complained to me several times that the CO would put undue strain on the ship by doing things that the machinery was not able to handle causing great wear and tear and break down.

m. Operation Officer downgraded by CO for trying to aid CO. The Operation Officer tried to talk to the CO about the church program he was conducting and to let him know that it was causing a big problem among the men. Instead of taking the help of his officer, the CO wrote him up in his files as being violently opposed to the command program for moral guidance. In addition, made threats to the operation officer to try and bring him under complete subordination so that he would make no further complaints. This was done by the fact that he said he would have the officer's spot promotion taken away. This information was received from the Operation Officer when he came to me asking if I could do anything about the forced religious program.

n. Required attendance at pseudo-church service. All hands aft is what the CO calls his command moral guidance program. It is conducted with prayers and the singing of hymns. At first it was conducted in lieu of protestant lay leader services, but it was required attendance for all hands. After many complained and the CO received some letters about this the program was changed slightly and protestant lay leaders services were conducted again. I talked with the CO on this and got nowhere except to plant the idea that if he were really interested in moral guidance he could look into the program the Navy had prepared for use in WestPac. CO maintains his right to hold such services on the basis that they are good for the men and the Navy thinks so because the Academy has required Church attendance.

o. The use of Recreation Fund. I received complaints that the CO uses Recreation funds in an illegal way. No one seemed to be questioning the CO's right to authorize the expenditure of funds but the feeling was that he did not have the right to take $500 when the ship was in Thailand and to spend it as he did. Only part of this money could be accounted for in any way when I was on board. The custodian could only account

for it in that it had been given to the CO. He did not know
what it had been spent for. The XO said that about half the
money could be accounted for for dinners and beer for the
crew at the EM Club. Some of the rest could be accounted for
in hotel rooms for the officers and CPO's and for the CO
himself and for free meals given by the CO to anybody he
wanted in Thailand.

4.   In addition to the complaints I received there are those things
that I became directly involved in for one reason or another or
formed an opinion on.

a.   Two men tried to go after the CO while I was on
board. One in a drunken state from a beach party that was
held, the other from a nervous state. One man had a shot gun
and was stopped by the medic and put under sedation. After
an interview with this man I told the medic to keep him under
mild sedation until a doctor could see him. The other man was
kept under control by shipmates and when he sobered up I
talked with him and felt he would not do anything for the
present.

b.   The CO got involved in trying to tell me how to run
my church service while on board the first Sunday. The problem centered around the choice of hymns. On Saturday night,
5 March 1966, he sent a memo to me with a list of four hymns
for Sunday Services. I took this to mean that he was suggesting
possible hymns that he knew were familiar to the men. My
order of worship has room for only three hymns so when I
gave the copy of the bulletin to the MO to be printed I had
used two hymns listed by the CO and one of my own choice
that fitted into the service. The CO saw the outline for the
service and added to it the other two hymns as special music
to be sung by a choir which he wanted the XO to form in a few
hours time. The XO told him that there just were not enough
singers on board or time to train any. So we sent the Bulletin
to the Ship Office to be typed without the two hymns. Next the
CO saw the bulletin without his hymns listed so added them
again as hymns in the service. The Chief Yeoman showed me
and I removed them and asked him to prepare the bulletins for
my service the way I had given it to him. The CO was upset
by this but did not say anything to me instead talked with the
XO for two hours in which the XO tried to tell the CO that
the Navy gives her Chaplain the right to conduct services

according to the way of his own church. The CO did not seem to understand and ended by ordering the XO that he would stand at the end of the service and start singing the hymn that he had chosen. I talked with the CO later in the week and made my position clear to him and my second service on board was conducted without interference.

c.   I made an attempt to talk with the CO about the morale problem I found on his ship and to try and help him understand what was happening. I could do little talking as in the four hours I [was] with him the CO did most of the talking, telling all the good he had done for the ship. He did not seem to be interested in my opinions at the time. By my talking to him however he began a program of trying to find out more about the morale on board the ship and at later times seemed really interested in the problem, but only his own interpretation of it, and not in what the XO or myself tried to tell him. In fact it seemed as if the CO was trying to say that the blame was on the XO.

d.   I was witness to a sorry display on the part of the CO when ABC TV newsmen were to use the VANCE as a photo ship for part of a feature on the Market Time Operation. He felt he had to work up a big display and disregarded the messages from the WPB bringing the Newsmen out to the VANCE that they wanted to come on board. Instead he had his Army type fire team firing and other such displays while the Newsmen sat on the bow of the WPB and laughed at us. When on board the VANCE finally the newsmen asked the CO what he had the fire team for and he said to fire on the junks to stop them. The Newsmen are surprised asked him how often he had to fire on a junk to stop them and the CO said almost all of the time, that they all try and run. The Newsmen showing a little familiarity with Market Time asked how come none of the other ships had that problem. The CO said he didn't know. In the talk with the Newsmen the CO made comment about the Liaison Officers from Vietnam saying that many of them were yellow and lazy, in direct violation of instruction that adverse comments would not be made about the people of Vietnam.

e.   I also observed that the CO does many things that there is no question about his authority to do. In fact things that he can be praised for such as having officers in clean uniforms, men with hair cut, shining brass and shoes, etc. The problem is that he goes about it in such a way as to create problems. One way is to fine each officer $.25 each time he fails to live up to his standard or each time the CO finds a man in his division out of order. No one seems to know what is done with the money except that the XO has it in a box.

    f.   This Officer does not appear to me to be as stable as an officer should be for Command. If any man or officer on the ship were to act the way this CO does I would at once tell the CO that he should be sent to a doctor for a complete mental check. This man just does not act like you would expect a natural man to act. The kindest thing I can say about him is that he needs help.

5.   I would like to emphasize that I have not known this officer before and certainly have no reason to degrade or embarrass him, but I feel it my duty to report a situation as I see it in all honesty to my superiors for such action, if any, as they may consider appropriate.

                                     G. W. DANDO
                                     Lieutenant, USNR

APPENDIX C

STATEMENT OF CAPTAIN RICHARD G. ALEXANDER, USN, TO THE SECRETARY OF THE NAVY ON BEHALF OF LCDR MARCUS A. ARNHEITER, USN.

Mr. Secretary—

This case concerning LCDR Arnheiter is a most important and delicate one. It is important because it goes to the roots of naval discipline upon which the authority of a Commanding Officer must ultimately rest. It also goes to the roots of the Administrative authority delegated to the Chief of Naval Personnel in entrusting officers with or removing officers from positions of command. The case is delicate because of the strong positions already taken by senior officers, because of the strong interest in the case by the officer corps of the Navy, and because of the impending treatment of the case in full by news media and others.

If LCDR Arnheiter was in fact an incompetent Commanding Officer, the authority of the Chief of Naval Personnel to remove him, and others, from command positions for the good of the service must be sustained, regardless of all other aspects of the case.

If however LCDR Arnheiter was in fact a competent Commanding Officer, whose relief was precipitated by the unfounded allegations of disloyal subordinates who succeeded in stampeding naval authorities into taking unjustified summary action against him, then redress is due not only to LCDR Arnheiter, but in a larger sense to every Commanding Officer in the Service because all of them are affected by this case.

Mr. Arnheiter contends that the record as it now stands is flawed and incomplete. It is flawed by a gross violation of his right as an interested party to be informed of the content and source of charges against him which had precipitated his relief and the ensuing investigation. This was the letter of Chaplain Dando which was used by the investigating officer but which was not furnished to Mr. Arnheiter until seven months later. The record is also flawed by its content, which was described by Rear Admiral Baumberger, who was the only reviewing authority who dealt with the allegations and the evidence in detail, as being unsubstantiated allegations by persons inimical to the Captain. The record is incomplete because the investigation was concluded before any specific findings of fault were stated to which rebuttal could be addressed. More important, it is also incomplete because new evidence has arisen since the case was concluded which weighs strongly on the side of Admiral Baumberger's two endorsements favoring LCDR Arnheiter, and against the conclusions reached by the Commander-in-Chief Pacific Fleet and the Chief of Naval Personnel.

This new evidence, in my opinion can achieve two vital things. It can throw serious doubt on, if not destroy, the veracity of the principal complainants against LCDR Arnheiter. In fact, it may well be prima facie evidence against several VANCE officers to support LCDR Arnheiter's previously submitted charges of nurturing collusion, false official statements and the like. In addition, this new evidence can give quite a different picture than was presented to the investigating officer of the conditions in USS VANCE with which LCDR Arnheiter was confronted, and of the relief with which his remedial efforts were greeted by many of the crew. Because of this, he requests that his case be made the subject of a Court of Inquiry in order that the full story can be brought to light under formal procedures prescribed by the Manual for Courts Martial, U.S. Navy.

I support LCDR Arnheiter in his request, Mr. Secretary; however, I go a step further to conclude that on the basis of the material now in existence in writing concerning the case—that is, the record of the investigation taken together with the Commanding Officer's rebuttal and submissions of new evidence; the detailed endorsement of the Cruiser-Destroyer Force Commander; the contradictory, general endorsements of a Fleet Commander-in-Chief and of the Chief of Naval Personnel which give unfavorable conclusions without specifying where in the record these conclusions are supported by uncontested fact; and the increasingly notorious and scandalous facts concerning the perpetration and acceptance of rumor and lies about a Commanding Officer—I conclude on the basis of all this that the case should be thrown out, redress given to LCDR Arnheiter, and charges preferred against those who willfully wronged him. Unless the Secretary is willing to submit this case to a Court of Inquiry, I am persuaded that this is the correct and just course to follow. If the case is given to a Court of Inquiry, I am equally persuaded the same result will ensue.

Mr. Secretary, when the conniving character, lack of veracity, deceitfulness, disloyalty, and premeditated attempts at character assassination on the part of several principal officers in USS VANCE, which can be established by documentary evidence and sworn testimony, are placed on one hand; and on the other hand one places the professional ability of the Commanding Officer, his consideration for subordinates, his zeal, his determination to correct the shortcomings of his new command, all of which are also matters which can meet the most stringent rules of evidence, there is now no doubt in my mind which party in this dispute was deserving of commanding support.

* * * * * * *

Mr. Secretary, let us consider what we can now establish about the officers who came forward with their grievances against Mr. Arnheiter.

The Executive Officer, LT Hardy, deflected a complaint concerning the Captain's character guidance program under General Order 21 so that the Captain never received it. LT Hardy advised the complaining officer, who was next senior on board, to seek help from outside the ship, thereby setting in motion the fatal cycle of clandestine complaints which eventually precipitated the Captain's relief. I shall deal with this aspect later. What is important here is that within two weeks of the Captain's assumption of command Mr. Hardy gave his next senior officer an impetus which was disloyal to the Captain. Later, LT Hardy was aware of attitudes and reactions in the wardroom which he never transmitted to the Captain. In fact quite the opposite was true. As the Captain's policies to improve the ship commenced to bring pressure on the Executive Officer he stooped to pleading with the junior officers to help make his life easier, by better performance. Contrary to the opinion of the investigating officer that the Executive Officer was loyal almost beyond the call of duty, the Type Commander found that the degree of support given to the Captain by his Executive Officer was less than he was entitled to expect.

The Operations Officer, LT Generous, within a month of the Captain's reporting and about one week after deploying from

Hawaii to WestPAC, was violently objecting to the Captain's program under General Order 21, and acting on the Executive Officer's advice "to seek outside help anonymously," was writing hysterically to a junior Chaplain in Pearl Harbor, invoking the Nuremberg Tribunal to support his acknowledged disloyalty. This program of the Captain's was later to receive the commendation of two senior 7th Fleet Chaplains and of the Navy Chief of Chaplains. Testimony now exists that LT Generous later induced an undetermined number of other men to write the same Chaplain complaining of compulsory non-Catholic services. At least two others are known to have done so, ENS Belmonte and HMC Cornejo. Other testimony is now available from a second class petty officer that LT Generous spoke openly to enlisted men on watch of the log being kept by certain officers concerning the Captain and stated that it would be used against the Captain at some future time. This log is described by one second class Petty Officer to whom it was shown as "a collection of fictitious and degrading remarks about the Captain." In addition there has now come to light copies of counterfeit family gram (ship's newspaper mailed to dependents) and a bogus plan-of-the-day which all evidence indicates were typed on LT Generous's personal typewriter, on forms normally in the custody of the Executive Officer. This family gram is utterly defamatory of the Captain in content. The plan-of-the-day is a childish attempt to ridicule the fast-paced activities of the ship. How many were mailed is unknown. It is certain that some were and that LT Generous was involved in their publication.

Other crew members have corroborated the Captain's testimony about LT Generous's open opposition to the Captain's tactics of taking VANCE where the action was; namely, close-in to the coast.

Finally, with regard to this officer, whose position at the heart of a disgruntled group is evident from the record and the later statements of crew members, it should be pointed out that LT Generous was not a stable person.

I have examined his record in company with a senior naval Medical Officer who has wide experience in the behavioral patterns of naval personnel. LT Generous was subject to an extreme emotional disorder which required his hospitalization, for about 35 days, while serving on board his first destroyer. His Commanding Officer indicated in his reports of fitness on this officer that his performance fluctuated so frequently from good to bad that he was impossible to evaluate. After hospitalization he was assigned to USS VANCE. Some 7 months later LCDR Arnheiter relieved command and commenced to correct glaringly low standards in the ship. Within a few weeks LT Generous began writing wildly to a junior Chaplain, invoking the Nuremberg Trials to support his disloyalty. Throughout the period of LCDR Arnheiter's command, he was openly opposed by LT Generous, who passed judgment on the Captain at every opportunity. The record does not end there. Seven months after LCDR Arnheiter's relief, LT Generous is again writing hysterically in his resignation that the Navy is not large enough: for himself and his former Captain, and that all naval authority stands condemned for complicity in placing Arnheiter, whom he has not seen in seven months, in command. Mr. Secretary, this suggests the pattern of paranoia, in the opinion of at least one naval Medical Officer. There is little doubt that this officer was instrumental in wrecking the career of a dedicated, professional officer. A senior petty officer who served in VANCE at the time has written: "Generous was the senior officer aboard who headed the conspiracy against the Captain. It is remarkable, except for a few instances that he was able to undermine the Commanding Officer so effectively."

To show how dangerous this open and flagrant disloyalty became, I also cite the case of ENS Belmonte, who testified that he was the initiator of the log being kept on the Captain. ENS Belmonte openly scoffed at the Captain's desire to bring the ship within gun range of VC coastal territory in order to more effectively prosecute the war. He ridiculed the few times the ship fired at shore targets and on one occasion when word was passed to take cover from hostile fire, ENS Belmonte ordered the CIC crew back to stations, saying that the word just passed was ridiculous. Yet the record shows that hostile fire was in fact observed by the Captain and confirmed by other bridge personnel.

One final comment, Mr. Secretary, on the veracity of certain officers in that ship. As I will mention in detail in a moment, the ship was visited by a young Chaplain sent to check on morale. This officer returned to his Commodore with six pages of hearsay complaints alleging grossly improper conduct and policies on the part of LCDR Arnheiter. It is obvious that these distortions and falsehoods were furnished by certain VANCE officers. Yet the investigation which ensued three weeks later substantiated only a few of them. Of these few, when reviewed by Rear Admiral Baumberger in the light of circumstances existing at the time, only two remained. These two Admiral Baumberger considered not significant. In my view, Mr. Secretary, this fact alone establishes that within the VANCE wardroom there were, by Mid-March, liars and disloyal officers bent on assassinating the Captain professionally. With this fact clear, how can the later testimony of this group be given the slightest credence?

If disloyalty and conspiracy to discredit their Captain becomes a strong suspicion in the case of at least three officers, what was the condition of the ship over which these officers had been presiding for up to a year prior to LCDR Arnheiter's arrival? Here the facts as testified to by former enlisted crew members, are shocking, Mr. Secretary.

At about the time LCDR Arnheiter's struggle with his officers reached a climax, there was a Congressional inquiry into a letter from a crew member, a second class petty officer, complaining of grossly unsatisfactory administration in the ship. The Cruiser-Destroyer Force Commander forwarded this man's letter to every ship in his force as an admonition to his Captains! He was aware of its source. Since publicity of LCDR Arnheiter's case on the West Coast, former crew members have come forward with sworn statements of conditions of brutal abuses of discipline, lack of officer attention to administration and other disgusting matters which vividly describe the situation which these disloyal officers were presiding over and tolerating. Several of the enlisted men's statements acknowledged that they were aware that Mr. Arnheiter's policies were temporarily successful in achieving improvement. One chief petty officer states that his tour in the ship was the worst in his 18 years service. The friends of yet another chief state that that man's emotional breakdown and retirement resulted from his tour in VANCE for the two years prior to LCDR Arnheiter's arrival. I shall quote selections from several of these statements in a moment.

Finally, as LCDR Arnheiter stated in his letter to you of 1 September, when he first assumed command of USS VANCE in Pearl Harbor he was vigorously instructed by the Rear Admiral commanding the Naval Base concerning the unsavory disciplinary record of his new command and the urgent need for the Captain's direct attention to the matter. It would appear, Mr. Secretary, that when LCDR Arnheiter undertook to achieve the improvements which his background and high standards, as well as Admiral

Person's admonitions told him were necessary, he had everything he needed to accomplish the task, except the support of key officers on board, and of his seniors at a later date when their support was vital.

In contrast to this dismal picture of a wretched ship under disloyal officers, what is the true picture of LCDR Arnheiter? The record of the investigation shows what was thought of him by disloyal liars and character assassins. Can we believe them? Should we care what they think? What did others think of him?

* * * * * * *

The record of the investigation alleges actions on LCDR Arnheiter's part which would constitute improper performance of duty if true. Rear Admiral Baumberger, as Type Commander, reviewed these allegations and found the vast majority unsubstantiated. The remainder, which had some basis in fact, were not considered significant by Admiral Baumberger when viewed in the light of the operations in which the ship was engaged. Admiral Baumberger twice recommended Arnheiter's restoration to command.

If LCDR Arnheiter's actions did not indicate deficiencies serious enough to warrant his abrupt dismissal, what about his behavior—that is, his conduct and relations with his officers and crew. Was he a bully? Was he slovenly and unkempt? Was he a drunk, a coward, a cheat? Did he cultivate favorites? Did he by-pass the chain of command below him? Was he overly severe in meting out punishment? Did he abuse his subordinate with recriminations and reprimand? Did he demand the impossible of his men? Did he exhaust them? These are some of the unsatisfactory traits of other Commanding Officers whose behavior and attitudes have made them unfit for command even though they had professional competence. The record of this investigation does not indicate that any of these descriptions is apt. What the record does indicate is that some of LCDR Arnheiter's officers, being unable to attack his character or behavior, assailed his professional competence; that is, shiphandling, selection of operational objectives, relations with coordinating commands, manner of making operational reports, and so forth. The so called "findings" of Captain Witter lie in this general area. Rear Admiral Baumberger demolishes them and other reviewing authorities have not taken issue with Admiral Baumberger's evaluation. What then, could have been bothering some of these VANCE officers?

In my opinion, which I am convinced available documents will now show, some of these officers were bothered by the fact that into their slovenly, unseamanlike lives there had arrived a new Captain whose attributes they wholly failed to understand or refused to accept. Mr. Arnheiter is an officer of great energy, ability and high standards. Bring these together in a situation offering the challenges of a "first command" and you can expect action. Make it a ship like VANCE and it is obvious there will be changes!

I want to illustrate the foregoing in two ways. First by showing you what kind of officer Mr. Arnheiter was before he went to VANCE. And secondly by showing you how he was appraised by some of VANCE's crew who realized the need for his efforts.

Before coming to USS VANCE, LCDR Arnheiter had been Executive Officer of USS INGERSOLL (DD-652). His Commanding Officer's official report of fitness is outstanding. However, the most remarkable evaluation of an officer by his subordinates that I have ever seen exists in letters written by INGERSOLL officers (including the Captain) after they had heard of his relief, almost a year after he had left their ship. Their letters are part of the record of the case. Mr. Secretary, I have seen thousands of officers' fitness reports. I have yet to see an officer's record which gives as clear a picture of a unique, respected, dedicated, competent, and successful officer as those letters do of LCDR Arnheiter. I submit that your personal understanding of this case will not be complete until you have read them. They indicate not only what Mr. Arnheiter's methods and objectives were, but the reaction of his subordinates—Initial opposition, followed by acceptance and cooperation, followed by loyal support and enormous respect. This one item selected from the detailed analysis of Mr. Arnheiter drawn by LT Forkash, MC, USNR, will illustrate the tenor of the evaluations reached by *all* of these officers:

"Of all the officers senior to me under whom I served, LCDR Arnheiter was able to lead and inspire his subordinates to higher levels of achievement than any other officer in executive of command authority. It was the consensus of my fellow junior officers that under LCDR Arnheiter we were working for an officer whose performance and potential would surely bring him to flag rank."

No doubt for INGERSOLL as well as for VANCE the impact of LCDR Arnheiter's drive and ability was felt with some discomfort. Here is a graphic description of this effect by one INGERSOLL officer, LTJG Novak, USNR:

"Commander Arnheiter met our ship, the U.S.S. INGERSOLL (DD-852), at Kaohsiung, Formosa. He relieved LCDR Lawler as Executive Officer and sweeping changes immediately occurred in daily routines. He vigorously attacked slovenly appearance (of officers, enlisted men and the ship), attitude and performance of duty. DUTY-HONOR-COUNTRY became words to live by. Ship's regulations, which had been conveniently overlooked, were enforced.

"The obvious result of such rapid changes was a severe reduction in morale. Personally, I have never seen morale fall to such a low ebb. Men were working hard and putting in extra hours. Gripes could be heard in almost all quarters.

"The officers (including myself) and chiefs objected most strenuously, as they were expected to set the example. The next loudest group was that of the lax petty officers who had spent the majority of their tours of duty on small ships. Only the new arrivals from Boot Camp, the efficient petty officers and the men who were recently transferred from large ships remained calm.

"The level of morale began to rise a few months later as new standards of watch standing, personal appearance and appearance of the ship became accepted. Pride in the Navy and in the ship became very noticeable. Rated men acted more like petty officers; junior officers began to act like professionals.

"During his tour on INGERSOLL, the ship literally 'pulled itself up by its bootstraps.' The ship evolved from a scroungy 'Tin Can' to a first-class fighting ship, staffed by competent and well trained men."

Well, this was the picture of Mr. Arnheiter six months prior to his reporting to USS VANCE. The record of the investigation gives quite a different picture of him during his short tour in command. We can explain this change by saying that once he was his own Commanding Officer, Arnheiter went too far. This is the official version. It makes a very neat explanation except that we now have reason to doubt the veracity of his detractors as well as their basic loyalty, and we also have new information which challenges the image which certain VANCE crew members created.

Keeping in mind the evaluation of INGERSOLL's officers and LT Novak's description of the "Arnheiter method," these evaluations by junior and senior VANCE sailors are most pertinent:

"Seaman Himebaugh: (8 April 1966)

"I felt proud when he (the Captain) held frequent inspections in order that the ship would be 'more squared away' . . . We had adventures that I know I will remember for many years to come . . . No matter what happens to CAPT ARNHEITER, there is no doubt in my mind that he was competent C.O. and that he deserved the respect of every crew member . . ."

"Radioman Striker Burkholder: (3 April 1966)

"He (the Captain) promised the crew that they would see some action and he tried to do just that. He did get some enemy targets for the VANCE to fire on. The men that went to the beaches are now up for commendations because the ex-Captain saw, as many others saw, that it could have been a dangerous mission even though the trip the men took was uneventful. My opinion is that the ex-Captain of the USS VANCE (DER-387), LCDR MARCUS A. ARNHEITER, was a Captain that looked out for the crew . . ."

"Second Class Petty Officer Matthews: (* April 1966)

"The ship was infested with roaches, the crew wore sloppy, torn, and dirty uniforms. When LCDR ARNHEITER came aboard all this changed. He had the welfare and appearance of the crew as two of his main concerns. He organized and arranged for recreation for the crew. He, I feel, wanted us to do our jobs as best we could, look smart, and get us as much enjoyment out of life and the Navy as possible . . . If LCDR ARNHEITER made any mistakes, it was probably trying too hard."

"Chief Yeoman Young: (3 April 1966)

"He instilled pride in her petty officers, conducted an effective leadership and character guidance program which included gathering the crew on the fantail to instill in them a sense of pride in themselves, their ship and their country . . . He constantly kept the crew informed on what was going on even at their G.Q. stations by use of the internal communications . . ."

As for a description of Mr. Arnheiter's methods in the VANCE we have a document which closely parallels LT Novak's letter. This was written by a Signalman First Class three months after Mr. Arnheiter was relieved:

"Signalman First Class Boson: (5 June 1966)

"I served on board USS VANCE for nearly 14 months, the last three of which were under the command of LCDR M. A. ARNHEITER, USN. During the first 9 months (before LCDR ARNHEITER assumed command) the ship was not the kind of warship you normally think of when you think of destroyers. In other words, the ship was lax. The barrier patrols lessened combat effectiveness. The ship went to GQ at the most from 4 to 8 times during all the time I was on board up to the time LCDR ARNHEITER came aboard. On the first Market Time Patrol under LCDR WRIGHT, the ship usually operated well out to seaward, and hardly ever came in close to shore, where on this past cruise LCDR ARNHEITER took us. The great majority of Vietnamese junks and sampans operate well within three miles of the coastline. LCDR ARNHEITER took the ship there to prosecute a visit and search effort all around the clock. When he was C.O., we had more operations because there were so many junks to search and inspect, LCDR ARNHEITER would have two forward and two aft alongside all at once, at the same time having the two boats in the water also looking for VC carrying contraband.

. . . "The Captain always seemed very concerned about the welfare of the crew. He talked to us at length both on the fantail, over the speaker, and individually as he walked around the ship. He was always asking for suggestions and ways to improve things. He wanted everyone to have pride in themselves and in their ship. He did so many things it was difficult for many of the officers and men to keep up with them all. *From suddenly being a ship full of people content to live quietly doing nothing and with not many requirements, the Captain changed all that to a lot of activity, something to do all the time, keeping people hopping, making*

them forget the boredom and making them get involved in the war
effort in every way he could think of. Some people thought he was
trying to do too much, and they compared what he was doing
with what the ship had done on the last cruise.

". . . *The morale of the ship, during the period LCDR ARN-*
HEITER was Captain, was good and getting better. The things
that he did for the crew were obvious and they appreciated it,
I think. The time he gave the crew the party in Guam and went
from table to table offering cigars made a big hit with the men. He
also learned about the ship's problems with all the fights and the
lack of discipline they had in the 1st Division. He promised to
do all he could to increase the authority of petty officers. One of
the things the Captain did to keep morale as good as it was during
his cruise was his keeping everyone informed about what was
going on, what was happening each day, before it happened and
while it was happening, so the crew wouldn't think they were
overworking all for nothing. The ship was full of cockroaches
until LCDR ARNHEITER took over. He was a man who believed
in getting things done. Once he started to do things, he never did
them half-assed. He always tried to do things better and more
completely than others. He did his duty. He had more junks
searched, he had a better armed crew, he had a ship that fired at
the enemy, he kept the ship looking more squared away than
before, kept the officers and men looking better, and so on.

". . . In my opinion, everything the Captain did, that I could
see or was aware of, that changed things in our routine or way
of doing things, was for the best interest of the ship so that the
ship could be more like a man of war. I believe the capability
of the ship to fight, and the overall spirit of the ship as a *warship,*
increased as a result of LCDR ARNHEITER's policies and actions.
He kept talking about VANCE being better than the rest of the
ships, and he tried hard to make this so. I believe he was suc-
ceeding."

Mr. Secretary, I will dwell no more on these comparisons.
I have only touched a selected few from a record which now contains many more.

Where did strength and where did weakness lie in that ship?
Who stood for DUTY, HONOR, COUNTRY, and who was disloyal? Whose standards would you commend to a young officer

today? Those of Hardy, Generous, and Belmonte? Whose efforts were deserving of command support and who should have been censored?

*　*　*　*　*　*　*

After this comparison of the qualities and actions of the disputants, if any doubt remains, that the full weight of command support should have been given to the Captain, one should then examine a separate but related aspect of the case—the manner in which the case was handled once credence was given to sheer rumor and hearsay. Here we find actions taken which not only violate U.S. Navy Regulations, to the terrible disadvantage of the Commanding Officer, but which also violate elementary common sense in pursuing impartial justice. I will describe these actions now. As I do so, I ask that you consider whether the picture of the Commanding Officer, in relation to the full picture of his accusers which has become visible, is such as to justify the acceptance of these incredible means to construct a case against him. These means could be acceptable only if the Captain could be proven culpable beyond any doubt.

While LCDR Arnheiter had command of USS VANCE, a little over 3 months, he had received one and only one mild caution from his Squadron Commander in Pearl Harbor. This was contained in a courteous, friendly, helpful and encouraging letter, which mentioned that religious services were a sensitive area and that religion must be kept out of any "all-hands" evolution to avoid the problem of compulsory attendance at worship. This letter was received by LCDR Arnheiter in WestPAC and was responded to promptly, with assurance being given to the Commodore that the problem was recognized and that the character guidance program of the command was being conducted accordingly. Aside from this straight-forward, friendly, manly, advice from a senior, LCDR Arnheiter received no other query or complaint regarding conditions in his ship until he received message orders on 31 March announcing his summary relief. Within twelve hours he was under guard in his cabin, having been relieved by another Escort Squadron Commander who gave no explanation. After a night under guard he was kicked off his ship. Four days later he was confronted in an investigation with an amazing chain of damning, ruinous allegations that were bewildering in scope and viciousness. Mr. Secretary, what all of your officers will demand to know is just how in hell this could happen in the United States Navy!

Here is what occurred, and this is a matter of record in a letter report by CDR D. F. Milligan, the Escort Squadron Commander who relieved LCDR Arnheiter—giving him no explanation and placing him under guard.

Several weeks prior to the actual relief, CDR Milligan in Subic Bay had received a telephone call from the VANCE's Squadron Commander in Pearl Harbor requesting that Milligan check on conditions in that ship since there were rumors among some dependents of a morale problem on board. Thereupon Commander Milligan arranged to have his staff Chaplain, LT Dando, a neophyte with less than 5 months in the Navy, visit VANCE to observe conditions. Upon his return LT Dando submitted a six page written report alleging horrendous problems in VANCE stemming from the conduct and policies of the Commanding Officer. Virtually all of these allegations were based on hearsay.

Another junior officer from CDR Milligan's staff embarked in VANCE and brought back an oral tale of low morale in the wardroom plus a scandalous allegation relayed from VANCE's Executive Officer concerning a Citation of LCDR Arnheiter for gallantry which the Executive Officer alleged he had been forced under duress to prepare and submit.

Armed with these reports CDR Milligan was in Subic Bay when VANCE arrived in Manila for rest and upkeep. CDR Milligan consulted members of the staffs of two destroyer flotilla commanders who were effecting a relief in Subic. Milligan was cautioned by a staff member to visit the ship, advise Commander Arnheiter of the allegations and check them on the spot before taking the matter to higher authority. He declined to do this, sought a hearing with the two Admirals, and persuaded them on the basis of his unverified information to obtain Bureau of Naval Personnel authority to relieve Arnheiter summarily. BuPers authority was obtained, and local orders were prepared ordering CDR Milligan to effect the relief and *to conduct a preliminary investigation of conditions in VANCE.*

CDR Milligan himself described his method of conducting his preliminary investigation. He placed a note in the ship's Plan-of-the-Day "stating that he was available to any man who had anything to say pro or con about events in the ship since 22

December," the date of LCDR Arnheiter's commencement in command. Under these circumstances, in which their Captain had been summarily relieved in amazing fashion, the crew of VANCE was alive with rumors. Certainly Arnheiter had done something scandalous! Into CDR Milligan's cabin came the ship's malcontents to unload their complaints. One would have expected those who respected Arnheiter to be stunned into silence. Amazingly, some brave souls came forward on his behalf. CDR Milligan then sent a selection of statements to CAPT Witter in Subic Bay, who by then had been designated to conduct an informal, one-man investigation.

Mr. Secretary, consider CDR Milligan's position! He had perpetrated an unheard-of relief of a Commanding Officer in violation of Article 1404 of U.S. Navy Regulations which requires that charges and complaints against an officer be given him in writing, and in violation of Article C-7801 of the BuPers Manual, which provides safeguards against the preemptory action Milligan initiated. His conduct was so unmanly as to inspire instant contempt. And now he had to justify what he had brought about. Mr. Secretary, was CDR Milligan competent to be an impartial investigator?

Now, sir, consider the officers in VANCE who had initiated the rumor and slander against the Captain. They had exceeded beyond their wildest expectations. The Captain was gone! But the show was not over. There would be an investigation. Having lied, exaggerated and misrepresented before, could they be expected now to be objective and truthful?

Then, Mr. Secretary, consider CAPT Witter. With no prior knowledge of this situation he was suddenly caught as investigating officer of an action which two flag officers in his chain of command had already perpetrated. Mr. Secretary, could CAPT Witter qualify as an impartial investigating officer?

There is more, Mr. Secretary. Consider now Rear Admirals Irvine and King, the two Flotilla Commanders who jointly authorized the relief. They had done so without a shred of substantiation. They had by-passed every one of the safeguards of the BuPers Manual. They had not enforced Navy Regulations Article 1404. Mr. Secretary, as convening authority of the investigation, Admiral King was its first reviewer. Was he competent to be objective?

In fact, Mr. Secretary, Admiral King reached his conclusions which roundly condemned LCDR Arnheiter and recommended disciplinary action, without having seen LCDR Arnheiter's rebuttal to the so-called findings of the investigating officer.

Suffice it to say, Mr. Secretary, that when this fantastic fishing expedition to support an improper, cowardly, preemptory action against a Commanding Officer, which passed as an investigation, reached Rear Admiral Baumberger, he had the good sense and courage to twice recommend in effect that the whole mess be thrown out and that redress be made to LCDR Arnheiter, if such was possible.

Again Mr. Secretary, I ask the question that your entire officer corps will soon ask. How is such a thing possible in the U.S. Navy?

* * * * * * *

Mr. Secretary, I offer a conclusion from this for your consideration—not as my own but because you should be forewarned that it will be embraced by all but the most charitable observer. It is that *because* the case was handled so badly by authorities in Subic Bay they *had* to justify their flawed and extra legal means by demolishing LCDR Arnheiter. The end had to be constructed to ensure acceptance of what they had done.

Well, sir, this brings me to the end of my statement on behalf of my friend LCDR Arnheiter. I make it on *his* behalf, but also on behalf of many silent officers, young and old, who will be diminished if LCDR Arnheiter stands here alone and unsupported by active duty officers.

It is an easy thing for rumor and falsehood, if uncontested, to destroy a reputation anywhere. In the Navy, our vulnerability is particular and peculiar. The fruits of many years of experience, and the sense of fair play and manliness which are inherent in the character of an officer lie behind the safeguarding regulations which were violated in this case. Only the most patent, proven dereliction on the part of the accused could justify this treatment. Far from proving this dereliction, the evidence in the case now points clearly in the opposite direction.

If I may end on a personal note: Last March, in the absence of the evidence which is now available to construct a more complete view of this episode, I concluded there was no effective way to challenge the decisions reached in the case. I withdrew my support. I went further and took a stand against Mr. Arnheiter. To have withdrawn my support was prudent. But to turn against him was pusillanimous. I hope my statement today, in addition to presenting the case for Mr. Arnheiter, will also encourage others to re-examine views and positions they have previously taken.

Thank you for the opportunity of presenting this statement.

ABOUT THE AUTHOR

NEIL SHEEHAN was born in Holyoke, Massachusetts on October 27, 1936. After graduating from Harvard in 1958 he went into the Army, and in 1962 joined United Press International's Tokyo bureau. He spent the next two years covering the war in Viet Nam as UPI's bureau chief there. In 1964 he went to work for *The New York Times* and served on its city staff before returning to the Far East to report from Indonesia and then to spend another year in Viet Nam for *The Times*. In the fall of 1966 he became the newspaper's Pentagon correspondent and in 1968 took over the White House beat. In 1971 he obtained the Pentagon Papers for *The Times*. He is at present a correspondent on political, diplomatic and military affairs. He is married to Susan Sheehan, the writer. The Sheehans live with their two daughters in Washington, D.C.